The Food of Southern Thailand

Also by

AUSTIN BUSH

The Food of Northern Thailand

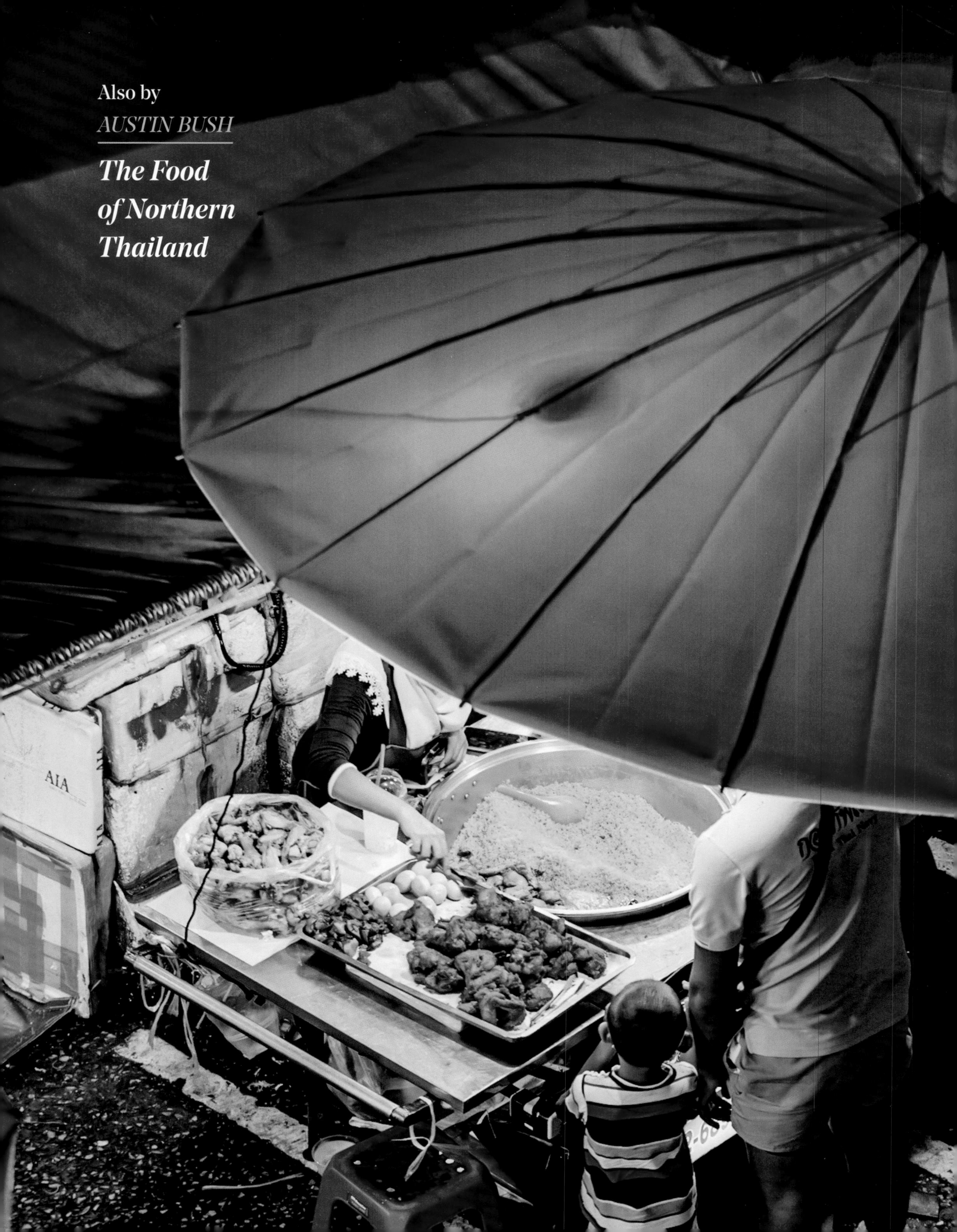

The Food of Southern Thailand

Written and
photographed by

AUSTIN BUSH

ILLUSTRATIONS BY CANDICE LIN

W. W. NORTON & COMPANY
Independent Publishers Since 1923

For information about permission to reproduce selections from this book, write to
Permissions, W. W. Norton & Company, Inc., 500 Fifth Avenue, New York, NY 10110

For information about special discounts for bulk purchases, please contact
W. W. Norton Special Sales at specialsales@wwnorton.com or 800-233-4830

Manufacturing by Imago
Book design by Toni Tajima
Production manager: Lauren Abbate

Library of Congress Cataloging-in-Publication Data available.

ISBN 978-0-393-54169-4

W. W. Norton & Company, Inc.
500 Fifth Avenue, New York, N.Y. 10110
www.wwnorton.com

W. W. Norton & Company Ltd.
15 Carlisle Street, London W1D 3BS

1 2 3 4 5 6 7 8 9 0

To all the
kind southerners

A vendor at Narathiwat's central market.

Contents

An Introduction to the Food of Southern Thailand

I have a rather shocking admission to make. In many, many visits—a total of several months that spanned more than three years—to southern Thailand to watch people cook, conduct interviews, do research, and take photos for this book, I never went to the beach.

Well, OK. Technically speaking, I did once.

One overcast morning, while on the island of Phuket, I rented a motorcycle and scaled hills; buzzed past Russian restaurants, seafood buffets, high-rise hotels, tour buses full of Chinese tourists, and billboards touting elephant shows; and briefly got stuck in traffic before reaching my destination, Kata Beach. I stepped off my bike and, wearing shoes and long pants, burdened with a massive bag full of camera gear, shuffled onto the sand and promptly felt out of place. I was probably there for ten minutes before I headed back to my hotel.

Admittedly, I'm not much of a beach guy. I didn't choose to write a book about the cuisine of southern Thailand so that I could stick my toes in the sand. I did it because the food is utterly unique and delicious, and because nobody else was writing about it.

That last part came as a surprise to me because in many ways, the food of southern Thailand fits the outside world's notion of Thai food. Revolving around intensely vibrant ingredients such as fire-truck-red chiles, orange Fanta–hued turmeric, and neon green bitter beans, it's incredibly colorful. It's also spicy: dishes pack a punch that comes not only from chiles but also from black pepper. There's a distinct emphasis on curries—everybody's favorite Thai dish. And, given southern Thailand's coastline, seafood and coconuts pop up a lot.

Yet if you've ever stayed at a resort or guesthouse in Thailand's south, it's unlikely you got to sample much of this. As I stood on Kata Beach that day, the food offerings were more Bangkok—or perhaps even more Boston, Berlin, or Beirut—than southern Thailand: fast-food chains, Chinese restaurants, kebab stalls. To understand southern Thai cuisine, I knew that I'd have to go deeper. Over the next few years, I bounded between big cities and sleepy provincial capitals, roadside stalls and restaurants, "floating" villages and rural homestays, markets, home kitchens, fishing ports, community groups, and libraries across

---

OPPOSITE: The lunch of a group of Buddhist monks, Trang.

the region. Not once, I am both proud and ashamed to say, was there a sunbathing session. But there was lots of amazing food.

■ □ ■ □ ■

I visited Thailand for the first time in 1998. I was an undergraduate linguistics student at the University of Oregon on an exchange program in Chiang Mai, in Thailand's north, and Luang Prabang, in Laos. The following year, I received a scholarship to study the Thai language at Chiang Mai University. I lived in Thailand for the next twenty-three years. I was based in Bangkok but always had a strong connection to the country's north, and when I had free time, I made every effort to visit that region, accumulating knowledge over two decades about its food and culture. I was drawn to the dishes and flavors of northern Thailand, but even a bigger part of what pulled me in was learning that Thai food is not one single entity. Just as we in the U.S. now know that dishes in Italy or France can vary tremendously from region to region, the same is true of Thailand. Indeed, I came to see that the variations between regional cuisines might be even greater in Thailand, where a fundamental staple like rice is cooked and eaten in completely different ways from north to south.

This interest culminated in 2018 with the release of my first book, *The Food of Northern Thailand*. Thanks to the buzz kicked off, in part, by my friend Andy Ricker's Pok Pok restaurants, northern Thai food was now on the radar of adventurous American cooks and eaters. Fans of Thai food clearly wanted to go deeper than green curry and phat Thai, and thanks to Andy and my book, home cooks and chefs in otherwise un-Thai places such as Colorado and Iceland were dry-roasting chiles and mincing pork for rustic southern Thai–style laap.

It was not long after *The Food of Northern Thailand* was published that I started to notice a low-level buzz around the cuisine of Thailand's southern region. In Bangkok, several new southern Thai restaurants had popped up, and arguably the city's toughest reservation was a restaurant doing a refined, upscale take on southern Thai cuisine. Jitlada, LA's (if not America's) most famous Thai restaurant, has its roots in Nakhon Si Thammarat, in southern Thailand. And the last time I was in New York, the city's most-talked-about new Thai restaurants all seemed to boast southern Thai menu items. I dug around and saw that there was virtually nothing written about the cuisine in English (and not a whole lot more in Thai). I saw yet another opportunity to share with the world the fact that Thai food runs deeper and takes more forms than most of us realize.

■ □ ■ □ ■

My approach to researching and writing is rooted in old-school journalism. I speak and read Thai fluently, and I take advantage of these skills to talk to people and to comb through books or the internet to uncover the ingredients, cooking techniques, and dishes that are unique to a place. I reach out to vendors, home cooks, restaurateurs, hawkers, academics, and writers. I interview these people and watch and record what they're cooking. Then I do my best to re-create these dishes at home. The recipes that stem from this process are not mine— rather, they are my effort to capture and share what the people of southern Thailand cook and eat. This dedication to journalistic documentation extends to the photographs of the dishes you see in this book, which I shot myself while on location in southern Thailand, not in a studio in the U.S. In doing my utmost to accurately record and share the dishes of southern Thailand, I hope to bring you with me beyond Kata Beach, past the well-worn ruts of the tourist trail, to the markets, stalls, home kitchens, and restaurants that lie just beyond. To a delicious, vibrant, full-flavored cuisine, and to the people who are keeping it alive.

The Roots and Influences of a Cuisine

A BRIEF HISTORY OF SOUTHERN THAILAND

The Malay Peninsula, the landmass that includes the region we know today as southern Thailand, has, for millennia, been a crossroads for Austronesians, Mon-Khmers, and Thais, as well as outside peoples, including the Chinese, South Asians, Europeans, Arabs, and Persians.

We don't know who the earliest people to have lived on the Malay Peninsula were, but they left behind some intriguing clues. Neolithic artifacts, in particular stone tools known in Thai as *khwaan faa*, "sky axes," have been found across the region. And the pottery, tools, hearths, food detritus, and human remains discovered in the so-called Lang Rongrian Cave, in Krabi Province in southern Thailand, which date back 27,000 to 38,000 years, are considered some of the oldest and most intact evidence of early human society in all of mainland Southeast Asia. The ancestors of those first inhabitants may have included hunter-gatherers such as the Mani (also known by the blanket Malay-language term *Orang Asli*, meaning "first people"). But with fewer than 1,000 of these people remaining in southern Thailand, in scattered groups in remote corners of Yala, Phatthalung, and Satun Provinces, their future is extremely precarious.

More sophisticated evidence of early society in the region has been found in the form of large ornamental brass drums, thought to be relics of the Dong Son, a culture based in what is present-day Vietnam between 300 BC and AD 200.

Loosely linked predominantly Mon-Khmer kingdoms dominated Southeast Asia from approximately AD 1 to AD 800. Archaeological evidence indicates that many of these cultures followed Hinduism, a faith imported by Indians who may have reached the area more than 2,000 years ago. In early Indian literature, Southeast Asia is referred to as *Suvarnabhumi*, meaning "Land of Gold," and it's possible that, in addition to religion, Indian traders also introduced the pepper plant to the region. The Greeks are thought to have visited Southeast Asia as long ago as the first century AD, with both *Periplus of the Erythrean Sea* and Ptolemy making references to "golden lands" located in the east. More reliable accounts left by Chinese traders indicate that as early as the third century AD. Southeast Asian cultures were conducting sea and transpeninsular land trade with outposts on the Malay Peninsula, name-checking at least ten different states located along the Gulf of Thailand.

The region's first expansive, long-standing, and influential civilization was Srivijaya, a Malay-Buddhist kingdom that ruled over parts of Southeast Asia, including much of the Malay Peninsula, from approximately AD 600 to AD 1400. Srivijaya was originally thought to have been based in Palembang, in modern-day Sumatra, Indonesia, but today that is debated; it likely had a number of capitals, one of which may have been Chaiya, located in what is present-day Surat Thani Province, in southern Thailand. Regardless, Srivijaya's general location between China and India meant that it was an important crossroads for trade, culture, and diplomacy. As ship and sailing technology improved, more boats were able to pass through the rough, narrow, pirate-infested Straits of Malacca, located between present-day Indonesia and the Malay Peninsula, rendering previous land routes across the peninsula increasingly obsolete and Srivijaya's control of the seas even more important. Srivijaya came to have an influence over ports on both sides of the Malay Peninsula, and it is thought that by the ninth century AD, its range extended as far north as Nakhon Pathom, located next door to Bangkok, in modern-day Thailand. Yet conflict with surrounding kingdoms keen to get a slice of trade led to a weakening of Srivijaya's virtual monopoly on sea routes, and thus its power, by the eleventh century.

The downfall of Srivijaya allowed for the ascent of Tambralinga, a Mon-Khmer kingdom based in Ligor, the modern-day city of Nakhon Sri Thammarat, in southern Thailand. Ligor had been a thriving maritime trade center for centuries; Hindu relics recovered in the area—among the oldest found in mainland Southeast Asia—suggest a long-standing relationship with India, and Chinese texts mention Tambralinga as early as 1001. In the post-Srivijaya power vacuum, Tambralinga's desirable location in the Gulf of Thailand became a point of conflict as Khmers, Malays, Burmese, Mons, and Indians sought to seize control of the lucrative sea trade conducted from the kingdom.

Tambralinga is also where ethnic Thais first enter the history of southern Thailand. The Thai people most likely originated in southern China, but by the middle of the thirteenth century, they had migrated as far south as the Malay Peninsula. Around this time, Tambralinga was battling with the Melayu Kingdom of Sumatra. This allowed Thais loyal to the Sukhothai Kingdom, in what is present-day northern Thailand, to seize power in Ligor and semi-linked states elsewhere along the peninsula. Eventually, King Ramkhamhaeng of Sukhothai, in northern Thailand, declared rule over Nakhon Sri Thammarat (as Ligor came to be known by the Thais) and, by extension, its vassal states, which reached as far south as the present-day Malaysia. This, more or less, established the southernmost extents of the Thai people and nation that exist today.

It was during this period that religion started to spread along lines that also still exist on the Malay Peninsula. By the middle of the thirteenth century, Nakhorn Sri Thammarat had become an important center for the spread of Theravada Buddhism, a transit point from which monks from Sri Lanka would bring the religion to states north, west, and east. Ships from Arabia and Persia had visited Southeast Asia as early as the seventh century, bringing aspects of their culture (including food) with them, but Islam didn't gain a significant foothold until the early fifteenth century, when a powerful, well-connected Hindu-Malay ruler of Malacca, in what is present-day Malaysia, converted to Islam. Over the subsequent centuries, Islam spread across Southeast Asia, including south to Indonesia and north along the Malay Peninsula, where it was adopted by smaller, predominantly ethnic Malay states.

The next significant Thai kingdom, Ayuthaya, was, to date, Thailand's most cosmopolitan and outward looking. Ayuthaya established diplomatic relations with Portugal—the first between the Thais and a European country—in 1511; it is thought that the Portuguese introduced chiles to Thailand around this time. With Japan, China, Persia, Arabia, and other European countries also clamoring to do business with Ayuthaya, the kingdom was able to assert more control over Nakhon Sri Thammarat, Phatthalung, Songkhla, Pattani, and other port states along the Malay Peninsula, effectively extending the range and influence of the Thai people.

Distance, diplomacy, conflict, and culture allowed the smaller vassal states of the Malay Peninsula to retain varying degrees of autonomy in the centuries that followed. But in the late nineteenth century, a Bangkok-based king appointed local commissioners to govern the territories that fell within the Thai sphere, thus centralizing power and leading to the end of semi-hereditary rule in these states. Around this time, colonial powers also influenced important political and territorial changes in Southeast Asia. On the Malay Peninsula, the Anglo-Siamese Treaty of 1909 ceded the predominately Malay-Muslim sultanate of Pattani to Siam (as Thailand was then known), and Kedah and Kelantan and other sultanates to British Malaya, creating the border with Malaysia that exists to this day.

THE GEOGRAPHY OF SOUTHERN THAILAND

- The region culturally and geographically known as southern Thailand begins approximately 300 miles south of Bangkok, in Chumphon Province, and extends south approximately 500 miles, spanning 27,303 square miles of land.

- Southern Thailand is generally considered to be comprised of fourteen provinces, which are home to a total of around 10 million people.

- The region has two international borders, one in the northwest, with Myanmar, and the other in the south, with Malaysia.

- Southern Thailand spans more than 1,200 miles of coastline across two distinct coasts, the Andaman Sea coast to the west and the Gulf of Thailand coast to the east.

- The Andaman Sea coast side is rugged, taking the form of mountain ranges that sometimes terminate in jagged limestone formations, while the eastern side is home to river valleys that flow to the Gulf of Thailand.

- The Isthmus of Kra, part of which is located in Rayong Province, is the narrowest point on the Malay Peninsula.

- Forests cover around 25 percent of southern Thailand.

- Southern Thailand is subject to a tropical monsoon climate and is influenced by three different monsoon systems, which means that the region has only two distinct seasons, wet and dry.

In 1932, a coup led to the end of absolute monarchy in Siam. In short time, the formerly semi-independent states along the Malay Peninsula were designated provinces and quietly integrated into the country that had recently been renamed Thailand. The exception to this was in the country's deep south, where people had lived with considerable autonomy for centuries. In the provinces of Pattani, Narathiwat, and Yala, where the vast majority of inhabitants were ethnic Malay, spoke a Malay dialect, and followed Islam, there was resistance to Bangkok-based rule. This sentiment was compounded when fascist-leaning Thai governments enacted policies meant to instill so-called traditional Thai values in the region's inhabitants, such as allegiance to the monarchy and Buddhism, and enforced the use of Thai language and dress while also outlawing Islamic-based education and law. The arrest of an influential local leader in Pattani in 1948 sparked protests, effectively kick-starting an insurgency that continues to this day. Since 2004, the beginning of the most recent phase of unrest, bombings, assassinations, drive-by shootings, and military and civilian raids have caused the deaths of more than 7,000 people. Although separatist groups have claimed responsibility for some of the violence, there is no clear, unified movement for autonomy, and both locals and other analysts note that insurgents seem more motivated by chaos and unrest, with local criminal elements also playing a role. Today the conflict is considered one of the longest-running and deadliest in Asia.

THE BUILDING BLOCKS OF SOUTHERN THAI FOOD

The food of southern Thailand is unmistakably Thai, yet it also exhibits countless foreign influences, coalescing in a cuisine with more blurred lines than clear divisions.

The cuisine's Thai roots can be seen most clearly in its love of curries and soups—indigenous cooking techniques that predate stir-frying or deep-frying. Indeed, the archetypical southern restaurant is the curry stall, where nearly all the day's offerings are served from pots. Another important indigenous cooking method is used for naam chup, dips made by pounding herbs and seasonings—inevitably including chiles—to a coarse paste with a mortar and pestle. Roughly equivalent to a Mexican salsa, naam chup run the gamut from dry to watery, and they are always paired with rice and raw and/or cooked vegetables.

Turmeric, native to South and Southeast Asia, makes frequent and liberal appearances in the southern Thai kitchen. The vibrantly colored fresh root—not the dried powder—is included in most southern Thai–style curry pastes, giving dishes a subtle, almost mustard-like aroma and a warm yellow or orange hue. Southern Thais absolutely adore their chiles, but these are a relatively new ingredient that weren't introduced until the sixteenth century. Peppercorns, with origins in South Asia, are also beloved, and they have been used for much longer. They are typically dried, but some dishes benefit from the vibrant, ginger-like buzz of fresh green peppercorns.

The role of coconut in southern Thai cuisine can't be understated: the rich meat from mature coconuts is grated and squeezed to make coconut milk, cream, and oil, or toasted and added to dishes; the water from young coconuts is drunk or sometimes added to sweet dishes; and coconut palms are tapped for their sap, which is made into sugar.

Distinctively pungent indigenous ingredients such as bitter beans (also known as "stink beans") almost singlehandedly define the cuisine for Thais from other parts of the country, who tend to associate southern Thai dishes with unabashedly bold flavors. And fresh herbs, many with names utterly unfamiliar beyond the region, and boasting flavors that range from sweet to astringent, are eaten at almost every meal.

A discussion of native ingredients in southern Thailand must also extend to the seafood that the largely coastline-bound inhabitants can access. This includes fish, of course, but it also means shellfish, cephalopods, and even various kinds of edible seaweed. Southern Thais have found numerous ways to extend the life of these items, from sun-drying to salt preservation and fermentation. Thailand's south is also home to an entire repertoire of condiments and seasonings made from preserved seafood—think fish sauce, shrimp paste, and more—some of which form the basis of its most well-known dishes.

The south is the most mountainous part of Thailand, and its jungly, rugged landscape has long been a source of scavenged and hunted edible ingredients such as wild ferns, mushrooms, game, and fruit, although these are seen less frequently nowadays in the southern Thai kitchen.

Perhaps the most fundamentally southern Thai ingredient of all is rice. It's thought that rice has been grown in Thailand's south since prehistoric times, and today the southern province of Phatthalung has earned a reputation as one of the country's premier rice-growing areas.

In terms of foreign influences on southern Thailand's food, the Chinese have probably had the largest impact. They were one of the first groups to trade with the early inhabitants of Thailand's south, and it was most likely later Chinese immigrants who introduced cooking techniques such as wok- and deep-frying, and who popularized ingredients such as pork, chicken, and duck, now almost entirely assimilated into Thai cuisine. The Chinese also introduced a variety of noodle dishes, today the basis of much of the region's restaurant and street food. And Chinese-origin condiments such as soy sauce are commonplace, if not staples, in much of southern Thailand. Additionally, in places such as Phuket and Trang, where Chinese immigrants and locals mingled, an entirely new cuisine emerged. Known as Baba or Peranakan, this combination of indigenous and Chinese ingredients, flavors, and techniques has resulted in unique and emblematic dishes such as muu hawng, pork braised in soy sauce, garlic, and black pepper.

Ingredients, dishes, and cooking techniques from the Islamic world have also had a massive impact on the culinary landscape of southern Thailand. The region's links with the Middle East are thought to go as far back as the seventh century, when outposts on the Malay Peninsula conducted trade with ships from Arabia and Persia. Today Thailand shares a border with predominantly Muslim Malaysia, although the two territories were not always so explicitly distinct. Centuries of exchange with Muslim cultures brought dishes such as satay, biryani, griddled flatbreads, and rich, meaty curries—dishes with roots in places as distant as the Middle East but that nowadays are more or less considered part of the greater Thai repertoire.

THE FLAVORS AND FRAGRANCES OF SOUTHERN THAILAND

With ample access to the sea, it's not surprising that the people of Thailand's south love salt. In many of the region's dishes, this salty flavor stems from preservation techniques used to extend the life of highly perishable seafood—as in salted fish or fish- and seafood-based condiments—but often it simply comes from the (typically generous) addition of salt. It's always there, a constant reminder of the ocean, and perhaps the most beloved flavor in the cuisine.

In a country of spicy regional cuisines, the food of southern Thailand is hands-down the spiciest. Vast amounts of chiles, dried or fresh (or dried *and* fresh), go into the herb pastes that are the basis for many curries and other dishes. Fresh chiles often feature in stir-fries, salads, soups, and chile-based dips. But in addition to the full-frontal assault of chiles, the southern Thais also like the subtler, lingering, ginger-like burn of black pepper, a sensation they describe as *phet rawn*, meaning, approximately, "hot spicy."

Southern Thais also love tart flavors. The region's signature dish is, arguably, *kaeng som*, literally "tart soup," a dish to which southern Thais will add a squeeze of lime and a spoonful or two of tamarind pulp, along with the other already mouth-puckeringly sour ingredients such as pickled bamboo or sour fruit. One unique source of sour flavor in southern Thailand is asam fruit, related to the mangosteen, which is sliced and dried before being added to soups.

The traditional source of umami in southern Thai cuisine is shrimp paste. It is present in most of the region's herb pastes and is sometimes added to stir-fries and rice dishes. But its rounded, savory flavor is typically a background note rather than a headliner. These days, additional umami flavor may come from the MSG-laden seasonings or bouillon cubes.

It's fair to say that, in general, bitter pops up more in Thai cuisine than it does in the U.S. or Europe, but bitter flavors aren't particularly common in southern Thai dishes. When that astringent, mouth-puckering flavor is there, it typically stems from herbs or vegetables.

A bit of sugar is often added to dishes to provide balance, but it's used conservatively, and sweet flavors are more likely to come from the addition of fruit or the natural sweetness of ingredients such as coconut cream. The exception to this is in the Muslim communities near the Malaysian border, where some savory dishes are seasoned with so much sugar that they can be almost candy-like in their sweetness.

Aroma is a very important aspect of Thai cooking, and various ingredients are added to dishes to ensure that they smell as well as taste good. Generally fresh herbs are the source of these fragrances. Aromatics such as galangal and lemongrass are frequently pounded up in curry pastes, and herbs such as the peppery leaves of the cumin plant or the sweet, green wild betel leaf are added, whole or sliced, to curries, soups, and stir-fries.

Southern Thais are particularly fanatical about what I can only describe as pungent flavors and fragrances. There's an entire repertoire of pale green, pod-like ingredients—bitter beans, krathin seeds, djenkol beans—that are distinctive to the region. Talk to anyone from another part of the country, and they will inevitably associate such ingredients with southern Thai cooking.

Apart from black peppercorns, dried spices feature occasionally, not commonly in southern Thai dishes, the exception being in Muslim communities, where ingredients such as cumin, coriander, and fenugreek play an important role.

GLOSSARY

The Ingredients That Shape Southern Thai Food

To aid you on your journey to cooking like a southern Thai, I've created this glossary, which spans ingredients ranging from the relatively familiar to the deeply regional.

If you have access to an Asian grocery store or a well-stocked supermarket with ingredients such as fresh lemongrass, galangal, and turmeric; a selection of fresh and dried chiles; shrimp paste; and non-Japanese soy sauce, you should have no problem in making most of the recipes in this book. For more obscure ingredients, good online sources include ImportFood.com, TempleofThai.com, H Mart, and, yes, Amazon.com.

If there's a substitution that I feel doesn't compromise the integrity of a dish, I've mentioned it in the recipes as well as below. But for many less-common ingredients, especially southern Thailand's fresh herbs and vegetables, there simply aren't alternatives.

ANNATTO, ACHIOTE SEED
kham ngoh, kham saet, dawk chaat
คำเงาะ, คำแสด, ดอกชาด
Also used in some Latin American cuisines, the dried seed of this tree gives dishes a bright red hue.

ASIAN PENNYWORT
bai bua bok
ใบบัวบก
Resembling a larger, rounder, paler four-leaf clover, this herb has a sweet, slightly astringent "green" flavor. It's standard on the trays of herbs that accompany southern Thai meals, and it is also used in salads, soups, and curries.

Bai man puu
ใบมันปู
The young buds of this member of the spurge family (with no colloquial English-language name) have a waxy appearance, a green/purple hue, and a slightly tart, rich flavor. They are often served as part of the platters of herbs and vegetables that accompany southern Thai meals.

Bai phaa hohm   ใบพาโหม

A member of the madder family of flowering plants (also with no colloquial English-language name), this finger-length, pale green leaf adds a pungent aroma to southern Thai–style rice salads.

BITTER BEANS, STINK BEANS, PETAI

sataw, luuk taw   สะตอ, ลูกตอ

The seeds of the Parkia tree are bright to pale green and almond-sized, with a pungent, almost garlic-like flavor and odor. For more on bitter beans, see page 216.

BOUILLON POWDER

sup kawn   ซุปก้อน

MSG- and salt-laden stock cubes or powders, such as those made by Knorr and RosDee, have become an increasingly common pantry ingredient in southern Thailand.

BUDU

naam buuduu   น้ำบูดู

This salty, moderately filtered, fermented fish–based condiment is common in Thailand's Muslim deep south. The standard is a relatively clear fish sauce–like liquid, but some recipes call for a thicker, less-filtered version (known in Thai as *naam buuduu khon*, "thick budu"). For more on budu, see page 279.

BUTTERFLY PEA FLOWERS

dawk anchan   ดอกอัญชัน

The resplendently purple yet flavorless and odorless fresh or dried flowers of this vine are used to give some foods—in particular, Thai-style sweets and rice dishes—a blue hue.

CHILES

The fresh chiles available in the U.S. can be much hotter and much less fragrant than those in Thailand, so proceed with caution. Some Mexican dried chiles serve as excellent substitutes for their Thai counterparts.

Dried Chiles

- **TINY SPICY DRIED CHILES**
  phrik khii nuu haeng, dii plii haeng
  พริกขี้หนูแห้ง ดัปลี้แห้ง
  These small (less than 1 inch long) dried chiles are pounded up and used as condiments or added to many southern Thai herb pastes.

- **MEDIUM SPICY DRIED CHILES**
  phrik haeng   พริกแห้ง
  Although there's some crossover in size with their smaller counterparts (they're generally around 2 inches long), these spicy chiles are used in herb pastes or to garnish dishes. Dried chiles de árbol make a reasonable substitute.

- **LARGE MILD DRIED CHILES**
  phrik chii faa haeng, dii plii mueang haeng
  พริกชี้ฟ้าแห้ง, ดีปลีเมืองแห้ง
  Usually at least 3 inches long, mild-tasting dried chiles are an essential ingredient in Thai herb pastes. Guajillo and Puya chiles aren't too far off. Those used in southern Thailand, especially in the deep south, are relatively squat and around 2 inches long, with thick skin; chiles costeño are a good substitute for these.

Fresh Chiles

- **TINY SPICY FRESH CHILES**
  phrik khii nuu suan   พริกขี้หนูสวน
  With a Thai name that translates as "mouse shit chiles," these red and green chiles (often less than ½ inch long) are the spiciest—and most fragrant—in the southern Thai larder, used in stir-fries and herb pastes. They aren't generally available outside the region; substitute the same amount of the tiniest, spiciest chiles you can find.

- **MEDIUM SPICY FRESH CHILES**
  phrik nak   พริกหนัก
  From around 1 inch to 1½ inches long, these red and green chiles are the workhorses of the southern Thai kitchen, used in just about every way possible, from spicing up soups to pounded into herb pastes. Chiles de árbol function well as a substitute.

- **LARGE MILD FRESH CHILES**
  phrik chii faa, dii plii mueang sot
  พริกชี้ฟ้า, ดีปลีเมืองสด
  These mild, long (around 3 to 4 inches), slender, thick-skinned chiles, both dark green and red, are commonly sliced and used as garnishes or, very occasionally, in curry pastes.

• LARGE MILD FRESH PALE GREEN CHILES

phrik yuak, dii plii yuak
พริกหยวก, ดีปลี่หยวก

Very mild in flavor, with a pale green hue, a chubby shape, and thin, slightly wrinkled skin, these chiles are common in Muslim areas of the deep south. Hungarian wax peppers are similar in appearance and flavor.

CHINESE CHIVES

kui chaai　กุยช่าย

These flat, dark green, grass-like leaves have a slightly astringent but sweet flavor. They're used in stir-fries and are commonly served in or alongside fried noodle dishes.

CHINESE KEY

krachaai　กระชาย

Also known as fingerroot, lesser ginger, or wild ginger, this rhizome is native to Southeast Asia. It takes the form of slender, pale yellow fingers that can be up to 4 inches long, with a taste and aroma like mild ginger.

CILANTRO

phak chii　ผักชี

The leaves of this herb, also known as coriander, are used as a garnish, while the roots are added to soups and stocks or included in herb pastes. The dried seeds, most often known as coriander seeds, find their way into various dishes and some herb pastes.

COCONUT MILK

kathi, naam the, naam thi
กะทิ, น้ำเท่, น้ำทิ

Coconut milk, an important southern Thai ingredient, is the liquid squeezed from the grated flesh of mature coconuts, not the clear, sweet water found inside young green coconuts. For more on coconut milk, see page 134.

DEEP-FRYING FLOUR

paeng thawt krawp　แป้งทอดกรอบ

A combination of wheat flour, tapioca starch, and seasonings (often including MSG), this flour is used to batter deep-fried items. Gogi is the most popular brand in Thailand.

DRIED ASAM FRUIT

som khaek　ส้มแขก

Related to the mangosteen, this fruit is native to Malaysia and Thailand. Sliced and dried, with a deep-red, leathery appearance, it gives dishes, in particular those in the deep south border regions, a sharp, aromatically tart flavor. Tamarind paste functions as a substitute.

DRIED TAMARIND PULP

makhaam piak, som khaam piak
มะขามเปียก, ส้มขามเปียก

Tamarind pulp is the fruit of the tamarind tree that has been dried and compressed into dark, sticky blocks; it generally includes seeds and coarse strands. To use it, it's diluted in hot water and the solids strained out and discarded; the thick liquid that results provides dishes with a tart, subtly sweet flavor and a distinct aroma.

FISH SAUCE

naam plaa　น้ำปลา

The liquid extracted from salted and fermented anchovies, this condiment adds a salty, savory flavor to many dishes. If you are outside of Thailand, avoid the cheapest brands, which are made from multiple "pressings" and can include seasonings and preservatives; instead, simply choose the most expensive bottle of Thai fish sauce you can find.

GALANGAL

khaa, hua khaa　ข่า, หัวข่า

A pale white/off-pink root with a pleasing aroma and a flavor that some describe as "soapy," this aromatic is often compared to ginger, for which it should not be substituted. It's added to broths and soups and is almost always present in southern Thai herb pastes. Mature galangal is the standard, but occasionally tenderer, more fragrant young galangal is called for. If you don't have access to the young stuff, be sure to slice mature galangal very thin, as it can be quite dry and woody. Avoid dried galangal, which retains little, if any, of its vibrant, fresh scent.

GARLIC

krathiam, hua thiam　กระเทียม, หัวเทียม

These days, large cloves of so-called Chinese garlic are the norm in Thailand, but for some of the recipes here, I call for the much smaller (sometimes only ¼ inch long), more fragrant Thai garlic cloves, which are used skin and all.

GREEN MANGOES

mamuang priaw, mamuang man
มะม่วงเปรี้ยว, มะม่วงมัน

Green mangoes—either tart and unripe or semisweet and semi-ripe—are used in a handful of salad-like dishes in southern Thailand.

GRAY MULLET

plaa krabawk, plaa bawk
ปลากระบอก, ปลาบอก

This fish, which lives in brackish water and has tender white flesh, is a favorite in southern Thailand. It is used in soups, grilled, and deep-fried.

KINGFISH

plaa insii ปลาอินทรี

A member of the mackerel family that averages around 3 feet long, with dark, slightly oily, firm flesh, kingfish is used fresh in a variety of soups, curries, and stir-fries in Thailand's south and is also salt-preserved.

Krathin, luuk taw bao กระถิน, ลูกตอเบา

The bright green, tiny, tender, immature leaves and seeds of this plant, which has no colloquial English name, have a pungent, almost garlic-like taste and odor. They are often eaten raw, as an optional ingredient, in or with noodle dishes.

LEMONGRASS

takhrai, khrai ตะไคร้, ไคร

These coarse stalks are used in soups and herb pastes to provide a citrusy aroma. Avoid dried lemongrass, which has little, if any, of the plant's vibrant, fresh scent.

To prepare lemongrass, peel away and discard the one or two outermost coarse, less fragrant layers. If using in a curry or herb paste, chop off and discard the hard end "cap" and thinly slice only the off-purple/white lower part of the stalk; discard the woody green remainder. If using lemongrass in a soup, cut off and discard the upper woody green part of the stalk and bruise the lower section with a pestle or the handle of a knife.

LONG PEPPER

diiplii ดีปลี

A dried spice in the pepper family, long pepper has a milder, sweeter aroma than black pepper. It's very occasionally used by Muslims in soups in Thailand's deep south.

MAKRUT LIME

makruut, luuk kruut มะกรูด, ลูกกรูด

Also known by the name kaffir lime (which is now usually considered a perjorative term), this lime-sized, knobbly, aromatic green citrus fruit features frequently in the southern Thai kitchen. The leaves are used in soups to add a subtle citrus fragrance, while the zest is sometimes used in herb pastes. The flesh is not generally used.

MELINJO

phak miang, bai miang, phak liang, bai liang
ผักเหมียง, ใบเหมียง, ผักเหลียง, ใบเหลียง

This evergreen tree is native to Asia. Its pale green, tender, slightly waxy young leaves are used fresh in soups and stir-fries in southern Thailand. The leaves don't have a great deal of flavor but, rather, contribute a subtle richness and pleasant mouthfeel that Thais refer to as *man*. Spinach, Swiss chard, or, best of all, beet greens, work as an approximate substitute.

MONOSODIUM GLUTAMATE (MSG)

phong chuu rot, paeng waan
ผงชูรส, แป้งหวาน

This seasoning gives dishes an umami, or round, meaty flavor. The Ajinomoto brand has a near monopoly in Thailand.

Most contemporary research has indicated that small amounts of MSG have no negative impact (the so-called "Chinese restaurant syndrome") on diners. That said, its ubiquity and overuse in Thailand has led to disparate dishes having an eerily similar flavor.

NIPA PALM VINEGAR

naam som jaak น้ำส้มจาก

Used only occasionally in southern Thailand, nipa palm vinegar is common in the Philippines, where it's known as *sukang sasa* or *sukang nipa*. For more about it, see page 307.

NONI LEAVES

bai yaw ใบยอ

The coarse, dark green, hand-sized leaves of the noni tree are sometimes added to khaao yam, southern Thai–style rice salads, to give the rice a fragrant aroma and a dark hue.

NOODLES

- **FRESH THIN ROUND RICE NOODLES**
khanom jiin, nom jiin
ขนมจีน, หนมจีน
These noodles, a breakfast staple in southern Thailand, are made by extruding lengths of fermented rice batter into boiling water and are used fresh, never dried. They are generally not available outside Thailand, but fresh or dried bún (medium-gauge round Vietnamese-style rice noodles) make an approximate substitute.

- **THIN ROUND RICE NOODLES**
sen mii เส้นหมี่
Thin round rice threads, available both fresh and dried, and sometimes labeled rice vermicelli, are common in southern Thailand, used in both soups and stir-fries.

- **THIN FLAT RICE NOODLES**
sen lek เส้นเล็ก
Narrow flat rice noodles, both fresh and dried, feature in soups and stir-fries in southern Thailand.

- **ROUND YELLOW WHEAT NOODLES**
sen mii เส้นหมี่
Thick round ropes of wheat flour, available both dried and fresh, are used in a handful of Chinese-origin dishes. Outside of Thailand, they're often labeled yakisoba noodles.

PANDAN LEAF
bai toei ใบเตย
Also known as pandanus or screw pine, the arm's-length, coarse, dark green leaves of this tropical plant provide sweets, coconut milk, and rice with a subtle but distinct aroma that calls to mind commercial white bread. Like bay leaves, the leaves are not consumed. Avoid dried pandan leaf, which will have lost much of its fragrance.

PEA EGGPLANT
makhuea phuang, luuk khuea phuang
มะเขือพวง, ลูกเขือพวง
Round, crunchy, and slightly astringent, these pale green eggplants are often seen on the platters of fresh herbs and vegetables that accompany meals in the south, as well as in the shrimp paste–based dips that may accompany them.

PICKLED MUSTARD GREENS
phak kaat dawng ผักกาดดอง
Lacto-fermented mustard greens, which can range in flavor from sweet to tart, are an accompaniment to a handful of southern Thai dishes.

RICE

- **LONG-GRAIN RICE**
khaao suay ข้าวสวย
The staple carb of southern Thailand is long grains of rice that are cooked in boiling water. Outside Thailand, the most commonly available variety is jasmine rice, a higher-quality, more fragrant strain. For more on southern Thailand's long-grain rice, see page 209.

- **SANGYOD RICE**
khaao sangyot ข้าวสังข์หยด
This long-grain heirloom rice varietal, grown in Phatthalung Province, was the first Thai product to receive Geographic Indication (GI) status. It's gained an almost cult-like following for its wealth of nutrients and antioxidants and its low glycemic index. Long-grain red rice works as an approximate substitute. For more on Sangyod rice, see page 209.

- **STICKY RICE**
khaao niaw ข้าวเหนียว
These short, stocky, ivory-hued grains of rice, sometimes labeled glutinous or sweet rice, are cooked by steaming them over water, not by boiling them in water. In southern Thailand, sticky rice (including black sticky rice) is typically paired with certain snacks, such as fried chicken, or used in desserts.

RICE FLOUR, STICKY RICE FLOUR
paeng khaao jao, paeng khaao niaw
แป้งข้าวเจ้า, แป้งข้าวเหนียว
Fine flour ground from long-grain or sticky rice is the basis for many southern Thai sweets. As the volume of this ingredient can vary, it's essential to measure by weight.

SALT
kluea เกลือ
Thais generally use fine-grained iodized table salt. These recipes were all tested with fine table salt.

SHALLOTS

hawm daeng, hua hawm   หอมแดง, หัวหอม

Shallots are ubiquitous in southern Thai cooking, used in soups and nearly all herb pastes. The shallots found in Thailand are generally round, small (around 1 inch in diameter), and purple; seek out the smallest shallots available and go by weight, not number of shallots.

SHRIMP PASTE

kapi, khoei   กะปิ, เคย

Made from salted, fermented krill, shrimp paste is an important ingredient in southern Thai herb pastes, and it provides dishes with a savory flavor, a pleasantly funky aroma, and salt. For more on shrimp paste, see page 289.

SIAMESE CARDAMOM

look krawaan, look krawaan khaao
ลูกกระวาน, ลูกกระวานขาว

Resembling garbanzo beans, this dried spice is a member of the cardamom family. It has a subtly camphoraceous aroma and is used in spice mixtures and various dishes in southern Thailand's Muslim community. The pale green dried leaves are also used, sometimes labeled, incorrectly, as bay leaves. Regular cardamom seeds, green or black, aren't substitutes.

"SKEWERED SHRIMP"

kung siap   กุ้งเสียบ

These are medium-sized shrimp that have been skewered and smoked over coals until dried. They are an ingredient associated with Phuket, but are largely produced in neighboring Phang-Nga Province. If you can't find "skewered shrimp," go with the highest-quality dried shrimp available. For more on "skewered shrimp," see page 289.

SNAKE GOURD

buap   บวบ

Also known as angled luffa, this vegetable has a thick, pale green exterior with coarse ridges and an interior that's similar to zucchini. It's typically used in soups and stir-fries or parboiled and served with Thai-style dips.

SOY SAUCE

Healthy Boy brand soy sauce has a near monopoly in the export Thai soy sauce market, and it works just fine in these recipes. Avoid Japanese-style soy sauce, which has an entirely different flavor and aroma.

- **LIGHT SOY SAUCE**

  sii iw khaao   ซีอิ๊วขาว

  Also known as "white soy" or "light soy," this type of soy sauce has a watery consistency and a salty, savory flavor.

- **BLACK SOY SAUCE**

  sii iw dam   ซีอิ๊วดำ

  Black soy sauce has a relatively thick consistency and a sweet, slightly bitter flavor that comes from the addition of molasses and a long fermentation. It is sometimes known as dark soy sauce.

- **SWEET SOY SAUCE**

  sii iw waan   ซีอิ๊วหวาน

  This soy sauce has a thick consistency and a sweet flavor that comes from the addition of sugar and molasses.

SUGAR

- **PALM SUGAR**

  naam taan tanoht, naam phueng, naam phueng waen
  น้ำตาลโตนด, น้ำผึ้ง, น้ำผึ้งแว่น

  In southern Thailand, sugar is produced from a variety of palms, including nipa palms and coconut palms, but the most prized is that from sugar palms. Sold in silver dollar–sized disks bordered by dried sugar palm leaves, with a distinctly dark hue and a subtly sweet, earthy fragrance, the sweetener is unique to the region. Coconut palm sugar, however, available at Asian markets, can be used as a substitute. As the volume of this ingredient can vary, it's essential to measure by weight. For more on palm sugar, see page 221.

- **RAW CANE SUGAR**

  naam taan saai daeng   น้ำตาลทรายแดง

  Unrefined cane sugar is used in some southern Thai dishes, both for its dark color and its molasses-like flavor. It's also known as natural brown sugar, raw sugar, or whole cane sugar; Domino brand dark brown sugar can be used as a substitute.

- **ROCK SUGAR**

  naam taan kruat   น้ำตาลกรวด

  These crystal-like lumps of refined sugar are used in soups of Chinese origin for their flavor, which is slightly less sweet than most sugars.

TAI PLAA

tai plaa, phung plaa   ไตปลา, พุงปลา

This emblematically southern Thai condiment is made from salted, fermented fish offal. It has no colloquial English-language name; outside of Thailand, it's generally sold as tai plaa, or another variant on that spelling. Tai plaa is extremely salty and funky, and it generally needs to be simmered with aromatics and then strained before being used.

THAI CHILE JAM

naam phrik phao   น้ำพริกเผา

This relatively mild, oily, dried chile–based condiment, with origins in central Thailand, can also be used as a seasoning.

TURMERIC

khamin, khiimin   ขมิ้น, ขี้มิ้น

A finger-sized rhizome with a bright orange color; an astringent flavor; and a distinct, almost mustard-like fragrance, turmeric is a staple in the southern Thai kitchen. Fresh turmeric is common in soups and herb pastes, while the dried powder features in a handful of dishes cooked in southern Thailand's Muslim communities. Turmeric leaf is sometimes included on the platters of fresh vegetables and herbs that accompany southern Thai–style meals.

Another member of the turmeric family, white turmeric has a pale yellow color and a sweeter flavor. Peeled and sliced thin, it's sometimes served with Thai-style dips.

THREADFIN BREAM

plaa saai daeng   ปลาทรายแดง

This saltwater fish has a pink/red body and delicate white flesh. It's used a variety of ways, from soups to deep-fried dishes, in southern Thailand. Snapper and grouper aren't too far off in terms of flavor and texture.

TORCH GINGER FLOWERS

dawk daalaa   ดอกดาหลา

The fist-sized, firm, resplendently pink petals of this flower have a subtly tart flavor and fragrance. They are added to a handful of dishes, including southern Thai–style rice salads.

VEGETABLE FERN

phak kuut   ผักกูด

This edible fern grows in abundance during southern Thailand's rainy season, and it is used in salads and stir-fried or parboiled and served with Thai-style dips. Young fiddlehead ferns can be substituted.

VIETNAMESE CORIANDER

phak phaew   ผักแพว

The small, slender, teardrop-shaped green leaves of this herb have a strong aroma and sweet flavor that almost crosses over to licorice. They are sometimes seen on the platters of fresh herbs that accompany meals in the south.

WATER CELERY

phak chii lawm   ผักชีล้อม

Similar to Chinese celery, this pale green plant, with its crispy, hollow stem and jagged, pointed leaves, is similar in flavor and aroma to the slightly more intense Chinese celery. It is sliced thin and included in southern Thai–style rice salads, or sometimes served on the platters of fresh herbs and vegetables that accompany southern Thai dishes and meals. Italian parsley can function as a rough substitute.

WILD BETEL LEAVES

bai chaphluu   ใบชะพลู

The size of a child's hand, with a green hue and an almost crispy texture, these fragrant leaves are related to pepper, not betel. They are eaten raw, as part of the platter of herbs and vegetables that accompany southern Thai–style meals, or sliced thin and added to curries.

WING BEANS

thua phuu   ถั่วพู

Similar to green or French beans but with a light, frilly exterior, these beans are often served raw on the platters of herbs and vegetables that accompany Thai curries.

Cooking and Eating Like a Southern Thai

Just as you no doubt know what to do if presented with a box of Cheerios, a handful of strawberries, and a carton of milk, southern Thai cooks know what to do with a stalk of lemongrass before tossing it into a mortar, or at what stage to add makrut lime leaves to a soup or curry. Likewise, a southern Thai cook knows how sweet a bowl of kaeng som should taste, or that kaeng phung plaa doesn't require any sugar at all.

If this is your first time cooking southern Thai food, though, there's no need to be worried. I'm going to assume that you've never cooked with items such as lemongrass before, and will coach you through the steps to prep and use these ingredients.

Where things get more complicated is in the seasoning. A single southern Thai dish can encompass a variety of flavors—not to mention a handful of aromas and textures. Southern Thais cook by repeatedly tasting their dishes, tweaking the seasonings until they reach a junction of the flavors, aromas, and textures a dish should have, and the flavors, aromas, and textures that an individual cook prefers. For someone who grew up in southern Thailand, this is relatively easy—perhaps even intuitive. If you're cooking these dishes for the first time, it's a challenge, and written text isn't the ideal way to convey subtle differences among these elements.

The work-around I've found is to employ a combination of technology, guidance, and personal preference. As you'll see, I strongly encourage everybody who cooks from this book to buy a digital scale.

Although nobody in southern Thailand uses one, in my experience it's the best way to ensure that you're at least starting in the same ballpark as a southern Thai cook. With your ingredients properly weighed out, the next step is tasting. I've done my best to describe in detail the primary and secondary flavors (and aromas) of every dish. Aim for these while also keeping in mind your own preferences. If you don't like sugar, for example, it's fine to use a bit less; if you're not a fan of heat, use fewer chiles. As long as you adhere, broadly, to the balance of flavors I've described, you'll have a dish that succeeds. This type of customization is essentially cooking southern Thai–style—that is, dipping in and out of the dish, evaluating and reassessing seasonings until you reach a balance of the flavors and aromas associated with the particular dish and a taste that makes you happy.

Using a Granite Mortar and Pestle

Curry pastes, finely ground mixtures of herbs, spices, and seasonings, are the basis for many southern Thai dishes. Traditionally these were made via pounding the ingredients together with a granite mortar and pestle. These days, however, the average southern Thai does not have the time to pound curry pastes by hand. Nor, frankly, do southern Thai restaurateurs, who rely on food processors and blenders, or commercially produced curry pastes.

So why am I asking you to break out a heavy

granite mortar and pestle set and embark upon the noisy, messy, time-consuming task of pounding herbs and spices if the locals don't do it? For one, if you're cooking these recipes outside southern Thailand, it's unlikely you'll have access to a market vendor selling a variety of herb pastes, so you don't have a choice. But above all, I'd argue that pounding herbs with a mortar and pestle, mashing, blending, and emulsifying the ingredients rather than processing them results in a superior texture and fragrance. It's also a great way to become familiar with the characteristics of ingredients such as lemongrass, galangal, fresh turmeric, chile, and shrimp paste, the building blocks of southern Thai cuisine.

Thais have a very specific way of using a mortar and pestle. To minimize splashing and to ensure that the ingredients are ground and distributed properly, they generally start with the dried chiles, often with a pinch of salt to aid in the grinding process. Next go in the predominantly coarse, woody, dry ingredients such as lemongrass and galangal. These are followed by the relatively coarse but slightly more "wet" ingredients such as makrut lime zest or leaves, fresh chiles, and/or fresh turmeric. After these go in the shallots and garlic. And lastly, to bring it all together, shrimp paste.

Place a damp dish towel underneath your mortar to minimize noise, to prevent it from shifting, and to lessen the chance that you'll damage your countertop or floor (in southern Thailand, curries are almost always pounded while the cook is sitting, cross-legged, on the ground). Use a spoon to scrape the ingredients from the sides of the mortar and pestle as you work. And, perhaps most important, don't be afraid to put your tools to work! Using a mortar and pestle the Thai way is more about pounding than grinding.

Cooking with Coconuts

Coconuts make their way into a huge variety of dishes in southern Thailand, in numerous forms. In this book, the word *coconut* almost always refers to mature coconuts, that is, those with a hard, shaggy, brown exterior; firm meat; and little or no liquid inside (if a recipe requires immature coconuts—those with the thick green shells, tender meat, and sweet juice—that is made explicit).

Before the meat of a coconut is toasted and added to a dish, or squeezed of its fat to make coconut milk, it must be grated. Nowadays in Thailand, this is done with electric contraptions that process the meat into almost needle-like thin shreds. But in the past it was done with a coconut "rabbit," a manual, stool-like contraption fronted with sharp metal teeth. It's possible to find handheld Thai-style graters, and these are what you should seek out if you plan on shredding coconut for sweets or for toasting (for these purposes, a Western-style box grater will generally result in strands of coconut that are too thick). When making coconut milk, rather than grating the meat by hand, which is time-consuming, I suggest using a blender or food processor to blitz chunks of coconut meat.

Despite being one of the most fundamental ingredients in the southern Thai kitchen, coconut milk is

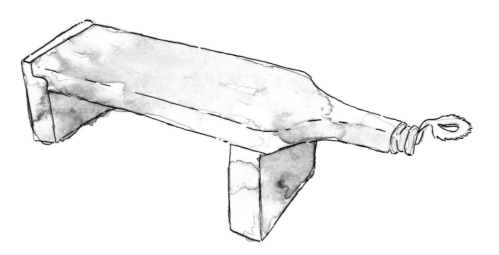

also hands-down the ficklest. Freshly pressed coconut milk can vary immensely in richness and quality, and it is extremely volatile, going off in hours, while UHT or canned coconut milk never quite behaves like the fresh stuff, and it needs to be diluted as well. Not to mention the fact that there are, practically speaking, three different types of coconut milk: thin coconut milk, thick coconut milk, and coconut cream. Additionally, the way coconut milk is used in southern Thailand can vary greatly. In certain curries, one must cook the coconut milk until the oil "cracks" or separates (something that, frustratingly, doesn't always happen if using canned or UHT coconut milk), while for other dishes, that is not done. I've made an effort to be as clear about this as possible in the recipes. Refer to page 134 for details on the different types of coconut milk and how to prepare them, from both fresh coconuts and the boxed stuff, if that's all you have access to.

Cooking with Chiles

Southern Thai food is undeniably spicy, and the chiles used to impart that heat take a variety of forms (both fresh and dried), colors (from bright red to pale green), sizes (from the size of your pinky fingernail to the length of your hand), and names. Because many of these chiles aren't available outside of Southeast Asia, and to avoid getting too bogged down in Thai language names, in these recipes I've opted to describe chiles in terms of broad parameters: size, freshness, and heat. For the Thai names of the chiles and, if appropriate, substitutions, refer to the Glossary.

It's worth noting that in my experiences in cooking with fresh chiles in the U.S., I've found them *much* spicier (and far less fragrant) than their counterparts in Thailand.

Cooking with Fresh Turmeric

Turmeric, the fresh rhizome, not the dried powder, is one of the most ubiquitous ingredients in the southern Thai kitchen. It's also one of the messiest. Fresh turmeric will stain all it comes in contact with—your hands, cutting board, knife, countertop, everything. Consider wearing latex gloves when prepping fresh turmeric. Likewise, you should be wary about exposing your favorite knife to turmeric, as the yellow stains and the sticky sap are almost impossible to remove (in my kitchen in Bangkok, I had a cheap but sharp knife that I used specifically for turmeric). You've been warned.

Folding Banana Leaves

Many southern Thai sweets and some savory dishes are served or steamed in banana leaf wrappers. In addition to making convenient (and environmentally friendly) packaging, banana leaves also lend these dishes a subtle aroma. Folding banana leaves properly involves a fair bit of experience and muscle memory, and the folds can be hard to describe via words, so for recipes that require them, I've included step-by-step illustrations.

In southern Thailand, banana leaves are ubiquitous and cheap. Elsewhere you may only have access to frozen banana leaves, which are limp and/or slimy when defrosted. If you do have access to fresh banana leaves, before folding them, wipe them clean and make any stiff leaves pliable by holding them a few inches above a flame for a second or two.

Substitutions

In my effort to cover as much ground as possible, some of the recipes in this book include ingredients that are not generally available outside southern Thailand. The good news is that I've kept those recipes to a minimum, and if you have access to a relatively well-stocked Southeast Asian market, one with items such as fresh turmeric, lemongrass, and fresh coconuts, you should be able make most of the dishes in this book. When there's a substitute that doesn't compromise the unique flavors, aromas, or textures of a dish, I've referred to it in the recipe and included it in the Glossary.

Investing in a few specific kitchen tools—both Thai-specific and otherwise—will make things easier for you on your journey to cook like a southern Thai.

Digital Scale

First and foremost, I encourage readers to take the distinctly un–southern Thai step of purchasing a digital scale. Because nearly all the ingredients in this book can vary in size, weight, not volume, is really the only way to ensure some element of consistency. The flavors of these ingredients can, of course, vary, but starting with weight as a baseline and working toward the flavor profiles described here is the best way I've found to re-create these dishes. As such, in this book, I've listed all weights in grams, which typically refer to ingredients before they're peeled, etc., unless otherwise stated.

Mortar and Pestle

Among the more traditional—and essential—southern Thai cooking tools you should consider purchasing is a granite mortar and pestle. Besides being the best way to make the herb- and spice-based pastes that are the basis of so many dishes, these are also handy for tasks such as crushing garlic or chiles and grinding dried spices.

Seek out a set that's carved from granite, rather than one made from compressed cement (and note that wood and/or clay mortar and pestle sets are meant for pounding Thai-style salads, not herb pastes). Look for a mortar with an opening that's approximately 6 inches in diameter; anything smaller than this is impractical, while anything larger will be too heavy, discouraging frequent use.

Wok

Stir-frying and deep-frying are commonplace cooking techniques in southern Thailand, and a wok is the ideal tool for both. A wok about 12 inches in diameter is big enough for most recipes in this book without being too unwieldy in a small kitchen. If you do buy a wok, you'll also want to pick up a wok spatula and perhaps a wire skimmer. Also known as a spider, a skimmer is handy for deep-frying and for procedures such as parboiling noodles.

A new wok will need to be "seasoned" with oil; there are many, many videos on YouTube that describe how to do this simple process.

Chinese-Style Steamer

While only a few of the savory recipes in this book are cooked by steaming, nearly all the sweet recipes are prepared this way. A stainless steel or aluminum Chinese-style steamer, with stacked inserts studded with holes, is cheap and convenient, and it allows for consistent steaming. You can improvise steam cooking with a large saucepan and a sieve suspended over simmering water, but as much of the steam will escape without a tight lid, cooking times can vary. Avoid bamboo steamers, which tend to be overpriced and will not last as long.

Thai-Style Sticky Rice Steaming Equipment

If you're going to cook sticky rice, it's worth investing in a Thai-style sticky rice steaming set, which takes the form of a tall aluminum pot and a cone-like basket woven from strips of bamboo. The height of the pot keeps the rice properly elevated above the boiling water (sticky rice that's too close to the steam will turn to mush), while the basket, when topped with a damp tea towel and saucepan lid, keeps the rice in the almost-pressurized environment required for it to steam properly. If you don't have access to these tools, sticky rice can be steamed using cheesecloth and a Chinese-style steamer, or, with even more tweaking and trial and error, a saucepan, sieve, and damp tea towel.

Grill

Although the grill isn't particularly associated with the southern Thai kitchen, it is common (and distinctly southern Thai) to grill fish or other seafood over coals before adding them to soups or curries. The traditional Thai stove, similar in shape and size to a large bucket, made from hardened clay and coated with a thin layer of metal, is cheap, convenient to use, and ideal for imparting that requisite smoke. Otherwise, an American-style barbeque or even an oven broiler will do. A peripheral tool worth considering is a hinged grilling basket, which makes grilling both large items such as whole fish and small items such as chiles much easier.

Electric Rice Cooker

If you plan on eating southern Thai food frequently, one of the best investments you can make is an electric rice cooker. These days, it's safe to say that the vast majority of Thais use this tool, which is the most consistent and convenient way to prepare long-grain rice. There's no need to blow your paycheck on one; I still use the sub-$20, one-button rice cooker I bought at a fresh market in Chiang Mai more than twenty years ago.

See page 215 for tips on cooking long-grain rice with and without an electric rice cooker.

Thai Coconut Grater

A handful of the desserts in this book are garnished or served with freshly shredded coconut. To obtain the requisite crunchy texture and strand-like form of this ingredient, the ideal tool is a Thai coconut grater, which takes the form of a small piece of wood with sharp metal teeth or perforated metal disks of varying finenesses. Using one is time-consuming, but you'll get better results than with a box grater or food processor, both of which tend to produce thick, flat, limp strands of coconut.

EATING SOUTHERN THAI-STYLE

Sitting down to a southern Thai meal, the first thing you'll probably notice is the variety of the dishes. Despite its spicy reputation, southern Thai food is ultimately about balance, and if there's a spicy meat or fish curry on the table, for example, it will most likely be countered with a mild, vegetable-centered stir-fry. A chile-forward soup might be paired with a rich omelet, while a deep-fried fish might be accompanied by a spicy Thai-style dip. Southern Thai cooks strive to include nearly the entire spectrum of flavors, textures, and types of dishes in every meal. A particularly southern Thai way of eating that speaks to this variety is the platter of fresh herbs and vegetables, along with tiny bowls of shrimp paste–based dip, that accompany just about every meal. The former provides a needed break from spicy, salty flavors, and the latter provides even more piquant saltiness. In southern Thailand, as you'll see, you can have it all.

Despite the variety at hand, the centerpiece of any southern Thai meal is quite one-dimensional: rice. Unless otherwise noted, every meal (and just about every dish) in this book is meant to be paired with Thai long-grain rice. When eating curries, stir-fries, and soups with rice, a Thai takes the equivalent of a bite or two (it's a distinctly Western move to take "your" entire portion) from the communal serving vessel, spoons it over part of his plate of rice, and then, using his fork, pushes that portion onto his spoon and eats it (the spoon-and-fork combo is standard in Thailand; chopsticks are generally used only for noodle dishes). Thai-style dips are eaten the same way: take an herb or vegetable from the shared tray, place it on top of your rice, drizzle this with whatever dip is served, and, with your spoon, eat the entire package—rice, vegetable/herb, and dip—in one go.

It's worth noting that by Western standards, at least, southern Thai serving sizes are relatively small. This is because the dishes are meant to function as part of a greater meal that includes two, three, or four items, shared among four people, and the recipes in this book reflect this. For street food–style dishes, one-plate meals, noodle dishes, and sweets, which typically require more preparation, I've generally upped the yield to six servings.

A SOUTHERN THAI MENU PLANNER

Feeling overwhelmed by the scope of southern Thai food? A good starting place is the very first recipe in this book, A Tart, Spicy Soup with Vegetables and Fish (page 39), quite possibly the most emblematic and beloved dish in the entire cuisine, and a recipe that includes both some uniquely Thai cooking techniques (such as pounding a curry paste with a mortar and pestle) and some distinctly southern Thai ingredients (chiles, fresh turmeric)—not to mention the chance to play with southern Thai flavors. Pair this with, of course, long-grain Thai rice (page 214).

With this dish under your belt, you can move to some of the more advanced preparations, and for that, I've suggested a few thematic meals below. As one should in a proper southern Thai meal, I've made an effort to balance each rich dish with a spicy one, and a soup with a stir-fry, and I've tried to include both seafood and vegetable-forward dishes, as well as rice.

A CLASSIC SOUTHERN THAI CURRY STALL MEAL

Pork Stir-Fried in a Spicy Herb Paste
(page 50)

Deep-Fried Fish with
Fresh Turmeric and Garlic (page 53)

A Soup of Coconut Milk and Melinjo Leaves
(page 136)

A Thai-Style Dip of Shrimp Paste
(page 58)

Long-Grain Thai Rice (page 214)

Simmered Black Sticky Rice with Taro and
Jackfruit (page 61)

or

Fish Belly Curry (page 269)

Bitter Beans Stir-Fried with Shrimp and Shrimp
Paste (page 219)

A Soup of Chicken and Turmeric
(page 40)

A Thai-Style Dip of Shrimp Paste
(page 58)

Long-Grain Thai Rice (page 214)

Sago Pearls Dressed
with Coconut Milk (page 245)

A SOUTHERN THAI STREET STALL MEAL

Chaiya-Style Phat Thai (page 260)

or

Fish Curry Served over
Thin Rice Noodles with Sides (page 138)

or

Yellow Noodles Fried with Pork,
Seafood, and Yu Choy (page 163)

or

Fried Thin Rice Noodles Served
with a Side of Pork Broth (page 165)

or

Betong-Style Curry Mee (page 74)

A PHUKET-STYLE MEAL

Pork Belly Braised with Soy Sauce, Black
Pepper, and Brown Sugar (page 160)

A Spicy Dip of Smoked Shrimp
and Shrimp Paste (page 295)

Phuket-Style Steamed Curry
with Fish (page 173)

Long-Grain Thai Rice (page 214)

A KO SAMUI-STYLE MEAL

Gray Mullet Grilled with Turmeric,
Black Pepper, and Garlic (page 189)

Fried Salt Pork (page 192)

A Dip of Green Peppercorns
and Grilled Fish (page 193)

Rice Cooked in Coconut Milk
with Mung Beans (page 188)

A THAI MUSLIM–STYLE MEAL

Thai Muslim–Style Oxtail Soup
(page 96)

Thai-Style Omelet (page 97)

Long-Grain Thai Rice (page 214)

or

Goat Biryani with Ajaat (page 108)

A SOUTHERN THAI SEAFOOD FEAST

Deep-Fried Prawns in Tamarind Sauce
(page 314)

Grilled or Boiled Seafood with
Seafood Dipping Sauce (page 315)

Deep-Fried Kingfish Served
with a Fish Sauce Dressing and
Green Mango Salad (page 316)

Squid Fried with Salted Egg Yolk
(page 304)

Long-Grain Thai Rice (page 214)

AN ISLAND-STYLE BREAKFAST

A Simple Thai-Style Rice Salad (page 142)

or

Steamed Packets of Sticky Rice
and Banana (page 144)

AN ALMOST VEGAN SOUTHERN THAI MEAL

A Simple Thai-Style Rice Salad (page 142)

Malay-Style Pineapple Curry
(page 114)

Sweetened Sticky Rice
with Cashews (page 271)

A THAI-MUSLIM STREET STALL MEAL

Thai Muslim–Style Grilled Chicken (page 253)

or

Hat Yai–Style Fried Chicken with Sticky Rice
and a Dipping Sauce (page 101)

or

Puyut-Style Murtabak (page 237)

or

Rice Salad with Budu Dressing (page 282)

or

Roti with a Fried Egg and Chicken Curry
(page 120)

The Towns and the Cities

Whenever people come together, so do ingredients and recipes. And in southern Thailand, this means that the towns and cities are home to the region's most abundant, sophisticated, and diverse food.

This abundance can be seen in the curry stalls in the city of Nakhon Si Thammarat, which feature dozens of curries, soups, stir-fries, and dips that take advantage of this vast province's agricultural wealth—dishes that unite seafood from the coast, rice from the plains, and vegetables from the rugged interior.

The hustle of urban life means that not everyone has time to cook, leading to a culture of street food that's both abundant and specific to the region: steaming bowls of oxtail soup in the provincial capital of Pattani, mobile stalls hawking deep-fried chicken in Hat Yai, and noodle soups with curry broths in the border town of Betong.

Southern Thai cities such as Trang, Satun, and Ranong are also where one finds the region's greatest diversity of people and cultures. This means curries that can be traced back to places such as India, Indonesia, and Malaysia; breakfast spreads that seem to have been dropped straight out of southern China; dishes that are a unique and delicious blend of local and Chinese ingredients and cooking styles; and Muslim holiday feasts with dishes with roots that lead back to the Middle East.

In short, the cities are a microcosm of the ingredients, influences, peoples, and cuisines that make up Thailand's south—the perfect starting point for our journey.

PREVIOUS SPREAD: A street scene in Songkhla.

Curry and Rice

Go ANYWHERE in the south—or just about anywhere in Thailand, for that matter—and inevitably you'll encounter signs for "Nakhon Si Thammarat–Style Curry and Rice." The cooks of this particular city have a virtual monopoly on what might be the most southern type of eatery: the curry stall.

Why Nakhon Si Thammarat? For one, the city is located in the largest province in the south, meaning that from inland mountains to coastline, its people have access to virtually the entire spectrum of southern Thai ingredients. But perhaps more important, after weeks of eating and watching people cook in Nakhon Si Thammarat, I came to understand how locals used these ingredients. Yes, dishes at a Nakhon-style curry stall include lots of chile and, at times, can be downright spicy. But that heat is almost always countered by a strategic dash of sugar, a splash of rich coconut milk, or a generous dollop of savory shrimp paste. This wealth of produce and emphasis on balance have resulted in a style of cooking that somehow manages to excel at both abundance and restraint, in effect setting the standard for southern Thai cuisine.

Nakhon Si Thammarat–style curry stalls can be proper restaurants. They can also be an extension of the chef/owner's living room. They exist at the side of the highway, and they're also found in town. They're almost always inexpensive. And they don't serve only curries; along with the more soup-like dishes, you'll also find stir-fries, Thai-style dips, deep-fried items, and even desserts. What's constant is that all the dishes are made in advance. A Nakhon-style curry stall almost never has a menu; rather, a counter or table covered with dozens of pots and trays of prepared dishes serves the purpose. You roll up, scan what looks tasty, perhaps ask a couple of questions, and, in seconds, your choices are served over a plate of rice. If you've ordered in the local style, with its emphasis on balance, perhaps you opted for a peppery curry countered by a mild vegetable-based stir-fry; or maybe a tart, fiery bowl of soup with a side of sweet, rich braised pork belly; or a crispy, garlicky deep-fried fish paired with an herbaceous coconut milk curry.

Once you sit down, your plate will be supplemented with the obligatory (and complimentary) tray of vegetables and herbs and a spicy dip based on shrimp paste. Between bites, you soothe your palate with a refreshing slice of cucumber or the astringent young leaves of the cashew tree, or you go in the opposite direction with a tiny spoonful of that shrimp paste dip drizzled over a Thai eggplant and some rice. You wash it all down with a glass of water—ideally given a subtle but pleasant aroma with the addition of pandan leaves—pay the equivalent of a dollar or two, and leave, lips likely burning, having had one of the most quitessential southern Thai culinary experiences possible.

OPPOSITE: Inside Khaao Kaeng Paa Eet, a curry restaurant in Nakhon Si Thammarat.

Yupha Ninphaya, right, and her daughter "Taem," the chef/owners of Khaao Kaeng Paa Eet, a curry restaurant in Nakhon Si Thammarat.

A pork curry simmering over coals at Khrua Laa Lang, a curry stall in Nakhon Si Thammarat.

A Tart, Spicy Soup with Vegetables
and Fish as served at Suwalee,
Nakhon Si Thammarat.

A Tart, Spicy Soup with Vegetables and Fish
Kaeng Som
แกงส้ม

Any book about southern Thai cooking needs to start right here. In addition to the fact that it is the region's most famous dish, the ingredients that go into this soup, known locally as *kaeng som* (outside of the region as *kaeng lueang*, "yellow curry"), and the balance required when adding them culminate in a sort of crash course in southern Thai cooking—an exercise in extreme ingredients and flavors that, when taken as a whole, aren't so extreme.

Like many southern Thai dishes, kaeng som starts with an herb paste, a combination of aromatics and seasonings pounded with a mortar and pestle. Small incendiary chiles, fresh turmeric, garlic, lemongrass, and shrimp paste are obligatory elements of this particular paste. But beyond these, the only other constants of the dish are a tart and spicy flavor, some sort of vegetable and/or fruit, and fish. The vegetable or fruit could be unripe green papaya, cauliflower, or finger-sized potatoes; the tart flavor could stem from lime juice, tamarind pulp, sour fruit, or pickled bamboo, or a combination of some or all of these; and just about any saltwater fish—or shrimp—will do. Also essential are meticulous adding and constant tasting—gauging and adjusting seasonings until a balance that fits how the dish is meant to taste along with a bit of wiggle room for your personal preference is reached. Yes, southern Thai–style kaeng som should be tart and spicy, but it should also be enjoyable and delicious.

Serves 4 as part of a southern Thai meal

FOR THE HERB PASTE

½ teaspoon table salt
28 tiny spicy fresh chiles (15 g total)
3 medium spicy fresh chiles (12 g total), sliced
2 stalks lemongrass (50 g total; see page 19 for instructions on how to prepare lemongrass for an herb paste)

3 fingers fresh turmeric (45 g total), peeled and sliced
5 cloves garlic (25 g total), peeled and sliced
1 tablespoon shrimp paste

FOR THE SOUP

150 g fresh pineapple, ½-inch-by-1-inch pieces
100 g heart of palm, 1-by-2-inch thin slices
6 tablespoons lime juice
3 tablespoons white sugar
400 g sea bass fillet, 1-by-2-inch chunks

The sweetness of the pineapple you have will have an impact on the flavor of the dish; season the soup to accommodate this.

UP TO 5 DAYS IN ADVANCE, MAKE THE CURRY PASTE: Pound and grind the salt, tiny chiles, and medium chiles to a coarse paste with a mortar and pestle. Add the lemongrass and pound and grind to a coarse paste. Add the turmeric and pound and grind to a coarse paste. Add the garlic and pound and grind to a coarse paste. Add the shrimp paste and pound and grind to a fine paste. (Alternatively, if using a food processor or blender, process the salt, tiny chiles, medium chiles, lemongrass, turmeric, garlic, and shrimp paste to a fine paste.) If making it in advance, remove the paste to an airtight container and store in the refrigerator.

MAKE THE SOUP: Bring 4 cups (1 l) water to a boil in a saucepan over high heat. Add the curry paste, stirring to dissolve. When the water reaches a boil again, add the pineapple and heart of palm. Bring to a boil, reduce the heat, and simmer until the pineapple and heart of palm are just tender, around 5 minutes. Add the lime juice and sugar, stirring to dissolve. When the soup reaches a simmer again, add the fish and simmer until it is just cooked through and opaque, around 2 minutes. Taste, adjusting the seasoning if necessary; the soup should taste equal parts bracingly tart and spicy, followed by subtly sweet and salty flavors. It should have a bright yellow, almost orange hue; a pleasant and distinct aroma from the fresh turmeric and lime juice; and a subtle crunch from the pineapple and heart of palm.

Remove to a serving bowl and serve warm or at room temperature with long-grain rice.

A Soup of Chicken and Turmeric
Kai Tom Khamin
ไก่ต้มขมิ้น

Not all the offerings at a Nakhon Si Thammarat–style curry stall are—or even should be—spicy. Ordering at one of these stalls is all about balance, and a spicy dish should, ideally, be countered by something mild. One of the most standard, and beloved, counters is this soup, a savory, fragrant, sun-yellow broth of chicken, fresh turmeric, and lemongrass. Using a scrawny free-range chicken like those in Thailand will result in a more savory-tasting, fragrant soup but will increase the cooking time.

Serves 4 as part of a southern Thai meal

**500 g free-range chicken, whole or any
desired bone-in parts, 1-inch pieces
5 cloves garlic (25 g total), peeled and bruised
8 shallots (80 g total), peeled and bruised
A 2-inch piece galangal (20 g), peeled,
¼-inch-thick slices
3 stalks lemongrass (75 g total; see page 19 for
instructions on how to prepare lemongrass for
a soup)
3 fingers fresh turmeric (45 g total), peeled,
¼-inch-thick slices
¼ cup (60 ml) pickled garlic liquid (see Note)
2 teaspoons table salt**

In Thailand, the liquid used to pickle garlic, typically a combination of vinegar and honey, is sometimes added to dishes to give them a subtly sweet/sour boost. If you can't find a jar of Thai-style pickled garlic, a combination of vinegar and honey will approximate the brine's subtle sweet/tart flavor.

Combine 5 cups (1.2 L) water and the chicken in a large saucepan and bring to a boil over high heat. Add the garlic, shallots, galangal, lemongrass, and turmeric, reduce the heat, and cook at a low simmer until the chicken is tender, at least 30 minutes but as long as an hour, depending on your chicken, and the broth is slightly reduced and concentrated.

Add the pickled garlic liquid and salt. Taste, adjusting the seasoning if necessary; the soup should taste savory and subtly salty and sweet, with a pleasant fragrance from the turmeric and lemongrass and a subtle yellow/orange hue.

Remove to a serving bowl and serve warm with long-grain rice.

ABOVE: A Soup of Chicken and Turmeric as served at Raan Khaao Kaeng Phuen Baan, in Nakhon Si Thammarat.
OPPOSITE: Serving up curry to go at Khaao Kaeng Paa Eet, a curry restaurant in Nakhon Si Thammarat.

A Curry with Cockles and Wild Betel Leaf

Kaeng Kathi Sai Hawy Khraeng Kap Bai Chaphluu

แกงกะทิใส่หอยแครงกับใบชะพลู

A mild, fragrant coconut milk–based curry is obligatory at any southern Thai curry stall, and this take is one of the more popular—and delicious. The bold aromatics in the curry paste and the wild betel leaf serve to counter any unpleasant "fishy" aromas from the cockles, while the palm sugar and the finishing drizzle of thick coconut milk serve to temper the heat of the chiles. The curry paste here is more or less standard for this type of rich coconut milk–forward curry. Yupha Ninphaya, a curry stall owner in Nakhon Si Thammarat and the source of this recipe, also uses the paste to make a curry that swaps out cockles and wild betel leaves for finger-sized local potatoes and slices of fatty pork belly, or slices of beef and Thai eggplants, and so can you.

Serves 4 as part of a southern Thai meal

FOR THE CURRY PASTE

½ teaspoon table salt
24 tiny spicy fresh chiles (12 g total)
12 medium dried chiles (6 g total)
2 teaspoons black peppercorns
3 stalks lemongrass (75 g total; see page 19 for instructions on how to prepare lemongrass for a curry paste)
2 makrut lime leaves, sliced
A 1-inch piece galangal (10 g), peeled and sliced
1 finger fresh turmeric (15 g), peeled and sliced
2 fingers Chinese key (10 g total; see Glossary), peeled and sliced
¼ teaspoon chopped makrut lime zest
4 shallots (40 g total), peeled and sliced
4 cloves garlic (20 g total), peeled and sliced
1 tablespoon shrimp paste

FOR THE CURRY

2 kg cockles, cleaned of mud
4 cups (1 L) thin coconut milk (see page 135 for instructions on how to make thin coconut milk)
24 wild betel leaves (24 g total; see Glossary), sliced
25 g palm sugar
½ teaspoon table salt
6 makrut lime leaves, torn
½ cup (125 ml) thick coconut milk (see page 135 for instructions on how to make thick coconut milk)
1 large mild fresh red chile (around 35 g), sliced

UP TO 5 DAYS IN ADVANCE, MAKE THE CURRY PASTE: Pound and grind the salt, fresh chiles, and dried chiles to a coarse paste with a mortar and pestle. Add the peppercorns and pound and grind to a coarse paste. Add the lemongrass and makrut lime leaves and pound and grind to a coarse paste. Add the galangal, turmeric, and Chinese key and pound and grind to a coarse paste. Add the makrut lime zest and pound and grind to a coarse paste. Add the shallots and garlic and pound and grind to a coarse paste. Add the shrimp paste and pound and grind to a fine paste. (Alternatively, if using a food processor or blender, process the salt, both chiles, the peppercorns, lemongrass, makrut lime leaves, galangal, turmeric, Chinese key, makrut lime zest, shallots, garlic, and shrimp paste to a fine paste.) If making it in advance, remove the paste to an airtight container and store in the refrigerator.

ON THE DAY OF SERVING, PREPARE THE COCKLES: Bring 2 quarts (2 l) water to a boil in a saucepan over high heat. Working in small batches, boil the cockles until they open, 1 to 2 minutes, transferring the cooked cockles to a bowl of cool water as they are ready.

When the cockles are cool enough to handle, open them and remove the meat, discarding the shells. Rinse the cockles in several changes of water to get rid of as much grit as possible. Cover the cockles with a few inches of cool water in a bowl and set aside.

OPPOSITE: Cooking at a curry stall inside Chumphon's market.

MAKE THE CURRY: Combine the thin coconut milk and curry paste in a large saucepan and bring to a rapid simmer over medium-high heat. Add the cockles, betel leaves, palm sugar, and salt, reduce the heat, and simmer until the mixture is reduced by approximately one-third, around 20 minutes.

Add the makrut lime leaves and thick coconut milk and return to a simmer. Taste, adjusting the seasoning if necessary; the curry should taste spicy and rich, with an herbaceous aroma from the curry paste (in particular, from the turmeric and pepper) and the wild betel leaves.

Remove to a serving bowl, garnish with the sliced red chile, and serve warm or at room temperature with long-grain rice.

A Dry Curry of Pork Ribs
Kaeng Khua Sii Khrohng Muu
แกงคั่วซี่โครงหมู

"This type of curry has to be spicy!" proclaims Phanida Sikhao, the source of the recipe, a thick, assertively piquant "dry" curry based on pork ribs. In uniquely southern Thai fashion, the herb paste for the curry unites fresh and dried chiles. But like many southern Thai dishes, a significant proportion of the heat—and aroma—comes not only from chiles but also from the liberal use of peppercorns.

The dish is a staple across southern Thailand, but Phanida and other cooks in Nakhon Si Thammarat Province give it a local twist with the addition of khrueang raa, a spice powder that can include as many as ten different items. Black pepper, coriander seeds, cumin, cinnamon, and star anise are more or less obligatory; if you can't find some of the more esoteric spices, they can simply be omitted.

Serves 4 as part of a southern Thai meal

FOR THE SPICE MIXTURE

1 teaspoon black peppercorns
½ teaspoon coriander seeds
A 1-inch piece cinnamon stick
1 Siamese cardamom pod (see Glossary)
2 star anise
4 cloves
A small piece of nutmeg (around 1/16 of a small one)
1 teaspoon cumin seeds
2 Siamese cardamom leaves

FOR THE CURRY PASTE

20 tiny spicy fresh chiles (10 g total)
15 tiny spicy dried chiles (5 g total)
1 tablespoon black peppercorns
3 stalks lemongrass (75 g total; see page 19 for instructions on how to prepare lemongrass for a curry paste)
2 makrut lime leaves, sliced thin

A 1-inch piece galangal (10 g), peeled and sliced
1 finger fresh turmeric (15 g), peeled and sliced
6 fingers Chinese key (30 g total; see Glossary), peeled and sliced
3 shallots (30 g total), peeled and sliced
3 cloves garlic (15 g total), peeled and sliced
2 tablespoons shrimp paste

FOR THE CURRY

500 g pork ribs, 2-inch pieces
250 g pork spareribs, 2-inch pieces
Table salt or fish sauce (optional; see Note)
1 large mild fresh red chile (25 g), sliced
4 makrut lime leaves, sliced very thin

In Phanida's recipe, the salty flavors of this dish stem from the generous amount of shrimp paste. If the shrimp paste you have isn't providing enough saltiness, compensate with a pinch of salt or a dash of fish sauce.

UP TO 5 DAYS IN ADVANCE, MAKE THE SPICE MIX: Dry-roast the peppercorns, coriander seeds, cinnamon, Siamese cardamom, and star anise in a wok or frying pan over medium heat until fragrant and toasted, around 2 minutes. Remove and set aside.

Add the nutmeg and cumin seeds to the pan and dry-roast until fragrant and toasted, around 1 minute. Remove and set aside. Add the cardamom leaves to the hot pan and dry-roast until fragrant and toasted, around 30 seconds. Remove from the pan.

Grind the toasted spices to a fine powder with a mortar and pestle or in a coffee grinder or food processor. If making it in advance, remove the spice mix to an airtight container.

ALSO UP TO 5 DAYS IN ADVANCE, MAKE THE CURRY PASTE: Pound and grind the fresh and dried chiles to a coarse paste with a mortar and pestle. Add the peppercorns and pound and ground to a coarse paste. Add the lemongrass and makrut lime leaves and pound and grind to a coarse paste. Add the galangal, turmeric, and Chinese key and pound and grind to a coarse paste. Add the shallots and garlic and pound and grind to a coarse paste. Add the shrimp paste and pound and grind to a fine paste. (Alternatively, if using a food processor or blender, process both chiles, the peppercorns, lemongrass, makrut lime leaves, galangal, turmeric, Chinese key, shallots, garlic, and shrimp paste to a fine paste.) If making it in advance, store the paste to an airtight container in the refrigerator.

MAKE THE CURRY: Combine the ribs, spareribs, and 6 cups (1.5 l) water in a wok and bring to a boil over high heat. Reduce the heat and cook at a rapid simmer, scooping off and discarding any scum that rises to the top, until the ribs are starting to become tender and

the water has reduced to the same level as the pork, about 25 minutes.

Add the spice mix and curry paste, stirring to combine, and cook at a rapid simmer until the liquid has reduced to just below the level of the pork and the pork is tender, about 20 more minutes. Taste, adjusting the seasoning with salt (or fish sauce) if necessary; the curry should taste intensely peppery and spicy, followed by salty, and have a strong aroma from the dried spices.

Remove to a shallow bowl, garnish with the sliced chile and makrut leaves, and serve warm or at room temperature with long-grain rice.

A Dry Curry of Pork Ribs as served at Raan Khaao Kaeng Phuen Baan, a curry stall in Nakhon Si Thammarat.

Serving up curries at Khaao Kaeng
Sawng Naam, a curry stall in
Nakhon Si Thammarat.

Minced Kingfish Stir-Fried in a Spicy Herb Paste, and Chinese Chives and Bean Sprouts Stir-Fried with Tofu and Duck Liver as served at Khrua Laa Lang, a curry stall in Nakhon Si Thamamrat.

Minced Kingfish Stir-Fried in a Spicy Herb Paste

Khua Kling Plaa
คั่วกลิ้งปลา

No Nakhon Si Thammarat–style curry stall would be complete without at least one tray of khua kling, minced (well, usually—see the next recipe for a different take on this dish) protein stir-fried with a spicy, turmeric-heavy herb paste, one of the most iconic southern Thai dishes. Jaruwee Jutikamol, a restaurateur in Nakhon Si Thammarat and the source of this recipe, prepares three different types of khua kling—pork, chicken, and fish—on a daily basis. Her kingfish khua kling, made with finely chopped fish and a heat-forward herbaceous paste, is a deliciously homey, unfussy, rustic version of the dish.

Serves 4 as part of a southern Thai meal

FOR THE HERB PASTE

½ teaspoon table salt

14 tiny spicy fresh chiles (7 g total; see Glossary)

20 medium spicy dried chiles (10 g total)

1 teaspoon black peppercorns

3 stalks lemongrass (75 g total; see page 19 for instructions on how to prepare lemongrass for an herb paste)

A 1-inch piece galangal (10 g), peeled and sliced

1 finger fresh turmeric (15 g), peeled and sliced

¼ teaspoon chopped makrut lime zest

6 cloves garlic (30 g total), peeled and sliced

1 tablespoon shrimp paste

FOR THE STIR-FRY

500 g kingfish steaks or fillets, any bones and skin removed and discarded

2 tablespoons vegetable oil

1 to 1¼ cups (250 to 300 ml) thin coconut milk (see page 135 for instructions on how to make thin coconut milk)

½ teaspoon table salt

20 tiny spicy fresh chiles (10 g total), bruised

4 makrut lime leaves, torn

FOR SERVING

A platter that includes leafy herbs and fresh vegetables such as cucumbers, cabbage, wing beans, Thai eggplants, pea eggplants, long beans, Thai basil, Asian pennywort, young cashew tree leaves, bai man puu (see Glossary), Vietnamese coriander, water celery, and/or young mango leaves

---

Khua kling is often served with a small platter of "cooling" items such as slices of cucumber and herbs that are eaten in between bites of the spicy dish.

UP TO 5 DAYS IN ADVANCE, MAKE THE CURRY PASTE: Pound and grind the salt, fresh chiles, and dried chiles to a coarse paste with a mortar and pestle. Add the peppercorns and pound and ground to a coarse paste. Add the lemongrass and pound and grind to a coarse paste. Add the galangal, turmeric, and makrut lime zest and pound and grind to a coarse paste. Add the garlic and pound and grind to a coarse paste. Add the shrimp paste and pound and grind to a fine paste. (Alternatively, if using a food processor or blender, process the salt, both chiles, the peppercorns, lemongrass, galangal, turmeric, makrut lime zest, garlic, and shrimp paste to a fine paste.) If making it in advance, remove the paste to an airtight container and store in the refrigerator.

MAKE THE STIR-FRY: Chop and mince the kingfish with a cleaver until it has the texture of coarsely ground beef. Set aside.

Heat the oil in a wok over high heat. Add the herb paste and fry, stirring frequently, until fragrant, around 1 minute. Add the kingfish and ½ cup (125 ml) of the coconut milk and simmer, stirring frequently, until most of the liquid has evaporated, then add another ½ cup (125 ml) coconut milk and repeat, simmering for a total of around 5 minutes. Add the salt, chiles, and makrut lime leaves, and fry for another 2 minutes or so, until the mixture is relatively dry in texture (if it risks burning, add more coconut milk, 1 tablespoon at a time). Taste, adjusting the seasoning; the dish should taste roughly equal parts spicy, herbaceous, and salty, and the fish should be tender.

Remove to a serving plate and serve warm or at room temperature with the platter of vegetables and herbs and long-grain rice.

Pork Stir-Fried in a Spicy Herb Paste
Khua Kling Muu
คั่วกลิ้งหมู

To most Thais, khua kling is a dish synonymous with two things: chile and a finely minced protein. Suraphon Phanusamphol has a different idea.

"This dish, when made elsewhere, is always chopped very fine, but this is boring!" says the second-generation chef/owner of Suwalee, a really excellent curry stall located near Nakhon Si Thammarat's train station.

Instead of the standard minced pork, Suraphon opts for strips of fatty pork collar. Additionally, he turns down the volume on the chile, instead giving the dish a layer of warmth through the addition of coarsely ground black pepper, as well as a bit of herbaceous crunch in the form of thin slices of young galangal and lemongrass. A closing drizzle of thin coconut milk mellows out his almost decadent and decidedly unboring take on this Nakhon-style curry stall staple.

Serves 4 as part of a southern Thai meal

FOR THE HERB PASTE

½ teaspoon table salt
30 tiny spicy fresh chiles (15g total)
2 stalks lemongrass (50 g total; see page 19 for instructions on how to prepare lemongrass for an herb paste)
A 1½-inch piece galangal (15 g), peeled and sliced
2 makrut lime leaves, sliced thin
1 heaping teaspoon black peppercorns
¼ teaspoon chopped makrut lime zest
2 fingers fresh turmeric (30 g total), peeled and sliced
6 cloves garlic (30 g total), peeled and sliced
1 tablespoon shrimp paste

FOR THE STIR-FRY

½ teaspoon black peppercorns
20 small cloves garlic (10 g total)

2 tablespoons vegetable oil
4 makrut lime leaves, torn, plus 4 leaves, sliced thin, for garnish
1 cup (250 ml) thin coconut milk (see page 135 for instructions on how to make thin coconut milk), or as needed
350 g pork collar, cut into thin 1-by-2-inch slices
A 1½-inch piece young galangal (15 g), peeled and sliced thin
1 teaspoon white sugar
2 stalks lemongrass (50 g total; see page 19 for instructions on how to prepare lemongrass for an herb paste)
5 medium spicy fresh chiles (15 g total), sliced
1 teaspoon fish sauce
1 large mild fresh chile (25 g), sliced on the bias
Fish sauce or white sugar (optional)

FOR SERVING

A platter that includes leafy herbs and fresh vegetables such as cucumbers, cabbage, wing beans, Thai eggplants, pea eggplants, long beans, Thai basil, Asian pennywort, young cashew tree leaves, bai man puu (see Glossary), Vietnamese coriander, water celery, and/or young mango leaves

---

Suraphon uses tender, immature galangal, an ingredient not typically available outside Southeast Asia. If you only have access to mature galangal, use just the bits that have retained some residual moisture and be sure to slice it very thin.

Because of its spicy nature, khua kling is often served with a small platter of "cooling" items such as slices of cucumber and herbs that are eaten in between bites of the dish.

UP TO 5 DAYS IN ADVANCE, MAKE THE HERB PASTE: Pound and grind the salt and chiles to a coarse paste with a mortar and pestle. Add the lemongrass, galangal, and makrut lime leaves and pound and grind to a coarse paste. Add the peppercorns and pound and grind to a coarse paste. Add the makrut lime zest and pound and grind to a coarse paste. Add the turmeric and pound and grind to a coarse paste Add the garlic and pound and grind to a coarse paste. Add the shrimp paste and pound and grind to a fine paste.

(Alternatively, if using a food processor or blender, process the salt, chiles, lemongrass, galangal, makrut lime leaves, peppercorns, makrut lime zest, turmeric, garlic, and shrimp paste to a fine paste.) If making it in advance, remove the paste to an airtight container and store in the refrigerator.

MAKE THE STIR-FRY: Pound and grind the peppercorns to a coarse powder with a mortar and pestle; remove and set aside. Pound and grind the garlic, skin and all, to a coarse paste.

Heat the oil in a wok over medium-high heat. Add the garlic and fry, stirring frequently, until golden and just starting to get crispy, around 10 seconds. Add half of the torn makrut lime leaves and the herb paste and fry until fragrant, around 1 minute. If the mixture becomes too dry, add some of the coconut milk 1 tablespoon or so at a time. Add the pork and galangal and fry, stirring occasionally and adding more coconut milk 1 tablespoon at a time if the mixture gets too dry, until the pork is almost cooked through, around 5 minutes.

Add the sugar and the remaining torn makrut lime leaves, stirring to combine. Add the lemongrass and medium chiles, stirring to combine. Add the fish sauce, ground black pepper, and 2 tablespoons of the coconut milk, stirring to combine, and cook until the liquid has reduced slightly. Add the sliced large chile, stirring to combine. Taste, adjusting the seasoning with fish sauce or sugar if necessary; the dish should be equal parts spicy (from both the chiles and the peppercorns) and rich (from the fatty pork, oil, and coconut milk), followed by herbaceous and salty, with a strong, distinct aroma from the makrut lime leaves; a subtle crunch from the galangal; and a slightly oily, relatively dry texture.

Remove to a serving plate, garnish with the thinly sliced makrut lime leaves, and serve warm or at room temperature with the platter of vegetables and herbs and long-grain rice.

Pork Stir-Fried in a Spicy Herb Paste as served at Suwalee, Nakhon Si Thammarat.

Deep-Fried Fish with Fresh Turmeric and Garlic
Plaa Thawt Khamin
ปลาทอดขมิ้น

This dish is a Nakhon-style curry stall standard, as well as an example of how southern Thais use ingredients with strong aromas such as turmeric, garlic, and, in this case, makrut lime leaves, to counter any potentially unpleasant "fishy" smells. It's also a recipe that emphasizes satisfyingly crispy textures; deep-frying tiny cloves of garlic, skin and all, results in a dish with an addictive crunch. And with the fish almost hidden below a virtual cloud of the golden, crispy fried garlic, it may also be one of the most impressive looking dishes in this book.

Serves 4 as part of a southern Thai meal

3 fingers fresh turmeric (45 g total), peeled and sliced
150 small cloves garlic (75 g total), not peeled
2 teaspoons shrimp paste
1 teaspoon table salt
4 makrut lime leaves, sliced thin
4 small threadfin bream (around 500 g total) or other fish (see Note), scaled and gutted
At least 4 cups (4 l) vegetable oil for deep-frying

In Thailand's south, threadfin bream (see Glossary), a small, delicate, white-fleshed saltwater fish, is considered the ideal fish to cook this way, but just about any fish—mackerel, mullet, or sillago—or cut—fillets or steaks—can be cooked this manner, although deep-frying times may vary.

Seek out the smallest cloves of garlic you can find and leave on the skin, which crisps up deliciously when deep-fried.

Try deep-frying the fish Thai-style in a wok; its shape means you'll use less oil. You'll also need a flat fine-mesh strainer (also known as a spider) to scoop fish out of the hot oil and to drain the crispy deep-fried topping.

OPPOSITE: Deep-Fried Fish with Fresh Turmeric and Garlic, Suwalee, Nakhon Si Thammarat.

THE NIGHT BEFORE OR A FEW HOURS BEFORE COOKING, MAKE THE MARINADE: Pound and grind the turmeric, garlic, shrimp paste, and salt to a coarse paste with a mortar and pestle. Stir in the makrut lime leaves.

Make two deep incisions on both sides of each fish and apply the paste with your hands, coating the entire fish. Remove the fish to a plastic container, cover, and marinate in a refrigerator for at least a few hours or as long as overnight.

FRY THE FISH: Scrape the marinade off the fish and reserve it. Allow the fish to reach room temperature.

Heat the oil to 340°F in a wok over medium-high heat. Slide 1 or 2 of the fish into the hot oil and deep-fry, flipping once, until crispy, golden, and cooked through, around 5 minutes. Remove the fish to paper towels to drain. Remove and discard any debris from the oil with a fine-mesh strainer. Repeat with the remaining fish.

When all the fish have been deep-fried, add the marinade to the hot oil and cook until it floats to the top of the oil and is crispy and fragrant, around 5 minutes. Remove the crispy marinade with the strainer and drain on paper towels.

Remove the fish to a large serving plate, top with the crispy marinade, and serve hot or at room temperature with long-grain rice.

Sweet Pork
Muu Waan
หมูหวาน

Even southern Thais need a break from all that chile and turmeric, and this dish, fatty pork belly braised with palm sugar and fish sauce, serves as the perfect counter to the standard repertoire of spicy curries and soups. Given the rich ingredients, a serving only requires a few slices of pork, so this recipe makes a relatively small amount.

Serves 4 as part of a southern Thai meal

36 small cloves garlic (18 g total), skin left on if tiny, peeled if larger
2 tablespoons vegetable oil
6 shallots (60 g total), peeled, halved lengthwise, and sliced
400 g skin-on pork belly, 1-by-2-inch slices
1 teaspoon white sugar
15 g palm sugar
1½ tablespoons light soy sauce
1 teaspoon sweet soy sauce
1 teaspoon oyster sauce

If you have access to fragrant Thai garlic, with its tiny (less than ½ inch long) cloves, there's no need to remove the skin.

Pound the garlic, skin and all if using tiny cloves, to a coarse paste with a mortar and pestle.

Heat the oil in a wok over medium-high heat. Add the garlic and shallots and fry, stirring frequently, until just starting to turn golden and fragrant, around 3 minutes. Add the pork, white sugar, palm sugar, light soy sauce, sweet soy sauce, and oyster sauce. Fry, stirring occasionally, until the pork has rendered some of its fat and the seasonings are lightly caramelized and fragrant, around 10 minutes (add a tablespoon or more of water if the mixture seems too dry). Taste, adjusting the seasoning with palm sugar or light soy sauce if necessary; sweet pork should taste sweet, followed by salty, with a pleasant oiliness and fragrance from the seasonings.

Remove to a small serving plate and serve warm or at room temperature with long-grain rice.

RIGHT: A Curry with Cockles and Wild Betel Leaf, left, and Sweet Pork, right, as served at Khaao Kaeng Paa Eet, a curry restaurant in Nakhon Si Thammarat.
OPPOSITE: Driving by a curry stall in Surat Thani.

Chinese Chives and Bean Sprouts Stir-Fried with Tofu and Duck Liver

Phat Kui Chai

ผัดกุยช่าย

Another respite from southern-style heat is this fried vegetable dish with a generous protein component. Chinese chives add a pleasantly bitter flavor and a grassy aroma, while duck livers and oyster sauce provide savory richness.

Serves 4 as part of a southern Thai meal

200 g Chinese chives (see Glossary)
4 duck livers (200 g total)
¼ cup (60 ml) vegetable oil
250 g firm white tofu, ¾-inch cubes
4 cloves garlic (20 g total), peeled and minced
1 tablespoon oyster sauce
1 tablespoon fish sauce
50 g bean sprouts

PREPARE THE CHINESE CHIVES: Trim the chives of their pale stalks and wispy ends and cut into 1½-inch-long pieces; you should have around 150 g sliced chives. Set aside.

PREPARE THE DUCK LIVERS: Bring 4 cups (1 l) water to a boil in a saucepan over high heat. Add the duck livers and parboil until just cooked through, 30 to 45 seconds. Remove the livers and discard the water.

When they are cool enough to handle, slice the livers into ½-inch-wide slices. Set aside.

FRY THE TOFU: Heat the oil in a wok over medium-high heat. Add the tofu and fry, turning occasionally, until golden and puffed up, around 7 minutes. Remove and drain on paper towels.

PREPARE THE STIR-FRY: Pour off all but approximately 2 tablespoons of the oil from the wok and set it over high heat. Add the garlic and fry until golden and fragrant, around 10 seconds. Add the reserved tofu and duck livers, the oyster sauce, and fish sauce, stirring occasionally, and cook until the ingredients are thoroughly combined and the proteins are heated through, 1 to 2 minutes. Add the chives and bean sprouts and cook, stirring occasionally, until just starting to become tender, around 3 minutes.

Taste, adjusting the seasoning if necessary; the dish should taste pleasantly salty and savory, with a crunchy texture and a slightly bitter flavor from the Chinese chives.

Remove to a serving plate and serve warm or at room temperature with long-grain rice.

OPPOSITE: Making Chinese Chives and Bean Sprouts Stir-Fried with Tofu and Duck Liver at Khrua Laa Lang, Nakhon Si Thammarat.

A Thai-Style Dip of Shrimp Paste

Naam Chup

น้ำชุบ

As odd as it might sound, it's conceivable that a southern Thai curry stall might not have a curry. Perhaps they didn't cook one that day, instead focusing on other types of soups or stir-fries, or they ran out early. But for a southern Thai curry stall not to serve this dish, a spicy, funky, salty, garlicky, tart dip based on shrimp paste, would be absolutely inexcusable.

Place an order at a Nakhon-style curry stall, and in addition to your curry, soup, or stir-fry, you'll receive a tray of herbs and vegetables and a small bowl of a shrimp paste–based dip, provided automatically, no charge. The vegetables and herbs, which can range from slices of cucumber to various astringent-tasting herbs with no colloquial English language names, serve different functions. Eaten on their own, they provide a respite from the spiciness of the main dishes. Paired with a drizzle of the dip and taken with a spoonful of rice, they offer yet another full-flavored bite.

Serves 4 as part of a southern Thai meal

FOR THE DIP

2 feet banana leaf (optional; see Note)
2 heaping tablespoons shrimp paste
10 tiny fresh chiles (5 g total; see Glossary)
1 clove garlic (5 g), peeled
15 g palm sugar
1 tablespoon lime juice
12 g pea eggplants (see Glossary)

FOR SERVING

A platter that includes leafy herbs and fresh vegetables such as Thai eggplants, lettuce, long beans, wing beans, cabbage, cucumber, Asian pennywort, Thai basil, bitter beans, tender cashew tree leaves, tender mango tree leaves, water celery, bitter beans, bai man puu (see Glossary), and/or Vietnamese coriander

Thai-style dips such as this one are made using a granite mortar and pestle, which lends them a pleasantly coarse, chunky consistency. A food processor or blender isn't a substitute for these tools and would result in a dip with too fine a consistency.

Source the most expensive Thai shrimp paste you can find; it won't cost much more than the cheap stuff, but the flavor will be disproportionally better.

Wrapping the shrimp paste in banana leaves and toasting or grilling it beforehand takes away some of its funk and mellows it, but you can skip this step if pressed for time if you want a more full-flavored version.

This version of the dish relies on the tiny (often less than ½ inch long), spicy, fragrant fresh Thai chiles known as *phrik khii nuu* (literally "mouse shit chiles"). If you don't have access to them, simply go with the smallest, hottest fresh chiles you can find.

To eat a Thai-style dip, take an herb, green, or vegetable, put it on your plate of rice, and top it with a bit of the dip, resulting in a bite that combines all three elements.

TOAST THE SHRIMP PASTE, IF DESIRED: Wrap the shrimp paste in a couple layers of banana leaf, seal with a toothpick, and toast, turning once, over low coals or under a broiler, or dry-roast in a wok or frying pan over low heat, until subtly fragrant but not completely dry, around 5 minutes on each side. Remove from the heat and unwrap the paste.

MAKE THE DIP: Pound and grind the chiles and garlic to a coarse paste with a mortar and pestle. Add the shrimp paste and palm sugar and pound and grind to a coarse paste. Add the lime juice, stir, and pound to a coarse paste. Add the pea eggplants, gently bruise them, and stir to combine. Taste, adjusting the seasoning with more sugar and/or lime juice if necessary; the dip should taste roughly equal parts spicy, salty, and funky, followed by sweet and tart, with a strong taste/aroma from the garlic, a pleasant crunch from the pea eggplants, and a just-watery texture. If the consistency of the dip is too dry to drip off a spoon, add a teaspoon or so of water.

Remove to a small bowl and serve with the platter of vegetables and herbs and long-grain rice.

A Thai-Style Dip of Shrimp Paste at Khaao Kaeng Paa Eet, a curry restaurant in Nakhon Si Thammarat.

Simmered Black Sticky Rice with Taro and Jackfruit

Khaao Niaw Dam

ข้าวเหนียวดำ

A Nakhon-style curry stall wouldn't be complete without a few desserts. Most commonly, these take the form of starchy items such as mung beans, sago pearls, or even corn simmered with a bit of sugar and a thickening agent. Served in a bowl, topped with a drizzle of coconut milk seasoned with a pinch of salt, these are a rich, subtly sweet way to end a southern Thai meal. My favorite take on this genre of dessert is grains of black sticky rice simmered until just bursting and supplemented with fragrant fruit. Often the latter is longan, but Jaruwee Jutikamol, who runs a curry stall in Nakhon Si Thammarat, opts for tender cubes of taro and almost ethereally fragrant slices of jackfruit. It's a relatively simple dessert (or snack) that spans a disproportionate number of textures, flavors, and even colors.

Serves 4

1¾ cups (150 g) black sticky rice
100 g taro, cut into ½-inch cubes
¾ cup (150 g) white sugar
¼ teaspoon table salt, plus ½ heaping teaspoon
2 to 3 pieces ripe jackfruit, depening on size
    (75 g total), sliced thin lengthwise
1 cup (250 ml) thick coconut milk (see page 135 for
    instructions on how to make thick coconut milk)
1 pandan leaf, tied in a knot

Seek out the most mature, fragrant jackfruit you can find for this; canned jackfruit, with its tender texture and concentrated flavor and aroma, could work well here.

AT LEAST 6 HOURS BEFORE SERVING, PREPARE THE BLACK STICKY RICE: Gently wash the rice in several changes of water. Remove to a bowl, cover with several inches of water, and soak for 4 to 6 hours.

PREPARE THE TARO: Combine the taro and 4 cups (1 l) water in a small saucepan and bring to a boil over high heat, then reduce the heat and simmer until the taro is tender, around 5 minutes. Drain the taro, discarding the water. Set aside.

MAKE THE STICKY RICE: Drain the rice, discarding the water. Combine the rice and 4 cups (1 l) water in a saucepan and bring to a boil over high heat, then reduce the heat and cook at a rapid simmer, stirring and scraping constantly to prevent the rice from sticking to the bottom of the saucepan, until the water has reduced to the level of the rice and the mixture has a relatively thick, glossy texture, around 30 minutes. Add the sugar and the ¼ teaspoon salt and simmer until the sugar has dissolved, 2 to 3 minutes.

Remove the saucepan from the heat and add the taro and jackfruit, stirring to combine. Allow the rice to cool to room temperature. The sticky rice should have a thick but still pourable consistency just short of a porridge, with a dark, glossy appearance, and it should taste subtly sweet with a pleasant and distinct fragrance from the jackfruit.

WHILE THE RICE IS COOLING, MAKE THE SALTED COCONUT MILK TOPPING: Combine the coconut milk, pandan leaf, and the remaining heaping ½ teaspoon salt in a small saucepan and bring to a boil over medium heat, then reduce the heat and simmer until the coconut milk has thickened slightly, around 30 seconds. Remove from the heat. The coconut milk should taste rich and just salty, with a subtle fragrance from the pandanus.

To serve, transfer around ½ cup (120 ml) of the sticky rice mixture to a small bowl and top with 1 to 1½ tablespoons of the thick coconut milk topping. Repeat with the remaining ingredients for a total of four servings.

OPPOSITE: Simmered Black Sticky Rice with Taro and Jackfruit at Khrua Laa Lang, a curry stall in Nakhon Si Thammarat.

The spread of breakfast options at Sin Jiw, a restaurant in Trang.

Steaming dim sum at Jip Khao, in Trang.

BREAKFAST IN TRANG

"The people of Trang have a reputation as serious eaters," explains Thanatip Boonyarat, a native of the city who runs a lauded restaurant. "People elsewhere eat three, maybe four times per day, but people in Trang eat nine times a day!"

It was only my second day in the city, and this obsession with eating was already apparent. It was scarcely 9 a.m., and the place where I'd taken my second breakfast was already winding down. The dim sum hall where I'd eaten breakfast number one had peaked by about 7:30 a.m. And Thanatip's restaurant, Khao Kaeng Ko Lay—ostensibly a lunch place—had already sold out of most items. The only amendment I would make to her statement would be to add the word "breakfast"—people in Trang seemed to be very, very serious breakfast eaters.

I've kicked off the day in just about every corner of Thailand, but I hadn't previously witnessed anything quite like breakfast in Trang. Cavernous dim sum halls;

decades-old restaurants selling steaming bowls of noodles and rice porridge; stuck-in-time cafés; streetside vendors hawking crispy, golden, deep-fried sticks of dough; and, most famously, stalls selling local-style roast pork by the kilogram—these are the standard morning dining options in Trang. It's fun, indulgent, delicious, overwhelming, and, perhaps most notably, almost entirely Chinese.

The urban centers along southern Thailand's Andaman Sea side have a palpable Chinese influence. But Trang just might be the most Chinese city in the country, a virtual melting pot of Chinese culture, with Hakka, Hokkien, and Teochew among the regional Chinese languages spoken there. Yet it's the Cantonese who have had the largest impact on the city's culinary culture. A rarity elsewhere in Thailand, the Cantonese, with their dim sum and roast pork, have almost single-handedly defined Trang's breakfast scene.

LEFT: An employee at Jip Khao, a dim sum restaurant in Trang.
RIGHT: Making deep-fried sticks of dough at Kun Chiang Bang Rak, a restaurant in Trang.

LEFT: Trang-style roast pork.
RIGHT: Deep-fried sticks of dough at Kun Chiang Bang Rak, a restaurant in Trang.

"In the old days, people would just come and drink tea," explains Yaowanee Thirakleela, the fourth-generation Cantonese owner of Jip Khao, the city's oldest and most revered venue for dim sum. "There weren't many things to eat with the tea; a couple of steamed dumplings, maybe deep-fried sticks of dough."

Yet over the decades, she tells me, Trang's teahouses started to offer more food, ultimately making the transition to full-fledged restaurants. Today the city is synonymous with vast dim sum halls that offer dozens of steamed and deep-fried options in addition to roast pork, noodles, and rice dishes. But Jip Khao is one of the few that have kept to a relatively simple repertoire of items, all made in-house and steamed in the traditional style: in wide trays rather than in tiny bamboo baskets. Cast aside any notions of delicate, jewel-like dumplings: Trang-style dim sum is homely and hearty, the almost exclusively pork-based fillings given a seemingly Thai-influenced oomph from generous additions of garlic and white pepper. And remnants of Chinese tea culture can still be seen in the drinks station standard at Jip Khao and its counterparts, where coffee and tea are made with a cloth filter that resembles a tiny wind sock. Yaowanee is proud that her restaurant is perhaps the only one in town that continues to serve proper Chinese tea.

"In the old days, in my father's time, they drank lots of tea," she tells me. "They could eat fatty food and still live long lives!"

Whereas the steamer draws locals to Jip Khao, bubbling oil is the pull at Sin Jiw, another long-standing Chinese-run dim sum hall. At a wok positioned outside the antique shophouse, a man slides almost ethereally soft, pale fingers of dough into hot oil, flipping them with long chopsticks until crispy and golden.

"The dough is our father's recipe," says Arjin Pornsinsiriruk, the restaurant's second-generation owner. "At other places, people use packaged mixes, but we use a starter—this is how our father made it."

The sticks are delicious, the levain-like rising allowing them to be graciously free of ammonium chloride, an ingredient used elsewhere in Thailand to encourage dough to rise quickly and to give it a crispy texture when deep-fried (leaving many versions with a sharp aroma not unlike that of Scandinavian black licorice). At Sin Jiw, the sticks are paired with an exceptionally rich, fragrant coconut custard or the standard porky, peppery dumplings, which in the local style can be inserted into the deep-fried dough, the package then topped with a slightly sweet chile sauce. ("It's how the old generation eats dim sum—like a sandwich!" Arjin tells me.) Such

is the ubiquity of deep-fried sticks of dough in Trang that on top of the dining table of any dim sum hall is a dispenser holding squares of thick, coarse gray paper; locals use these to dab excess oil from the sticks of dough and, it's said, to jot down figures while talking business over dim sum.

Yet undoubtedly the most famous element of Trang's breakfast culture is the roast pork. Although the dish has its origins in Chinese festivals and celebrations, it has become synonymous with Trang, sold from stalls at the morning market and dim sum halls alike, a staple indulgence for locals and a must-eat item for visitors.

Roast pork is found across Thailand, but a few things make Trang's take on the dish unique. For starters, the city is one of only a handful of places in the world where entire adult pigs are roasted whole in ovens the size of a Tokyo apartment (for more on this, see page 68). The pigs, deboned, scored, and basted with a sweet five spice–based marinade before being roasted, emerge with almost tooth-shatteringly crispy skin; firm, candy-like lean meat; and a fat layer that, ideally, is at the verge of melting.

"It should be crispy on the outside with a tender interior," explains Thanatip, the restaurateur who, along with a team of fellow restaurateurs in Trang, went on a fact-finding trip to Penang, Malaysia, another city with a strong Chinese influence. She pulls out her iPad and shows me photos of the roast pork she encountered there.

The city's larger dim sum halls have dedicated roast pork stations out front. Diners pair tiny plates of roast pork with steamed buns or deep-fried sticks of dough, eaten to a background track of the discursive, thumping sound of meat being hacked apart with a giant cleaver. Streetside, a brisk trade is done in take-away roast pork, with customers pulling up on motorcycles, shouting an order for a kilogram or two, and speeding away without even having disembarked.

It is on morning three, at venue number two, when I felt like I finally got into the swing of Trang-style breakfast. At a vast dim sum hall decked out with a statue of dugong (the marine mammal is a symbol of the province) and a coffee cup theme, I close with a combination of roast pork; a sweet, steamed cake made of lightly fermented rice flour; and a glass tumbler of impossibly dark coffee, and I don't eat again until around 8 p.m. In Trang, I finally realize, it's all about breakfast.

OPPOSITE: The interior of Pong O Cha, a dim sum restaurant in Trang.
LEFT: Preparing coffee the traditional way at Sin Jiw, a dim sum restaurant.
ABOVE: Dim sum stuffed inside deep-fried dough and drizzled with chili sauce, a food hack known among diners in Trang.

Roasting Pork Trang-Style

In Trang, at producers such as Ko Jiw, pictured here, roasting is done in ovens approximately eight feet high and six feet wide that can accommodate up to three pigs. Typically located underground, the ovens are made with bricks held together with a mortar that includes sugar, the fires fueled with rubber tree wood—a plentiful resource in southern Thailand. In witnessing the roasting at Ko Jiw, not once did I see a thermometer used; experience and clocks guided the workers in the roasting process.

1 At around 10 a.m., two adult pigs of around 150 pounds each were slaughtered on-site, their hair and organs removed.

2 The pigs were shifted to a table where nearly all their bones, except their ribs but including their skulls, were removed.

3 The meat and fat were scored deeply, checkerboard-style, without piercing the skin.

4 A rub of sugar, five spice powder, MSG, and salt was applied to the meat, and the pigs were left to marinate for 6 to 8 hours.

5 At around 10 p.m., the fire was started. As the wood reduced to coals, the rub was rinsed off the pigs, wire was used to maintain their cylindrical shape, and meat hooks were inserted.

6 At 10:50 p.m., the pigs were lowered into the oven, where they hung suspended from metal bars to roast for exactly 10 minutes.

7 The pigs were removed from the oven and immediately rinsed with water, then their feet and ears were removed and their skins pierced with a brush-like tool embedded with nails. The fire was stoked with additional wood, and metal buckets were put in the bottom of the oven to catch dripping fat and prevent flare-ups. The interior cavities of the pigs were lined with paper, and the pigs were returned to the oven at 11:30 p.m. to roast for an additional 15 minutes.

8 The pigs were removed again and a layer of paper applied to their exteriors. They were returned to the oven at midnight, and then, after a final 30 minutes of roasting, were removed, having spent a total of only about an hour in the oven.

9 The pigs were hung on meat hooks and the paper and wire removed. When they were cool enough to handle, the pigs were shifted to the tables, and the pork was cut into approximately 2-foot-square sections and loaded into baskets to be sold at Trang's morning market.

Diners at Thai Xee Hee, a 50-year-old dim sum restaurant in Betong.

Border Food

Betong, the country's southernmost city, is, without a doubt, part of Thailand. But culturally speaking, it's a Chinese town—one of the most resolutely Chinese outposts in the whole country. And, located less than five miles from the border with Malaysia, Betong transforms each weekend into something of a Little Malaysia, a playground for Malaysians who cross international lines to shop, take selfies, sing karaoke, and eat. If you've just arrived from Bangkok—or anywhere else in Thailand, really—it feels utterly foreign and discombobulating.

Betong is a border town in the literal sense, but in southern Thailand, borders can be more ephemeral. The mixing of cultures due to migration, trade, and colonization has led to several border towns across the country's south, many not located anywhere near an international boundary. These unique exchanges of culture—as well as ingredients and cooking methods—have also led to dishes that couldn't have appeared anywhere else in the world.

ABOVE: Making coffee the old-school way at a stall in Betong.
RIGHT: A soy sauce factory in Betong.

A Dry Curry with Pork Spareribs and
Green Banana simmering at Yay Puad, Chumphon.

Ingredients for a curry paste at Yay Puad, Chumphon.

Betong-Style Curry Mee

Mii Kaeng

หมี่แกง

"It's a Malaysian dish that we've adapted," explains Sangdow Duangkam, of mii kaeng, the signature dish at her restaurant in Betong, Thailand's southernmost town.

Known in Malaysia as curry mee (the Thai name is a literal translation of this), the dish takes the form of a coconut milk curry–based broth served with noodles. But in making the short journey across the border to Betong, the dish gained a slight Thai accent.

"In Malaysia, it includes curry powder, but we don't use any—it's too strong," Sangdow tells me. Additionally, whereas the Malaysian version typically includes protein such as shrimp, cockles, or puffs of deep-fried tofu, in landlocked Betong, Sangdow opts for chicken supplemented with tender, barely sweet, almost melting chunks of winter gourd.

"Malaysians who eat here say they like this even more than the version at home!" she says with pride, and I have to say that I feel the same way; her take adds a distinctly Thai element of richness and boldness that I'd always felt was lacking in the original.

Serves 6

FOR THE CURRY PASTE

20 medium spicy fresh red chiles (60 g total), sliced
3 stalks lemongrass (75 g total; see page 19 for instructions on how to prepare lemongrass for a curry paste)
A 3-inch piece galangal (30 g), peeled and sliced
½ teaspoon chopped makrut lime zest
1 finger fresh turmeric (15 g), peeled and sliced
10 shallots (100 g total), peeled and sliced
10 cloves garlic (50 g total), peeled and sliced
¼ cup (50 g) shrimp paste

FOR THE CURRY BROTH

2 tablespoons vegetable oil
1.5 kg chicken parts of your choice, 1½-inch bone-in pieces
2 quarts (2 l) thin coconut milk (see page 135 for instructions on how to make thin coconut milk)
1 kg winter gourd, peeled, quartered lengthwise, seeded, and cut into 1-inch-thick pieces
1 cup (250 ml) thick coconut milk (see page 135 for instructions on how to make thick coconut milk)
1 tablespoon white sugar
½ teaspoon MSG (optional)
Table salt (optional)
1 small bunch Thai basil, leaves only

FOR SERVING

180 g thin round dried rice noodles
250 g bean sprouts
Condiments such as fish sauce, sugar, and chile powder

If you're not up for pounding a curry paste from scratch, you can get away with a store-bought red curry paste supplemented with shrimp paste and fresh turmeric.

Sangdow prefers to serve this dish with the eponymous thin round rice noodles, but Betong's thick, round, yellow wheat noodles are also a popular option. If you can't make up your mind, you could always cross back to Malaysia, where the dish is typically served with both types of noodles.

UP TO 5 DAYS IN ADVANCE, MAKE THE CURRY PASTE: Pound and grind the chiles to a coarse paste with a mortar and pestle. Add the lemongrass and pound and grind to a coarse paste. Add the galangal, makrut lime zest, and turmeric and pound and grind to a coarse paste. Add the shallots and garlic and pound and grind to a coarse paste. Add the shrimp paste and pound and grind to a fine paste. (Alternatively, if using a food processor or blender, process the chiles, lemongrass, galangal, makrut lime zest, turmeric, shallots, garlic, and shrimp paste to a fine paste.) If making it in advance, remove the paste to an airtight container and store in the refrigerator.

recipe continues →

At a night market in Betong.

ON THE DAY OF SERVING, MAKE THE CURRY BROTH: Heat the oil in a wok over medium-low heat. Add the curry paste and fry, stirring frequently, until it is concentrated and fragrant, around 5 minutes. Add the chicken and 1 cup (250 ml) water and simmer, stirring occasionally, until the chicken is cooked through and the paste is fragrant, around 15 minutes.

Meanwhile, bring the thin coconut milk and winter gourd to a boil in a stockpot over medium-high heat. Reduce the heat to a simmer and cook until the winter gourd is just starting to become tender, around 10 minutes.

Add the chicken mixture to the stockpot and simmer until the chicken and gourd are both tender, about 10 minutes. Add the thick coconut milk and bring to a simmer. Add the sugar and MSG (if using) and taste, adjusting the seasoning with salt if necessary; the broth should taste rich, savory, and salty, with a background of spice and fragrance from the curry paste and a subtle sweetness from the gourd. Add the Thai basil leaves and stir to combine, then reduce the heat and cook at a low simmer while you prepare the noodles.

PREPARE THE NOODLES: Soak the rice noodles in a bowl of room-temperature water for 15 minutes. Drain in a sieve or colander.

Bring 4 cups (1 l) water to a boil in a large saucepan over high heat. Add around 75 g of the soaked noodles and 40 g of the bean sprouts. When the water reaches a boil again, remove the noodles and bean sprouts with a strainer, allowing them to drain, then add to a serving bowl and top with some of the curry broth. Repeat with the remaining ingredients to make five more bowls.

Serve hot with the condiments of your choice.

Betong-Style Curry Mee as served at Phii Daw Mii Kaeng, Betong.

A Peranakan Salad of Thin Rice Noodles
Yam Mii Hun
ยำหมี่หุ้น

As far back as the fifteenth century, commerce and labor have drawn Chinese immigrants to the Andaman Sea side of the Malay Peninsula. In cities such as Singapore, Melaka, and George Town, those immigrants married locals, and after multiple generations of cultural exchange, the result was a unique blend of indigenous and Chinese language, dress, and cuisine known as Peranakan or Baba culture. This cross-cultural heritage extended north to present-day Thailand as well, most notably to Phuket. Yet as in Singapore and Malaysia, one of the only aspects of Peranakan culture that remains today in Thailand is food.

Khanaporn Janjirdsak was born to a Peranakan mother, and her restaurant, Trang Ko'e, is Thailand's only eatery entirely dedicated to this unique fusion cuisine.

"Thais who love spicy food might find Peranakan food bland," says Khanaporn. We are in her kitchen in Trang, a lesser-known outpost of Peranakan culture, where she is making yam mii hun, a salad of thin rice noodles and squares of firm tofu—the dish's Chinese elements—seasoned with fragrant calamansi limes, shrimp paste, chile, and herbs such as lemongrass—its Southeast Asian half.

Admittedly, yam mii hun doesn't provide the full-frontal assault of flavor associated with many southern Thai dishes, but "bland" isn't a word I would use to describe the dish, which is savory and tart, sweet and spicy, crunchy, and fragrant all at the same time—not to mention one of the handsomest dishes I've ever photographed.

Serves 4, or 4 to 6 as part of a southern Thai meal

2 eggs

1 cup (75 g) finely grated coconut (see page 24 for tips on grating coconut)

16 medium head-on shrimp (500 g total)

180 g thin round dried rice noodles

1 tablespoon vegetable oil

1 block (around 180 g) firm tofu, halved and sliced

2 tablespoons shrimp paste

10 shallots (100 g total), peeled and sliced thin

4 cloves garlic (20 g total), peeled and sliced

5 medium spicy fresh chiles (about 15 g total)

20 g dried shrimp

30 g palm sugar

15 calamansi limes (about 150 g total; if not available, season to taste with 3 or 4 regular limes)

3 stalks lemongrass (about 75 g total), exterior tough layers peeled away, green sections cut off and discarded, pale sections sliced very thin

4 makrut lime leaves, sliced very thin

1 small bunch mint (about 25 g), leaves only

100 g bean sprouts

3 large mild fresh red chiles (about 75 g total), halved, seeded, and sliced lengthwise into thin strips

3 tablespoons light soy sauce

85 g toasted cashews

PREPARE THE HARD-BOILED EGGS: Bring a few cups of water to a boil in a saucepan over high heat. Add the eggs and boil for 8 minutes. Drain the eggs.

When they are cool enough to handle, peel the eggs and quarter them lengthwise. Set aside.

PREPARE THE TOASTED COCONUT: Dry-roast the grated coconut in a wok over medium-low heat, stirring frequently, until light brown in color and fragrant, about 15 minutes. Remove from the heat and let cool.

Transfer the coconut to a mortar and pestle (or food processor or blender) and pound (or process) to a coarse powder. Set aside.

PREPARE THE SHRIMP: Remove the heads from the shrimp and peel the shrimp; reserve the heads and shells. Combine the shrimp, shells, and heads in a saucepan, bring to a simmer over medium heat, and simmer until the shrimp are cooked through and

recipe continues →

fragrant and have released some juices, about 5 minutes. Remove from the heat and let cool slightly.

Drain the shrimp in a sieve set over a bowl; reserve the liquid and discard the shells and heads.

PREPARE THE NOODLES: Bring 4 cups (1 l) water to a boil in a saucepan over high heat. Add the noodles and parboil for about 5 seconds. Drain the noodles in a sieve or colander, rinse in a couple changes of cool water, and set aside to drain further.

PREPARE THE TOFU AND SHRIMP PASTE: Heat the oil in a nonstick frying pan over medium heat. Add the tofu and fry, turning occasionally, until uniformly golden and crispy, about 10 minutes. Remove to a paper towel to drain.

Reduce the heat to low and add the shrimp paste. Toast in the residual oil, flipping once, until fragrant, about 4 minutes. Remove from the heat.

MAKE THE DRESSING: Pound and grind half of the shallots, the garlic, and chiles to a coarse paste in a mortar and pestle. Add the tofu and shrimp paste, half of the dried shrimp, and the palm sugar and pound and grind to a coarse paste. Add 2 of the shrimp and the reserved cooking liquid, pounding, grinding, and stirring to combine.

Juice 11 of the calamansi limes and add the juice to the shrimp mix, pounding, grinding, and stirring to combine. Taste, adjusting the seasoning if necessary; the dressing should taste equal parts salty, funky, and tart, followed by equal parts spicy and sweet, with a pleasant pungency from the garlic and a distinct fragrance from the calamansi.

PREPARE THE NOODLE SALAD: Combine the noodles and dressing in a bowl, mixing well to ensure that the dressing is evenly distributed. Add the lemongrass, makrut lime leaves, three quarters of the mint leaves, the bean sprouts, chiles, light soy sauce, the remaining dried shrimp, the toasted coconut, the remaining shrimp, the tofu, and the remaining shallots, mixing well to combine. Taste, adjusting the seasoning if necessary; the salad should taste equal parts savory, salty, and tart, with a bit of chile heat and some crunch from the lemongrass and fresh herbs, and fragrance from the herbs and calamansi.

Divide the noodles among four individual plates and garnish each with one-quarter of the cashews, the remaining mint leaves, and the hard-boiled eggs, and a calamansi lime. Alternatively, serve on a platter garnished with the cashews, mint leaves, hard-boiled eggs, and calamansi limes. Serve with long-grain rice.

OPPOSITE: A Peranakan Salad of Thin Rice Noodles as served at Trang Ko'e, Trang.

Trader's Rice
Nasi Dagae
นาซิดาแฆ

"It's from a lot of countries—Indonesia, Malaysia, Thailand," says Hameedah Cheuma when I ask her to explain the origins of nasi dagae, a dish that she and her sisters serve in the deep-south city of Pattani.

Nasi dagae consists of three types of rice that are studded with fenugreek seeds and steamed with coconut milk, then topped with a rich, fragrant curry revolving around chunks of longfin tuna and hard-boiled eggs. Of all the countries Hameedah listed, it seems to have the fewest links with the one we were in. Its name is Malay in origin (it's a local pronunciation of the Malay *nasi dagang*, meaning "trader's rice"). It's found across the South China Sea in Indonesia. And one would struggle to find nasi dagae anywhere else in Thailand.

Present-day Pattani does not share a border with another country, yet it existed as an independent kingdom for more than 300 years, and it continues to have closer historical, cultural, and religious links with states in Malaysia than it does with Bangkok. And although this former kingdom was incorporated into Thailand at the beginning of the twentieth century, it's fair to say that was only reluctantly (for background on the long-running insurgency in Thailand's deep south, see page 14). Even today, entering Pattani feels a lot like crossing a border to a place that's not quite Thailand but also not quite Malaysia.

This otherness is manifest in nasi dagae, a dish allegedly brought to the Malay Peninsula by Indonesian sailors and one that emphasizes the rich, coconutty, slightly sweet, pleasantly oily, and fishy flavors so beloved by people in northern Malaysia. In Pattani, it's become a breakfast staple, and Hameedah and her sisters start selling it at 6 a.m., sometimes selling out by 8 a.m.

"We make the curry the day before and cook it over a very low heat overnight, which allows all the ingredients to meld together and be more concentrated," Hameedah tells me. Although this lengthy cooking time is unnecessary for the scaled-down version of the dish, because it has so many elements,

I'd still recommend spreading the prep over three or four days.

Serves 6

FOR THE CURRY PASTE

5 large mild dried chiles (25 g total)

1 tablespoon coriander seeds

½ teaspoon table salt

A 2½-inch piece galangal (25g), peeled and sliced

3 stalks lemongrass (75 g total; see page 19 for instructions on how to prepare lemongrass for a curry paste)

7 shallots (70 g total), peeled and sliced

8 cloves garlic (35 g total), peeled and sliced

2 teaspoons mild Malay/Indian-style chile powder (or cayenne pepper)

1 teaspoon turmeric powder

1 tablespoon shrimp paste

FOR THE SHRIMP TOPPING

2 large mild dried chiles (10 g total)

A ¾-inch piece ginger (7 g), peeled and sliced

3 shallots (30 g total), peeled and sliced

3 cloves garlic (15 g total), peeled and sliced

75 g peeled shrimp, chopped

½ cup (125 ml) thin coconut milk (see page 135 for instructions on how to make thin coconut milk)

10 g palm sugar

½ teaspoon table salt

1 slice dried asam fruit (see Glossary)

FOR THE RICE

1¼ cups (250 g) long-grain white rice

¼ cup (50 g) sticky rice

1 tablespoon Sangyod rice (see Glossary and Note)

¼ cup (60 ml) thin coconut milk (see page 135 for instructions on how to make thin coconut milk)

½ cup (125 ml) thick coconut milk (see page 135 for instructions on how to make thick coconut milk)

½ teaspoon table salt

2 teaspoons white sugar

4 shallots (40 g total), peeled and sliced thin

A ¾-inch piece ginger (7 g), peeled and julienned

1 heaping teaspoon fenugreek seeds

500 g longtail tuna, 6 pieces

¼ cup (60 ml) white vinegar

15 g palm sugar

1 teaspoon table salt

6 eggs

4 cups (1 L) thin coconut milk (see page 135 for instructions on how to make thin coconut milk)

2 cups (500 ml) thick coconut milk (see page 135 for instructions on how to make thick coconut milk)

4 slices dried asam fruit (see Glossary)

6 large mild fresh pale green chiles (around 200 g total)

2 tablespoons white sugar

½ teaspoon table salt

FOR SERVING

12 medium spicy fresh chiles (36 g total)

If you don't have access to longtail tuna, albacore tuna or kingfish can serve as substitutes.

If you can't find Sangyod or other "red" rice, simply substitute a tablespoon of white long-grain rice.

The most efficient way to steam sticky rice is with a Thai-style pot and a conical bamboo basket. If you don't have access to these tools, a steaming set can be improvised with a sieve elevated over boiling water, or a Chinese-style steamer lined with cheesecloth, although the cooking time may vary.

UP TO 5 DAYS IN ADVANCE, MAKE THE CURRY PASTE: Put the dried chiles and enough water to cover by an inch or two in a saucepan and bring to a boil over high heat. Remove the saucepan from the heat, cover, and soak the chiles for 15 minutes.

Drain the chiles, discarding the water, and when they are cool enough to handle, remove and discard the seeds and stringy membranes. Slice the chiles and let drain in a sieve or colander.

Dry-roast the coriander seeds in a wok or saucepan over medium heat until toasted and fragrant, about 2 minutes. Remove from the heat and process the seeds to a fine consistency with a mortar and pestle, coffee grinder, or food processor. Set aside.

Pound and grind the drained chiles and the salt to a coarse paste with a mortar and pestle. Add the galangal and lemongrass and pound and grind to a coarse paste. Add the shallots and garlic and pound and grind to a coarse paste. Add the ground coriander seeds, the chile powder, and turmeric powder and pound and grind to a coarse paste. Add the shrimp paste and pound and grind to a fine paste. (Alternatively, if using a food processor or blender, process the chiles, salt, galangal, lemongrass, shallots, garlic, coriander, chile powder, turmeric powder, and shrimp paste to a fine paste.) If making it in advance, remove the paste to an airtight container and store in the refrigerator.

UP TO A FEW DAYS IN ADVANCE, MAKE THE SHRIMP TOPPING: Put the dried chiles and enough water to cover by an inch or two in a saucepan and bring to a boil over high heat. Remove the saucepan from the heat, cover, and soak the chiles for 15 minutes.

Drain the chiles, discarding the water, and when they are cool enough to handle, remove and discard the seeds and stringy membranes. Slice the chiles and drain in a sieve or colander.

Pound and grind the drained chiles to a coarse paste with a mortar and pestle. Add the ginger and pound and grind to a coarse paste. Add the shallots and garlic and pound and grind to a coarse paste. Add the shrimp and pound and grind to a fine paste. (Alternatively, if using a food processor or blender, process the chiles, ginger, shallots, garlic, and shrimp to a fine paste.)

Combine the chile paste, thin coconut milk, salt, palm sugar, and dried asam fruit in a wok or large nonstick frying pan and bring to a simmer over medium-low heat. Simmer, stirring occasionally, until the liquid has entirely evaporated and the mix has a dry, crumbly texture and is a light brown color, around 45 minutes. Taste, adjusting the seasoning if necessary; the topping should taste equal parts savory and rich, with a subtle background of sweetness. If making it in advance, remove to an airtight container and store in the refrigerator.

AT LEAST 4 HOURS BEFORE SERVING, PREPARE THE RICE: Combine the three types of rice and rinse in several changes of water until the water remains clear, then cover with a few inches of fresh water. Soak for 4 to 6 hours.

recipe continues →

AT LEAST 3 HOURS BEFORE SERVING, MAKE THE CURRY AND HARD-BOILED EGGS: Combine 1½ quarts (1.4 L) water, the tuna, vinegar, sugar, and salt in a saucepan and bring to a boil over high heat. Add the eggs, reduce the heat, and simmer for 10 minutes. Remove the saucepan from heat, remove the eggs and tuna, and set aside. Reserve ½ cup (125 ml) of the liquid.

When they are cool enough to handle, peel the eggs; set aside.

Bring the thin coconut milk to a rapid boil in a wok over high heat. Add the thick coconut milk and return to a rapid boil. Add the curry paste and bring to a boil, then reduce the heat to a rapid simmer and cook, stirring constantly, to allow the ingredients to become amalgamated and fragrant and the liquid to reduce slightly, around 15 minutes.

Add the tuna, the reserved boiling liquid, the peeled eggs, and the dried asam fruit and cook at a rapid simmer until the curry is slightly reduced and a layer of oil has formed on the surface, around 30 minutes.

Add the chiles and simmer until they are tender, another 30 minutes or so. Add the sugar and salt. Taste, adjusting the seasoning with more sugar and/or salt if necessary; the curry should taste rich, with equal parts tart and sweet flavors, and it should be thick, with a generous layer of red oil on top and a subtle herbaceous aroma.

WHILE THE CURRY IS SIMMERING, STEAM THE RICE: Drain the rice, discarding the water. Bring a couple quarts of water to a boil in a Thai-style sticky rice steaming pot (or in a saucepan or a Chinese-style steamer; see Note). Put the rice in the bamboo steaming basket (or in a sieve or a Chinese-style steamer lined with cheesecloth) positioned a few inches above the boiling water. Cover with a tea towel and then a lid, creating a relatively tight seal that allows as little steam as possible to escape, and steam for 25 minutes.

Remove the rice to a bowl and, using a spatula or spoon, gently combine with the thin coconut milk. Return the rice mixture to the steamer and steam for another 25 minutes.

Remove the rice to a large bowl and, using a spatula or spoon, gently mix with the thick coconut milk, salt, sugar, shallots, ginger, and fenugreek seeds. Taste, adjusting the seasoning if necessary; the rice should taste rich, just barely sweet, and pleasantly oily. Allow the rice to rest for 10 minutes before serving.

To serve, place a scant ¾ cup of rice on a small serving plate and top with a piece of tuna, a drizzle of curry, and a heaping tablespoon of the shrimp garnish. Add a hard-boiled egg, 1 of the large mild green chiles from the curry, and 2 of the medium spicy fresh chiles. Repeat with the remaining ingredients to make five more plates. Serve warm or at room temperature.

LEFT: The various elements of Trader's Rice, Baan Nasi Dagae, Pattani.
OPPOSITE: Trader's Rice as served at Baan Nasi Dagae, Pattani.

Salted Kingfish "Fried" in Coconut Milk
Plaa Khem Thawt Kathi
ปลาเค็มทอดกะทิ

Chumphon is, officially at least, as far north as one can go in Thailand's south. The province is known as the "Gateway to the South," and it's where culture, accents, and, unsurprisingly, food all start to become more southern.

"The flavors in Chumphon are subtler here than elsewhere in the south," says Patanan Petpirun, the chef and second-generation owner of Yay Puad, a restaurant in Chumphon that specializes in local dishes. "We use more sugar. Our food isn't that spicy and not as salty as the rest of southern Thailand."

At Yay Puad, the emphasis is on subtly sweet, rich flavors, much like those one would find in Bangkok. Yet the dishes revolve around ingredients—rich coconuts, vibrant herbs, high-quality seafood—that any southerner would recognize. That intersection of sensibilities and product is most apparent in this dish, salt-preserved kingfish cooked in coconut milk. To make it, Patanan boils the fish in coconut milk until its water has essentially evaporated, leaving the coconut solids and fish to deep-fry and ultimately caramelize in the residual oil. And because this is (almost) southern Thailand, the mild dish is paired with strong-tasting ingredients, including chiles and garlic, although in this case they're served on the side.

Serves 4 as part of a southern Thai meal

FOR THE SALTED FISH

150 g salted kingfish
3 cups (750 ml) thick coconut milk (see page 135 for instructions on how to make thick coconut milk)
8 shallots (80 g total), peeled and sliced
3 tablespoons light brown sugar

OPPOSITE: A Dry Curry with Pork Spareribs and Green Banana, left, and Salted Kingfish "Fried" in Coconut Milk, right, Yay Puad, Chumphon.

FOR SERVING

20 small cloves garlic (10 g total), peeled (or 3 big cloves, peeled and sliced)
18 medium spicy fresh chiles (6 g total), sliced
3 long beans (40 g total), cut into 2-inch pieces
70 g pickled mustard greens, drained and sliced
2 small cucumbers (100 g total), sliced
2 sprigs bai man puu (see Glossary; optional)

Seek out the most expensive salted kingfish, ideally oil-packed, that you can get your hands on.

The strong odor of salted fish and the fishy/coconut oil splatters that result when making this dish means it may not be ideal for apartment cooking.

Remove and discard the skin and bones from the kingfish; this should yield around 100 g of fish. Mince the kingfish.

Bring the fish and thick coconut milk to a rapid simmer in a wok over medium-high heat and simmer, stirring and scraping the bottom of the wok frequently, especially toward the end of the process. After 10 minutes of rapid simmering, the fish should be completely disintegrated and the mixture should be thick and porridge-like. After 20 minutes, the mixture should be slightly gelatinous in texture, the solids and oil just starting to separate. Add half of the shallots to the wok.

After another 10 minutes, the solids and oil should be completely separated and the mixture should have the consistency and appearance of panfried ground beef or pork, with a strong but pleasant fragrance that blends fish, coconut, and shallots. Add the sugar.

After another 5 or 10 minutes, the mixture should have a toasty brown hue and the sugar should be completely dissolved. Remove from the heat and immediately pour into a metal or ceramic bowl. Allow the mixture to cool slightly and then pour off and discard as much of the excess oil as possible.

When the fish mixture has reached room temperature, remove to a small plate and serve with the remaining shallots, the garlic, and chiles. Accompany with another plate of the long beans, pickled mustard greens, cucumbers, and bai man puu leaves (if using). Serve with long-grain rice.

A Dry Curry with Pork Spareribs and Green Banana

Kaeng Khua
Kraduuk Awn Luuk Kluay
แกงคั่วกระดูกอ่อนลูกกล้วย

This curry, also from Yay Puad in Chumphon, unites the cooking of central and southern Thailand. The former appears in the form of pork and the rich, fragrant, relatively mild, barely sweet flavors, while the south can be seen in ingredients such as turmeric and the headlining fruit. Known as *kluay lep mue naang*, "ladyfinger bananas," these are finger-sized and sweet. Growing in dense, almost comblike bunches, they are the agricultural product most associated with Chumphon. In this recipe, firm, fully unripe green bananas seemingly magically transition to rich and tender—almost avocado-like—as they simmer in the curry, with none of the mouth-puckering astringency one would expect.

Serves 4 as part of a southern Thai meal

FOR THE CURRY PASTE

½ teaspoon table salt
20 tiny spicy fresh chiles (10 g total)
3 stalks lemongrass (75 g total; see page 19 for instructions on how to prepare lemongrass for an herb paste)
A 1-inch piece galangal (10 g), peeled and sliced
½ teaspoon chopped makrut lime zest
1 finger fresh turmeric (15 g), peeled and sliced
2 fingers Chinese key (10 g; see Glossary), peeled and sliced
40 small cloves garlic (20 g total), skin left on if tiny cloves, peeled if larger
4 shallots (40 g total), peeled and sliced
1 tablespoon shrimp paste

FOR THE CURRY

400 g meaty pork spareribs, cut into 2-inch pieces
2 large, firm, unripe green bananas (300 g total)
1 cup (250 ml) thin coconut milk (see page 135 for instructions on how to make thin coconut milk)
1 tablespoon white sugar
½ cup (125 ml) thick coconut milk (see page 135 for instructions on how to make thick coconut milk)
6 citrus leaves, sliced thin (optional)

Those cooking outside of Thailand won't have access to Chumphon's famous ladyfinger bananas, but unripe green supermarket-standard bananas can be used as a substitute.

Patanan finishes the curry with bai som paen, the leaves of a mandarin orange–like citrus that are not available outside the region. I've used young lime leaves instead, and they work as an acceptable substitute. You can also skip the leaves entirely if you don't have access to a citrus tree.

UP TO 5 DAYS IN ADVANCE, MAKE THE CURRY PASTE: Pound and grind the salt and chiles to a coarse paste with a mortar and pestle. Add the lemongrass and pound and grind to a coarse paste. Add the galangal and makrut lime zest and pound and grind to a coarse paste. Add the turmeric and pound and grind to a coarse paste. Add the Chinese key and pound and grind to a coarse paste. Add the garlic and shallots and pound and grind to a coarse paste. Add the shrimp paste and pound and grind to a fine paste. (Alternatively, if using a food processor or blender, process the salt, chiles, lemongrass, galangal, makrut lime zest, turmeric, Chinese key, garlic, shallots, and shrimp paste to a fine paste.) If making it in advance, remove the paste to an airtight container and store in the refrigerator.

ON THE DAY OF SERVING, PREPARE THE SPARERIBS: Bring the spareribs and 2 cups (500 ml) water to a boil in a large saucepan. Reduce the heat, cover, and simmer until the ribs are tender, around 45 minutes. Remove from the heat.

When they are cool enough to handle, remove the spareribs and set aside. Reserve ¼ cup (60 ml) of the cooking liquid.

recipe continues →

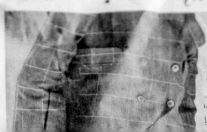

Curry paste being pounded with a mortar and pestle at Yay Puad, a restaurant in Chumphon.

WHILE THE SPARERIBS ARE SIMMERING, PREPARE THE BANANAS: Using a vegetable peeler, remove the stringy exterior of the bananas. Use a knife to chop the ends off the bananas. Using a Chinese roll cut, cut the bananas into roughly equal-sized triangular chunks around 1 inch long, immediately transferring them to a bowl of water as you go to prevent discoloring. You should have around 250 g banana chunks.

MAKE THE CURRY: Combine the thin coconut milk and bananas in a wok and bring to a boil over high heat, then reduce the heat and simmer rapidly until the bananas start to become tender, around 1 minute. Add the curry paste, stirring to combine, and cook at a rapid simmer until the paste is amalgamated and fragrant, around 1 minute. Add the spareribs, the reserved cooking liquid, and the sugar and simmer until the bananas and pork are tender and the ingredients are amalgamated, around 3 minutes.

Add the thick coconut milk and half of the citrus leaves (if using) and return to a simmer. Taste, adjusting the seasoning with additional salt if necessary; the curry should taste rich and herbal, followed by spicy and subtly sweet.

Remove to a serving bowl and garnish with the remaining citrus leaves (if using). Serve warm or at room temperature with long-grain rice.

Unripe "ladyfinger" bananas, Yay Puad, Chumphon.

Indian-Style Chicken Curry with Soybeans
Kaeng Karii Kai Sai Thua
แกงกะหรี่ไก่ใส่ถั่ว

Meena Leangjirakan was born in southern Thailand, but she can trace her ancestors back to a village near Hyderabad in India. Her great-grandparents came to Thailand via then-Burma, seeking work in the tin mines and rubber plantations. They eventually settled in a quiet village near a hot spring, just outside Ranong, where they also raised goats and cows and sold milk and spices. The small but visible Indian community they and others established still exists today, complete with dozens of residents of Indian heritage, a Hindu temple, the Telugu language as a lingua franca, and, of course, Indian food.

"They took their culinary traditions from home and found a way to earn money from them here in Thailand," explains Jaran, Meena's brother, of his great-grandparents. "We still follow this tradition by making their curry powder."

Under the brand name Mary Curry, Meena and Jaran make and sell a masala powder based on the family recipe, grinding the spices the old-school way, with a massive wooden mortar and pestle. It's spicy—I like to think of this as the southern Thai influence—and is an essential ingredient in kaeng karii, an Indian-style curry supplemented with dried soybeans that also stems from a family recipe. Meena suggested pairing the rich, meaty dish with the tart soup known in parts of southern India as *rasam*, and in this corner of southern Thailand as *sup makhaam*, Thai for "tamarind soup," and I've included her recipe for the dish.

Meena and Jaran wouldn't share the exact combination of spices that goes into their masala, but it has a distinct emphasis on chile, turmeric powder, and fenugreek, and I've re-created it as faithfully as I can.

Serves 4 as part of a meal with the tamarind soup

Meena and Jaran Leangjirakan at their home in Ranong.

FOR THE MASALA POWDER

½ teaspoon coriander seeds
½ teaspoon cumin seeds
¼ teaspoon black peppercorns
4 cloves
1 star anise
½ teaspoon fenugreek seeds
¼ teaspoon fennel seeds
⅛ teaspoon grated nutmeg
1 Siamese cardamom pod
5 teaspoons turmeric powder
2½ teaspoons chile powder
¼ teaspoon ground cinnamon

FOR THE CURRY

125 g dried split soybeans
½ cup (125 ml) vegetable oil
3 Siamese cardamom leaves
8 shallots (80 g total), peeled and sliced thin
6 cloves garlic (30 g total), peeled and minced
500 g chicken parts of your choice, skin-on or skinless, 2-inch pieces
1¼ teaspoons table salt
¼ teaspoon MSG (optional)

Tamarind Soup (recipe follows)

Meena and Jaran use skinless chicken thighs and breasts; I suggest skin-on thighs. Feel free to use whatever parts you prefer, being aware that this can affect cooking time.

UP TO A WEEK AHEAD, MAKE THE SPICE MIX: Dry-roast the coriander seeds, cumin seeds, peppercorns, cloves, and star anise in a wok or frying pan over medium heat, stirring frequently, until fragrant and toasted, around 2 minutes. Remove and set aside.

Add the fenugreek, fennel seeds, nutmeg, and Siamese cardamom to the wok and dry-roast, stirring frequently, until fragrant and toasted, around 1 minute. Remove from the heat.

Grind the turmeric powder, chile powder, cinnamon, and dry-roasted spices to a fine powder with a mortar and pestle, coffee grinder, or food processor. If making it in advance, remove the spice mix to an airtight container.

EARLY IN THE DAY OR THE NIGHT BEFORE COOKING, SOAK THE SOYBEANS: Cover the dried soybeans with a couple inches of water in a bowl and soak for at least 8 hours or as long as overnight.

MAKE THE CURRY: Heat the oil in a saucepan over medium-low heat. Add the cardamom leaves and shallots and fry, stirring frequently, until the shallots are just starting to turn golden and fragrant, around 5 minutes. Add the garlic and fry until fragrant and golden, 1 minute. Add 3 tablespoons plus 1 teaspoon of the masala powder and stir frequently until combined with the oil and fragrant, around 1 minute.

Drain the soybeans, discarding the soaking water. Add the soybeans and 1 cup (250 ml) water to the pan, increase the heat to high, and cook at a simmer until the soybeans are just starting to get tender, around 10 minutes.

Add ¾ cup (175 ml) water, the chicken, salt, and MSG (if using) to the pan, increase the heat, and bring to a simmer. Cover and simmer, stirring occasionally, until the chicken is cooked through and the soybeans are tender, around 20 minutes. Taste, adjusting the seasoning with salt if necessary; the curry should taste equal parts rich and spicy, followed by salty and savory, with a distinct aroma from the dried spices and a pleasantly oily but relatively dry consistency.

Remove to a serving bowl and serve warm with long-grain rice and the soup.

OPPOSITE: Indian-Style Chicken Curry with Soybeans, foreground, Tamarind Soup, background, as made by Meena Leangjirakan, Ranong.

TAMARIND SOUP
Sup Makhaam
ซุปมะขาม

Serves 4 as part of a meal with the chicken curry

50 g dried tamarind paste
1 tablespoon vegetable oil
16 fresh curry leaves
¼ teaspoon masala powder (from the recipe in Indian-Style Chicken Curry with Soybeans, page 89)
¼ teaspoon cumin seeds
¼ teaspoon fenugreek seeds
4 medium spicy dried chiles (2 g)
4 shallots (40 g total), sliced thin
1 teaspoon table salt

PREPARE THE TAMARIND BROTH: Bring 4 cups (1 L) water to a boil in a saucepan over high heat. Remove the pan from the heat, add the dried tamarind paste, and mash with a spoon to combine. Cover and set aside for 15 minutes.

Pour the tamarind mixture through a sieve set over a bowl, pushing on the solids to extract as much of the pulp as possible; discard the solids. Set aside.

MAKE THE SOUP: Heat the vegetable oil in a wok over medium-low heat. Add the curry leaves, masala powder, cumin seeds, fenugreek, and dried chiles and fry, stirring frequently, until fragrant, around 1 minute. Add the shallots and fry until just golden, around 5 minutes. Add the tamarind paste and salt, increase the heat to high, and bring to a simmer. Taste, adjusting the seasoning if necessary; the soup should taste tart, followed by equal parts spicy and salty, and there should be a distinct aroma from the curry leaves.

Transfer the soup to small serving bowls and serve warm or at room temperature.

Vendors preparing beef soup at a stall in Yala.

BEEF SOUP AND AN OMELET

In Yala, a city in Thailand's predominantly Muslim deep south, there's an entire alley lined with restaurants that serve beef soup. Down the dark, narrow lane, diners, pedestrians, and motorcyclists vie for space with at least six different places that specialize in the dish, each with a noodle stall–like vat of bubbling broth and a glass display case hung with offal. Order a bowl and a few slices of tripe, and a fistful of mung bean sprouts will be parboiled and topped with the beefy broth and the bowl given a boost from a last-minute seasoning of white pepper, MSG, sugar, fish sauce, lime juice, and chiles.

In Pattani, another city in Thailand's deep south, beef soup is also popular, and one restaurant there, Maksu Soup Chormalee, maintains a cauldron the size of a kiddie pool of the stuff. On a daily basis, it's topped up with oxtails, feet, shank, bones, lungs, and liver, not to mention herbs and dried spices. Choose your preferred cut—the people of Pattani are fans of the slightly gelatinous slices of skin from the feet—and your bowl will also be supplemented with those salty, fragrant, spicy, sweet, and tart seasonings.

Thai Muslims love their beef soup. And in Yala, Pattani, and elsewhere in the region, those bowls of beef soup are, almost without exception, paired with two items: rice and an omelet. Given that this is Southeast Asia, the rice is a no-brainer. But the omelet?

"Soup and an omelet? I don't know why, it's hard to say," says Shukree, a beef soup vendor in Yala, who only shared his first name, when I ask him to explain the reasoning behind this very specific, unique, and, to me at least, incongruous combination.

Cheusman Chetahey, the co-owner of Maksu Soup Chormalee, has a simpler reason: "For local people, if there's beef soup, then there has to be an omelet!"

Left to my own theories, I reached the conclusion that it works because the two dishes compensate for what each other lacks. Beef soup, it doesn't need to be said, is a liquid; one with meaty, tart, slightly sweet flavors and herbaceous dried spice aromas. An omelet is, by contrast, a solid dish with rich, oily, salty flavors. With rice as a centerpiece and a side of crunchy vegetables and herbs, the two coalesce in a meal that spans just about every texture and flavor imaginable while also managing to feel both light and satiating.

LEFT: The massive vat of beef soup at Maksu Soup Chormalee, in Pattani.
RIGHT: Offal on display at a stall that sells beef soup in Yala.
OPPOSITE: Thai Muslim–Style Oxtail Soup, Maksu Soup Chormalee, in Pattani.

Thai Muslim–Style Oxtail Soup

Sup Haang Wua
ซุปหางวัว

Cow's feet and stomach are, most likely, tough to source, so I'm sharing a version of this soup that is made with oxtails, another popular cut in Thailand's deep south.

Serves 4 as part of a meal with the Thai-Style Omelet

FOR THE SOUP

2 star anise
4 Siamese cardamom pods
A 3-inch cinnamon stick
4 cloves
2 long pepper seeds
1 teaspoon coriander seeds
1 cup (250 ml) vegetable oil
16 shallots (160 g total), sliced
1 small white onion (60 g), peeled and quartered
4 cloves garlic (20 g total), peeled and halved
1 small carrot (50 g), peeled and roughly chopped
1 medium tomato (90 g), halved and seeds removed
1 kg oxtails, cut into 2-inch pieces
2 teaspoons table salt
1 pandan leaf, tied in a knot
A 6-inch piece ginger (60 g), peeled and cut into thick slices
A 6-inch piece galangal (60 g), peeled and cut into thick slices
4 cilantro roots
1 teaspoon white pepper, plus more for serving

1 tablespoon fish sauce, plus more for serving
2 teaspoons white sugar, plus more for serving
¼ cup (60 ml) lime juice, plus more for serving
Scant ¼ teaspoon MSG (optional)
10 medium spicy fresh chiles (25 g total)
4 scallions (50 g total), chopped

FOR SERVING

A platter that includes greens such as sliced cucumber, small Thai eggplants, scallions and/or cilantro sprigs, and/or long beans, along with the remaining deep-fried crispy shallots, a few sliced limes, and the remaining crushed chiles

Thai-Style Omelet (recipe follows)

Skinless or skin-on (the latter is standard in southern Thailand) oxtails can be used here. With skinless, you'll get more meat, but the broth will have less lip-smacking collagen. If using skin-on oxtails, score the skin deeply lengthwise to make the meat easier to get at.

The dish is garnished with shallots, slowly simmered in oil until golden, sweet, and crispy. Don't rush the deep-frying here, or the shallots will taste unpleasantly bitter.

UP TO A WEEK BEFORE SERVING, PREPARE THE SPICES: Heat a wok or frying pan over medium heat. Dry-roast the star anise, cardamom, cinnamon, cloves, and long pepper seeds until fragrant and toasted, around 2 minutes. Remove and set aside. Dry-roast the coriander seeds until fragrant and toasted, around 2 minutes. Remove from the heat.

Grind the coriander seeds to a fine powder with a mortar and pestle, coffee grinder, or food processor. If preparing them in advance, remove the spices to an airtight container.

UP TO A DAY OR TWO BEFORE SERVING, MAKE THE DEEP-FRIED CRISPY SHALLOTS: Combine the oil and shallots in a small wok set and heat the oil to 250°F over medium-low heat. Cook at a low simmer, stirring occasionally, until the shallots are golden, fragrant, and toasted, around 45 minutes.

Drain the shallots in a fine-mesh sieve set over a bowl and transfer to a plate lined with paper towels to drain; reserve 2 tablespoons of the frying oil. Shift the shallots to another set of paper towels to drain further. When they are cool, dry, and crispy, remove the shallots to an airtight container.

AT LEAST 4 HOURS BEFORE SERVING, MAKE THE SOUP: Process the onion, garlic, carrot, and tomato to a paste in a blender or food processor. Set aside.

Bring 2 quarts (2 L) water to a rapid boil in a stockpot over high heat. Working in batches, blanch the oxtails in the boiling water and then transfer to a sieve or colander to drain. Discard the water.

Heat the reserved shallot oil in a large stockpot over medium heat. Add the pureed vegetables and fry, stirring frequently, until fragrant, around 5 minutes. Add the oxtails, salt, and 3 quarts (3 L) water, increase the heat to high, and bring to a rolling boil for a few seconds. Reduce the heat and simmer until the oxtails are just starting to get tender when tested with a fork, around 1 hour.

Add the pandan leaf, ginger, galangal, cilantro roots, white pepper, and the reserved spices to the pot, cover, and simmer until the meat is tender enough to easily be pulled apart with a fork, 3 to 4 more hours. Add the fish sauce, sugar, lime juice, and MSG (if using). Taste, adjusting the seasoning if necessary; the soup should taste tart and savory, with a strong but pleasant fragrance from the dried spices and aromatics.

Using a mortar and pestle, crush the chiles to a coarse paste. Set aside. Add a pinch of sugar, a few drops of fish sauce, a dash of white pepper, a squeeze of lime, and some of the crushed chiles to each of four small individual bowls, or slightly more to a large serving bowl. Pour the soup into the bowl(s) and garnish with the chopped scallions and some of the deep-fried shallots. Serve hot with the platter of greens and the additional garnishes, the omelet, and long-grain rice.

Thai Muslim–style beef soup, an omelet, and sides, Maksu Soup Chormalee, in Pattani.

THAI-STYLE OMELET
Khai Jiaw
ไข่เจียว

In Thailand, omelets are essentially deep-fried, resulting in crispy folds and layers. If the oil you've used seems to have magically disappeared, don't be alarmed; the eggs soak it all up. This recipe is courtesy of Andy Ricker.

Serves 4 as part of a meal with the oxtail soup

4 eggs	**6 drops white vinegar**
2 teaspoons fish sauce	**¼ cup (60 ml) vegetable oil**

Beat the eggs, fish sauce, and vinegar together in a bowl.

Heat the oil in a wok over high heat. When the oil is smoking, pour in the egg mixture in a slow, thin stream from at least 1 foot above the pan. When the omelet is golden and crispy on the bottom, after about 1 minute, flip and continue to fry until golden, crispy, and puffed up, a total of around 2 minutes.

Remove to a serving plate and serve hot.

INTO THE DEEP FRYER

Mention Hat Yai, a landlocked urban center in far southern Thailand, to any Thai and it's likely you'll get one response: fried chicken. The city is synonymous with the dish, which is sold from dozens of carts and stalls in the city center—as well as in just about every corner of Thailand.

Although each stall has its own signature elements, in Hat Yai, fried chicken is sold almost exclusively by Muslims. The dish is generally only available at night, typically from mobile stalls, and is usually sold to-go. And the chicken is almost always accompanied by three elements: a sweet, slightly tart, slightly spicy, very gloopy dipping sauce; a hillock of crispy deep-fried shallots; and sticky rice. Silverware never makes its way near this dish: diners eat the chicken with their hands, tearing the bird apart and plunging it into the dipping sauce, pinching off mounds of sticky rice and pressing them into the deep-fried shallots, and, in general, making a delicious, fun, hands-on mess.

OPPOSITE: A busy exchange of fried chicken and money, Kai Thawt Bat Khiw, a stall in Hat Yai.
ABOVE: Buying fried chicken to-go at Khao Mok Rot Sing, a stall in Hat Yai.

Hat Yai–Style Fried Chicken with Sticky Rice and a Dipping Sauce as served at Kai Thawt Bat Khiw, Hat Yai.

Hat Yai–Style Fried Chicken with Sticky Rice and a Dipping Sauce

Kai Thawt Haat Yai
ไก่ทอดหาดใหญ่

Serves 4

FOR THE CRISPY DEEP-FRIED SHALLOTS

30 shallots (300 g total), peeled and sliced lengthwise
½ teaspoon table salt
4 cups (1 L) palm oil

FOR THE DIPPING SAUCE

1 teaspoon table salt
10 medium spicy fresh red chiles (30 g total)
9 cloves garlic (45 g total), peeled
1 cup (200 g) white sugar
6 tablespoons white vinegar
1 teaspoon tapioca starch

FOR THE CHICKEN

2 tablespoons plus 2 teaspoons table salt (40 g total)
2 tablespoons plus 2 teaspoons light soy sauce
⅓ cup (60 g) white sugar
26 cloves garlic (130 g total), peeled and smashed
¼ cup coriander seeds
2 teaspoons white pepper
4 teaspoons MSG (optional; see Note)

2 kg bone-in chicken parts, such as wings, drumsticks, thighs, and/or breasts (breasts or thighs halved)
4 cups (1 L) palm oil

FOR THE STICKY RICE

2 cups (400 g) sticky rice

Vendors in Hat Yai wouldn't use the term, but essentially they're seasoning their chicken via a brine. This recipe is based on a 5 percent brine (5 g table salt per 100 g water, or 1 teaspoon table salt per ½ cup/125 ml water), with light soy sauce for color and aroma; MSG for flavor and color; and some aromatics. (You can omit the MSG if you want, but your fried chicken won't have the requisite flavor and color.)

Palm oil allows for deep-frying at a lower heat, resulting in a crispier product.

The most efficient way to steam sticky rice is with a Thai-style pot and a conical bamboo basket. If you don't have access to these tools, a steaming set can be improvised with a sieve elevated over boiling water, or a Chinese-style steaming set lined with cheesecloth, although the cooking time may vary.

UP TO A DAY AHEAD, MAKE THE DEEP-FRIED CRISPY SHALLOTS: Combine the shallots and salt in a bowl, tossing to mix. Transfer the shallots to a small wok, add the oil, and heat the oil to 250°F over

medium-low heat. Cook at a low simmer, stirring occasionally, until the shallots are golden, fragrant, and toasted, around 45 minutes.

Drain the shallots in a fine-mesh wire sieve set over a bowl, then transfer to a plate lined with paper towels to drain (reserve the oil for frying the chicken). Shift the shallots to another set of paper towels to drain further. When the shallots are cool, dry, and crispy, remove to an airtight container.

ALSO UP TO A DAY AHEAD, MAKE THE DIPPING SAUCE: Pound the salt, chiles, and garlic to a coarse paste with a mortar and pestle. Set aside.

Combine the sugar, vinegar, and ½ cup (125 ml) water in a saucepan and bring to a boil over high heat, then reduce to a simmer and cook, stirring occasionally until the sugar has dissolved and the mixture has reduced slightly, around 5 minutes. Add the chiles and garlic and simmer until the sauce has reduced by about half and is starting to thicken, around 10 minutes.

Whisk together the tapioca starch and 1 tablespoon water in a small bowl. Add to the simmering sauce, stirring to combine, and simmer for 1 to 2 more minutes. Taste, adjusting the seasoning if necessary; the dipping sauce should taste sweet and spicy and have a syrupy texture. If making it in advance, remove the dip to an airtight container and store in the refrigerator.

recipe continues →

THE DAY BEFORE—OR AT LEAST 5 HOURS AHEAD—PREPARE THE BRINE FOR THE CHICKEN: Combine the salt, soy sauce, sugar, garlic, coriander seeds, white pepper, MSG (if using), and 2 quarts (2 L) water in a large bowl, stirring to dissolve the salt and sugar. Score each piece of chicken one or two times to the bone. Transfer the chicken to a plastic container, add the brine, cover, and marinate in the refrigerator for at least 5 hours, or up to overnight.

AT LEAST 8 HOURS BEFORE SERVING, PREPARE THE STICKY RICE: Gently rinse the sticky rice in several changes of water until the water remains clear. Cover with about 2 inches of fresh water and soak for 4 to 6 hours.

A COUPLE HOURS BEFORE SERVING, STEAM THE STICKY RICE: Drain the rice, discarding the water. Bring a couple quarts of water to a boil in a Thai-style sticky rice steaming pot (or in a saucepan or a Chinese-style steamer). Put the rice in the bamboo steaming basket (or in a sieve or a Chinese-style steamer lined with cheesecloth) positioned a few inches above the boiling water, cover with a tea towel and a then a lid, creating a relatively tight seal that allows as little steam as possible to escape, and steam for 20 minutes.

Flip the entire mass of rice and steam for another 5 minutes, or until the grains are entirely cooked through, tender, and visibly stuck together. Remove the rice from the heat, transfer to a bowl or large plate, and gently stir with a wooden spoon to release steam for around 10 seconds. Remove the rice to a Thai-style sticky rice basket (or a cooler or Tupperware container lined with cheesecloth; cover to keep warm). Set aside.

FRY THE CHICKEN: Combine the 4 cups (1 L) oil and the reserved shallot oil in a wok and heat to 350°F over high heat. Set up a rack for draining the fried chicken.

Remove the chicken from the brine, wiping away and discarding any garlic or coriander seeds and patting the chicken dry with paper towels. Put a few pieces of chicken (if using different cuts of chicken, cook pieces of the same cut together) in the oil and deep-fry. Initially the heat will drop; increase the heat to boost the temperature, or turn off the heat or add more oil to reduce the temperature, to maintain an oil temperature of between 335°F and 350°F after around 5 minutes of frying. Fry the chicken until it's fragrant and cooked through (remove a piece and slice it to the bone to check) with crispy, orange skin, 8 to 12 minutes, depending on the cut (thighs tend to fry quickly, while wings take a bit longer). Remove the chicken from the oil with tongs or a flat mesh strainer (also known as a spider) and drain on the rack. Repeat with the remaining pieces.

Remove the fried chicken to a platter and serve hot or at room temperature with the sticky rice, dipping sauce, and crispy deep-fried shallots.

OPPOSITE: Inside a cafe in Pattani.

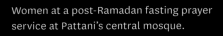
Women at a post-Ramadan fasting prayer service at Pattani's central mosque.

Fasting and Feasting

I T'S RAMADAN, the holy month, when Muslims fast between sunrise and sunset, and Hameedah Cheuma, who provided some of the recipes in this book, has invited me to take part in her family's *iftar*, or post-fasting meal. I arrive at the family home in Pattani, in Thailand's far south, and find it busy with the bustle of cooking: a sister pounding herbs with a mortar and pestle, another peeling and shredding tiny mangoes, yet others peeling shrimp and deep-frying shallots until golden and crispy. It looks like a normal afternoon for this friendly, food-obsessed family, although, of course, nobody is tasting any of the dishes that are in progress at this point.

Close to sunset, family members bring the dishes to the living room, distributing them between two mats: one for men and one for women. There is a salad-like dish of shredded beef in a dressing that combines coconut milk and palm sugar; tiny shrimp pounded in a mortar and pestle and paired with deliciously tart green mangoes; a vegetable-forward soup; salted eggs and sun-dried fish; a platter of fresh vegetables; and fried chicken, along with another couple of prepared dishes and sweets bought from the market. We sit on the mats, clutching dates in our hands, waiting for the *azan*, or the signal from the mosque that it is, officially, sunset.

"Yesterday we ate at 6:26 p.m., today we eat at 6:25 p.m.," says Adam, Hameedah's brother, looking somewhat fidgety and impatient.

With the green light from the mosque, there is a brief prayer before people slam down their dates, take massive gulps of water (many Muslims in Pattani also refrain from drinking any liquids during the daytime), and dig in. The eating that follows is not gluttonous but it is rapid, and by 6:45 p.m., all of the men have cleared their plates and are on their way to the mosque.

I ask Hameedah and Adam if there are any particular dishes associated with post-fasting meals.

"Dates are the food most associated with Ramadan," Adam tells me of the ingredient that's used to break the fast across the Muslim world, adding, "If you eat dates, you get even more merit!" Perhaps anticipating yet another string of food-related questions from me, he goes on to explain, "Ramadan is about fasting, so there aren't any special dishes during this period. It's more about making food and sharing with others or people who don't have so much."

Hameedah adds, "You should try fasting! Just for a day. Then you'll know how people who don't have food to eat every day feel."

It was a reminder to me that, although many Muslim celebrations revolve around special, often decadent, dishes—some of which I share below—Ramadan is about sacrifice and giving, rather than feasting. A reminder that more of us could use these days.

LEFT: Hameedah Cheuma and her family breaking the Ramadan fast, Pattani.
ABOVE: Muslim vendors at a curry stall on Ko Yao Noi, Phang-Nga Province.

Goat Biryani with Ajaat
Khaao Mok Phae
ข้าวหมกแพะ

When it comes to celebratory feasts among southern Thailand's Muslim community, goat rules. Many Muslims in the deep south keep goats—they're a common sight wandering the villages of the region—and when it's time for an occasion such as a wedding or birth, they are slaughtered and included in some sort of decadent communal dish. A massive wok of goat curry is standard. Another favorite for this treatment is goat biryani.

"Goat is expensive, so we only make this dish on special occasions," says Aisamaae Tokoi, the chef at Luukrieang, an orphanage and community center in Yala, who shared his recipe for goat biryani with me. "We only cook it at big festivals. We'll slaughter a goat and cook enough to serve many people."

Although time-consuming, Aisamaae's biryani is not particularly difficult to make, and the golden, fragrant rice and the obligatory tart/spicy quick pickle (the eponymous ajaat) are enough to win over even those who might be intimidated by the thought of eating this particular meat.

Serves 6

FOR THE BIRYANI

2 tablespoons coriander seeds
½ teaspoon black peppercorns
2 long pepper seeds
Two 3-inch cinnamon sticks
4 star anise
6 Siamese cardamom seeds
6 cloves
2 tablespoons vegetable oil
8 shallots (80 g total), peeled and sliced thin
8 cloves garlic (40 g total), peeled and sliced thin
2 tablespoons turmeric powder
1½ kg bone-in goat parts, in 6 equal portions, excess skin removed

A 3½-inch piece ginger (35 g), peeled and sliced
A 2-inch piece galangal (20 g), peeled and sliced
1 tablespoon table salt
15 g palm sugar
2 tablespoons ketchup
3 cups long-grain white rice

FOR THE AJAAT

½ cup (100 g) white sugar
1¼ teaspoons table salt
¼ cup (60 ml) white vinegar
4 small cucumbers (300 g total), halved lengthwise and sliced thin
4 large mild fresh chiles (100 g total), sliced
6 cherry tomatoes (100 g total), halved
13 shallots (130 g total), peeled and sliced
2 cloves garlic (10 g total), peeled and sliced thin

FOR THE DIPPING SAUCE

3 tomatoes (300 g total), halved and seeded
3 cloves garlic (15 g total), peeled and sliced
4 cilantro roots (2 g total), chopped
16 tiny spicy fresh chiles (8 g total)
1 teaspoon white sugar
½ teaspoon table salt
2 tablespoons lime juice
2 sprigs cilantro, chopped (including stems)

FOR SERVING

A platter that includes crunchy lettuce leaves, scallions, bai man puu (see Glossary), large mild fresh chiles, and/or cucumbers

---

Among southern Thai Muslims, the most prized cut for goat biryani is foreleg, because it offers the most meat with the least bone. However, any cut or mix of cuts works (ribs are especially delicious), but be sure to remove as much excess skin as possible.

Using a wide (rather than tall) pot to cook the rice will help distribute the heat so all the grains of rice cook evenly.

---

recipe continues →

Dry-roast the coriander seeds, black pepper, long pepper, cinnamon, star anise, Siamese cardamom, and cloves in a wok or frying pan over medium heat until fragrant and toasted, around 2 minutes. Remove from the heat.

Transfer half of the spices to a plate and set aside. Grind the remaining toasted spices to a fine powder with a mortar and pestle, coffee grinder, or food processor. If making them in advance, remove the spices to two airtight containers, keeping the whole and ground spices separate.

AT LEAST 4 HOURS BEFORE SERVING, PREPARE THE GOAT: Heat the oil in a stockpot over medium heat. Add the shallots and garlic and fry until fragrant and golden, around 5 minutes. Add the reserved ground spices and the turmeric powder and fry until combined and fragrant. Add 2 quarts (2 L) water, the goat, ginger, and galangal and increase the heat to high. Bring the mixture to a rolling boil for around 5 seconds, then reduce the heat to a simmer, cover, and cook for 30 minutes.

Add the salt, sugar, and ketchup to the pot and stir. Cover and simmer until the goat is just short of falliing-off-the-bone tender when pierced with a fork, 2½ to 3 hours.

WHILE THE GOAT IS SIMMERING, PREPARE THE AJAAT: Combine the sugar, salt, and ½ cup (125 ml) water in a saucepan, bring to a boil over high heat, and boil for 5 seconds or so, then reduce the heat and simmer, stirring frequently, until the sugar and salt have dissolved, around 1 minute. Remove from the heat and let cool.

Combine the cooled sugar mixture, the vinegar, cucumbers, chiles, cherry tomatoes, shallots, and garlic in a bowl. Taste, adjusting the seasoning if necessary; the ajaat should taste sweet and then tart, with faint background flavors of salty and spicy. Remove to a small serving bowl and set aside in the refrigerator.

MAKE THE DIPPING SAUCE: Process the tomatoes, garlic, cilantro roots, chiles, sugar, salt, lime juice, and 2 tablespoons water to a puree in a blender or food processor. Taste, adjusting the seasoning if necessary; the dipping sauce should taste tart, spicy, and a bit salty and be fragrant from the cilantro root and garlic. Stir in the chopped cilantro, remove to a small serving bowl, and set aside in the refrigerator.

AT LEAST 1 HOUR BEFORE SERVING, MAKE THE RICE: Drain the goat in a sieve set over a bowl. Retain the broth and goat meat and discard any other solids.

Gently wash the rice in several changes of water until the water runs clear. Combine the rice, goat, 4 cups (1 L) of the reserved broth, and the toasted spices in a wide stockpot and bring to a rolling boil over high heat for 5 seconds or so. Cover, reduce heat to as low as possible, and cook the rice for 20 minutes.

Turn off the heat and remove the lid for 5 seconds to allow excess heat and steam to escape, then cover and allow the rice to rest for 20 minutes. Uncover and gently stir the contents of the pot, then cover again and let rest for 5 more minutes.

Remove the biryani to plates and serve warm, with the ajaat, dipping sauce, and platter of vegetables.

Jutharat Birangrot, right, and her colleagues form a collective that promotes the food of Satun, their home province.

Beef Kurma
Kaeng Kurumaa Nuea
แกงกุรุม่าเนื้อ

Southern Thailand's Muslims are big fans of meat, but protein-centered dishes gain even more prominence during celebrations such as weddings, births, and ordinations. In the region, when it comes time for a special feast, it's obligatory for the host to purchase and slaughter a goat or cow—or, at the very least, shell out for a generous amount of meat from the butcher—and share it with everyone in the family, and often the community, as a gesture of generosity. Curries are a common vehicle for this meal, mostly because they're delicious, but also because they're relatively easy to scale up for as many as dozens of diners.

"This is a dish we'd eat at weddings," says Jutharat Birangrot, a native of the southern province of Satun, who shared with me her recipe for kaeng kuruma nuea, a mild beef curry. "You can use goat or chicken, but for celebrations, we tend to use beef."

It's likely that kurma, a dish with origins in Mughal, India, arrived in Satun via its neighbor to the south, Malaysia, a former British colony. Mughal-style kurma gets its mild, creamy taste from the addition of yogurt; in Satun, this comes from coconut milk. Countering this creaminess is an herb paste made from fragrant mild green chiles and a mix of dried spices that includes dill and fennel, the latter rarities in the Thai kitchen. The result is a sophisticated, almost delicate centerpiece dish that Jutharat suggests pairing with tart, sweet, rich Malay-Style Pineapple Curry (page 114).

Serves 4 as part of a southern Thai meal

recipe continues →

Two 3-inch sticks cinnamon

6 Siamese cardamom pods

2 star anise

1 tablespoon coriander seeds

2 teaspoons cumin seeds

1 teaspoon dill seeds

1 teaspoon fennel seeds

½ teaspoon table salt

4 large mild fresh green chiles (100 g total), sliced

10 shallots (100 g total), peeled and sliced

10 cloves garlic (50 g total), peeled and sliced

A 1½-inch piece ginger, peeled and julienned

FOR THE CURRY

2 tablespoons vegetable oil

5 cups (1.2 L) thin coconut milk (see page 135 for instructions on how to make thin coconut milk)

250 g lean boneless beef (such as round steak), sliced against the grain into 3-inch-long strips

1½ cups (350 ml) thick coconut milk (see page 135 for instructions on how to make thick coconut milk)

1 potato (180 g), peeled, halved lengthwise, and cut into ½-inch-thick slices

3 small white onions (100 g total), peeled and halved lengthwise

20 g palm sugar

1 teaspoon table salt

2 large mild fresh red chiles (50 g total), sliced on the bias

UP TO 5 DAYS IN ADVANCE, IF DESIRED, MAKE THE CURRY PASTE: Dry-roast the cinnamon, Siamese cardamom, and star anise in a wok or frying pan over medium heat until fragrant and toasted, around 2 minutes. Remove and set aside. Add the coriander seeds to the pan and dry-roast until fragrant and toasted, around 2 minutes. Remove to a plate. Add the cumin, dill, and fennel seeds to the pan and dry-roast until fragrant and toasted, around 1 minute. Remove to the plate.

Grind the coriander, cumin, dill, and fennel seeds to a fine powder with a mortar and pestle, coffee grinder, or food processor. Set aside.

Pound and grind the salt and chiles to a coarse paste with a mortar and pestle. Add half of the shallots, garlic, and ginger and pound and grind to a coarse paste. Add the ground spices and pound and grind to a fine paste. (Alternatively, if using a food processor or blender, process the salt, chiles, half the shallots, half the garlic, half the ginger, and the ground spices to a fine paste.) If making it in advance, remove the paste to an airtight container and store in the refrigerator.

MAKE THE CURRY: Heat the oil in a wok or saucepan over low heat. Add the remaining shallots, garlic, and ginger and the cinnamon, Siamese cardamom, and star anise and fry, stirring frequently, until the aromatics are fragrant and golden, around 1 minute. Add the curry paste and 1 cup (250 ml) of the thin coconut milk and fry, stirring frequently, until fragrant and a thin layer of oil has emerged, around 10 minutes.

Add the beef, stirring to combine. Add the remaining 4 cups (1 L) thin coconut milk and increase the heat to a rapid simmer. Reduce the heat to low and simmer, checking occasionally, until the beef is tender, around 1 hour.

Add the thick coconut milk, potatoes, onion, and palm sugar, bring to a simmer, and simmer until the potatoes are tender, around 15 minutes. Taste, adjusting the seasoning with salt and palm sugar if necessary; the curry should taste rich and just barely sweet from the coconut milk and be fragrant from the cumin and green chiles.

Remove to a serving bowl, garnish with the sliced red chiles, and serve warm or at room temperature with long-grain rice.

OPPOSITE: Beef Kurma as prepared by Jutharat Birangrot, Satun.

Malay-Style Pineapple Curry
Kaeng Patcharii
แกงปัจรี

Even Muslim-style feasts occasionally take a break from all that protein. An example is this meat-free curry, made from thick slices of pineapple braised in coconut milk with herbs and dried spices.

"In Satun, we live near the border," explains Jutharat Birangrot, who provided this recipe, of her home province. "People cross over to relatives' weddings and other events in Malaysia, and they probably brought dishes like this back."

To reach the proper confluence of fork-tender pineapple and amalgamated flavors and aromas, Jutharat tells me, cooks in Satun might simmer a massive pot of pineapple curry overnight before a festival or celebration. This scaled-down recipe doesn't require that much time, but it does involve a braise that can't be rushed. Jutharat suggests pairing the dish with Beef Kurma (page 111), the mild, fragrant, meaty curry providing a sharp contrast with the dish's predominantly sweet, rich flavors.

Serves 4 as part of a southern Thai meal

FOR THE CURRY PASTE

5 large mild dried chiles (25g total)
4 star anise
Three 2-inch cinnamon sticks
1 teaspoon coriander seeds
1 teaspoon cumin seeds
⅔ cup finely grated coconut (75 g; see page 24 for tips on grating coconut)
1 teaspoon table salt
16 shallots (160 g total), peeled and sliced
10 cloves garlic (50 g total), peeled and sliced
A 7-inch piece of ginger (65 g), peeled and sliced into very thin matchsticks

FOR THE CURRY

1 large pineapple (around 1.5 kg)
1 tablespoon vegetable oil

4 cups (1 L) thin coconut milk (see page 135 for instructions on how to make thin coconut milk)
1 cup (250 ml) thick coconut milk (see page 135 for instructions on how to make thick coconut milk)
30 g palm sugar
1 tablespoon fish sauce (optional)
2 teaspoons table salt

Select a slightly tart, slightly unripe, "crunchy" pineapple for this curry.

The seasoning of this dish depends on the sweetness of your pineapple and so can vary. Fish sauce is an optional seasoning here; if you only use salt, the recipe is entirely vegan.

UP TO 5 DAYS IN ADVANCE, IF DESIRED, MAKE THE CURRY PASTE: Combine the dried chiles and enough water to cover by an inch or two in a saucepan and bring to a boil over high heat. Remove the saucepan from the heat, cover, and soak the chiles for 15 minutes.

Drain the chiles, discarding the water, and when they are cool enough to handle, remove and discard the seeds and stringy membranes. Slice the chiles and drain in a sieve or colander.

Dry-roast the star anise and cinnamon in a wok or frying pan over medium heat until fragrant and toasted, about 4 minutes. Remove and set aside. Add the coriander seeds and cumin seeds to the pan and dry-roast until fragrant and toasted, around 2 minutes. Remove and set aside. Add the grated coconut and dry-roast, stirring frequently, until golden, fragrant, and toasted, around 15 minutes. Remove and set aside.

Grind 2 of the star anise, 2 pieces cinnamon stick, the coriander seeds, and cumin seeds to a fine powder with a mortar and pestle, coffee grinder, or food processor (reserve the remaining star anise and cinnamon for the curry). Set aside.

Pound and grind the chiles and salt to a coarse paste with a mortar and pestle. Add half of the shallots and garlic and pound and grind to a coarse paste (reserve the remaining shallots and garlic for the curry). Add one-third of the ginger and pound and grind to a fine paste (reserve the remaining ginger for the curry). Add the toasted coconut and ground spices and pound and grind to a fine paste. (Alternatively, if using a food processor or blender, process the chiles, salt, half of the shallots, half of the garlic, one-third of the ginger, the toasted coconut, and ground spices to a fine paste.) If making it in advance, remove the paste to an airtight container and store in the refrigerator.

A COUPLE HOURS BEFORE SERVING, MAKE THE CURRY: Peel the pineapple, removing the "eyes." Cut into rings approximately ¾ inch thick, removing the tough central core as you go. You should have approximately 750 g of pineapple rings.

Heat the oil in a wok over medium-low heat. Add the reserved garlic, shallots, and ginger and fry, stirring frequently, until fragrant and golden, about 1 minute. Add the curry paste and ¼ cup (60 ml) of the thin coconut milk and fry until fragrant, around

5 minutes. Add the pineapple, the reserved star anise and cinnamon, and the remaining 3¾ cups (900 ml) thin coconut milk, increase the heat, and cook at a rapid simmer, stirring occasionally, until the pineapple is tender, the liquid has reduced to just below the level of the pineapple, and a thin layer of oil has emerged on the surface, about 1 hour.

Add the thick coconut milk, palm sugar, fish sauce (if using), and salt, bring to a simmer, and simmer for 30 minutes. Taste, adjusting the seasoning if necessary; the curry should taste rich and equal parts sweet and tart, followed by slightly spicy and salty, with a strong, almost concentrated pineapple fragrance and a background of aroma from the spices.

Remove the curry to a serving bowl and serve warm or at room temperature with long-grain rice.

Malay-Style Pineapple Curry as prepared by Jutharat Birangrot, Satun.

Vendors at Satun's central market.

SOUTHERN THAILAND'S FLATBREAD

In restaurants and stalls across southern Thailand, cooks expertly manipulate balls of dough, pulling and twisting them into layered disks and then frying them in oil or margarine until they are as crispy and flaky as a croissant. At this point, the roti, as they are known across Thailand, resemble flatbreads or pancakes. But at Roti Thaew Nam, a decades-old restaurant in Phuket, one more important step remains. After they are fried, the cook pins one edge of a roti down to a work surface and hacks away at it with a stainless steel plate, shredding and ripping apart those layers, resulting in a hillock of what can only be described as irregular, crispy noodles. As a final flourish, the shreds are then slapped between two sheets of paper to puff them up and create even more surface area. The roti is then topped with a fried egg—a particularly Phuket touch—and served with a small bowl of a mild, almost soup-like chicken curry. The result is less a flatbread and more a deconstructed curry noodle soup that's one of the tastiest breakfasts in southern Thailand.

OPPOSITE: Roti with a Fried Egg and Chicken Curry at Roti Thaew Nam, in Phuket Town.
ABOVE: Frying roti, Thai-Muslim flatbeads, at Roti Thaew Nam, in Phuket Town.

Roti with a Fried Egg and Chicken Curry

Roti Khai Daao Kaeng Kai

โรตี ไข่ดาวแกงไก่

Serves 6

FOR THE ROTI DOUGH

¼ cup (60 ml) melted butter or margarine

1 egg

2 tablespoons sweetened condensed milk

½ teaspoon table salt

300 g all-purpose flour, plus more if needed

FOR THE CHICKEN CURRY

A 3-inch stick cinnamon

4 star anise

6 cloves

½ teaspoon black peppercorns

½ teaspoon coriander seeds

½ teaspoon cumin seeds

½ teaspoon fennel seeds

1 teaspoon mild chile powder (or cayenne pepper)

1 tablespoon vegetable oil

A 3-inch piece ginger (30 g), peeled and sliced into very thin matchsticks

400 g boneless chicken thighs, cut into 1-inch pieces

2 cups (500 ml) thin coconut milk (see page 135 for instructions on how to make thin coconut milk)

1 heaping teaspoon table salt

2 teaspoons white sugar

¼ teaspoon MSG (optional)

FOR THE ROTI

Oil for handling

8 ounces (225 g) butter or margarine for frying

6 eggs

THE DAY BEFORE SERVING, MAKE THE ROTI DOUGH: Combine 2 teaspoons of the melted butter, the egg, sweetened condensed milk, salt, and ½ cup (125 ml) water in a bowl. Beat with a fork or whisk to combine.

Measure the flour into another bowl. Slowly add the liquid mixture, using your hands to combine. The dough will be wet and sticky; if it's too sticky to handle, add another 25 g to 50 g flour. Gather the dough into a ball, turn it out onto a clean work surface, and knead vigorously, folding the dough onto itself, until it is warm, smooth, and elastic, 15 to 20 minutes. Return the dough to the bowl, cover with plastic wrap, and allow to rest in a warm place for 1 hour.

Remove the dough and, coating your hands liberally with the remaining melted butter, pinch off pieces of dough that

weigh 70 g and shape them into balls around the size of a golf ball; in the process, generously coat them with melted butter. You should have 7 balls of dough—1 for practice and 6 for serving. Put the balls of dough in a plastic container, close the lid, and allow to rest in a warm place overnight.

UP TO A DAY AHEAD, PREPARE THE SPICE MIX FOR THE CHICKEN CURRY: Dry-roast the cinnamon, star anise, cloves, peppercorns, and coriander seeds in a wok or frying pan over medium heat until fragrant and toasted, around 2 minutes. Remove and set aside. Add the cumin seeds and fennel seeds to the pan and dry-roast until fragrant and toasted, around 1 minute. Remove and set aside.

Grind the toasted spices and chile powder to a fine powder with a mortar and pestle, coffee grinder, or food processor. If making it in advance, remove the spice mix to an airtight container.

AN HOUR BEFORE SERVING, MAKE THE CHICKEN CURRY: Heat the oil in a large saucepan over low heat. Add the ginger, stirring until fragrant and soft, around 30 seconds. Add the spice mix and the chicken, increase the heat to medium, and sauté the chicken until it is just firm, around 2

recipe continues →

minutes. Add the thin coconut milk and 2 cups (500 ml) water, increase the heat, and simmer for 15 minutes, or until the chicken is cooked through and tender. Add the salt, sugar, and MSG (if using). Taste, adjusting the seasoning if necessary; the curry should taste mild and slightly salty, with a distinct aroma of star anise and cinnamon, and should have a soup-like consistency. Remove from the heat and cover to keep warm.

MAKE THE ROTI AND FRIED EGGS: Rub a thin layer of oil over a flat surface with lots of space to work, such as a clean kitchen counter or dining table, and prepare the roti one at a time, following the directionson page 123. Melt 2 tablespoons butter in a cast-iron or other heavy frying pan over medium-low heat. Transfer the shaped roti to the pan and fry slowly, flipping it occasionally, until it is golden, crispy, and fragrant, around 4 minutes (if the heat is too high, the roti will cook too quickly, burning on the exterior but remaining undercooked and doughy on the inside). Return the hot roti to the work surface and, using a spatula to pin one side of it down, use the edge of a plate held upside down (or another spatula) to tear the roti apart, starting at the opposite side, creating noodle-like shreds. With a paper towel in each hand, slap the pile of shreds a couple times to puff them up and remove excess oil. Add another tablespoon of butter to the pan, add an egg, and fry sunny-side up until it is crispy at the edges but the yolk is still liquid.

Transfer the roti to a plate, top with the fried egg, and serve with a small bowl containing around a cup of the curry. Repeat with the remaining roti and ingredients, adding more butter to the pan as you cook the roti and then the eggs, to make five more servings.

HOW TO PREPARE ROTI DOUGH

1   Coat your fingers with a generous amount of oil, put one ball of dough on a lightly oiled work surface (remember, the first ball is your tester, so use it to practice your technique), and smear it as thin as possible. Working from the center to the perimeter, fingers oiled enough to glide on the surface of the dough, to form a circle around 8 inches across whose center is just barely thicker than its perimeter.

2   Pick up the dough with both hands: your right hand, palm down, on the edge of the dough nearest to your body and your left hand, palm up, on the left edge of the dough. Using your left hand, fling the dough away from your body, allowing its farthest edge to stick to the work surface. Subsequently, use your right hand to pull the circle toward your body to stretch it.

3   Shift the position of your hands on the dough a few degrees clockwise and repeat this motion three or four times, the circle growing larger with each fling, and pull until you have a circle (or oblong) of very thin dough around 12 inches in diameter (it's OK if there are some small holes or tears).

4   Lift up one edge of the dough, pulling it into a long strip, and return it to the work surface in the shape of a coil.

5   Squash and manipulate the coil into a disk around 4 inches across.

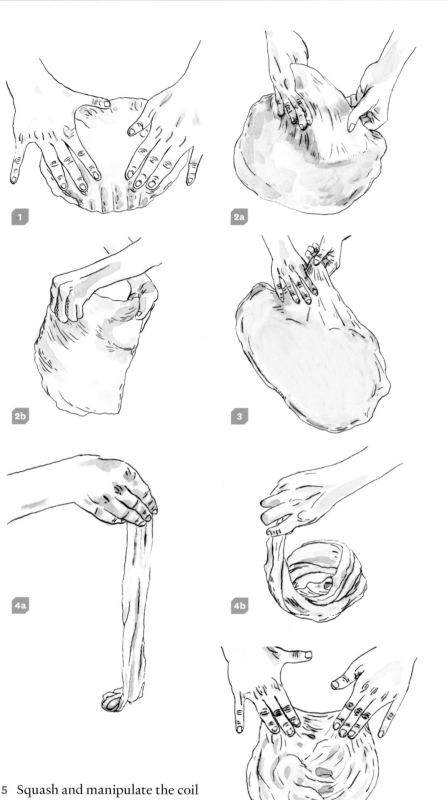

122

ตรงข้ามโลตัส
หาดใหญ่ใน
073 255590

A stall selling noodles at Pattani's night market.

The
Islands

I slands are the destination of many, if not most, of the people who visit Thailand. Yet I'll wager that few of these visitors will experience the dishes native to southern Thailand. On Thai islands, often the only food options available to nonlocals are resort-based restaurants serving Bangkok-style Thai dishes or tourist-oriented eateries selling Western food. When there is local food, the utter informality of island life means any restaurants or stalls can be hard to distinguish from private homes, and ordering is made difficult by the language barrier.

But southern Thailand's islands do indeed have their own cuisine. Although we don't tend to think of them as such, islands tend to be rural places, and the food there typically follows suit: rustic and simple, based on natural yet vibrant ingredients that are grown or gathered nearby, such as chiles, peppercorns, turmeric, and coconuts. This larder also includes, unsurprisingly, seafood. Thailand's islanders aren't eating the arm's-length prawns or giant squid you saw on display at your resort's seafood buffet. Instead, they're most often relying on the type of shellfish, crustaceans, and other creatures and plants that can be gathered by hand in shallow water, or on smaller and less sexy, but no less tasty, fish.

Many of the inhabitants of Thailand's islands are Muslim, which means that the food is often halal. And when a southern Thai island does have an urban center, there's typically a Chinese population, adding another cultural layer to the mix. The recipes in this chapter reflect this culinary spectrum, touching on the multicultural blend of ingredients, influences, and dishes of cosmopolitan island-bound cities such as Phuket Town; the type of rustic dishes made from items plucked from a garden on a farm on the back hills of Ko Samui; and the almost exclusively island-based cuisine of the Moken, a formerly nomadic ethnic group that lives in southern Thailand.

PREVIOUS SPREAD: A beach on the island of Ko Yao Noi, in Phang-Nga Province.

Cracking the Nut

On a rare cool tropical morning, I find myself in the middle of a coconut grove, dwarfed by towering top-heavy trees. I'm waiting for Phiphat Kepsap, a coconut gatherer, who eventually makes his entrance on a motorcycle with a sidecar occupied by two monkeys. Phiphat hops off his bike, leads one of the monkeys to the base of a tree, and grunts a command. The monkey shimmies up to the top: work has begun. Within seconds, it is raining coconuts, the bowling ball–sized orbs striking the ground with frightening yet satisfying thuds.

For Phiphat and his monkeys, this is just another day of work on Ko Yao Noi. Located a mere half hour by speedboat from Phuket, the island couldn't be more different from its flashy neighbor. It's quiet and mostly agricultural, with a dense, hilly inland of rubber plantations, rice fields, and villages ringed by an occasional narrow, rocky beach. The vast majority of its inhabitants—mostly farmers, fishermen, and rubber tappers—are, like Phiphat, Muslims. As on Phuket, coconut trees form a ever-present backdrop. But on Ko Yao Noi, they're more than just an exotic element of the scenery. Coconuts are an essential part of the local cuisine, with one or more finding their way into nearly every meal.

"He picks only mature coconuts," Phiphat tells me of the monkey. Indeed, the animal had beelined for the brown-colored nuts, spinning them furiously with his hands and feet to dislodge them. "I've had that one only a year or so," he goes on. "I bought it from somebody else who trained him. He cost me 50,000 baht"—around $1,600. With the occasional tug on the monkey's leash, Phiphat directs him toward specific coconuts or to an adjacent tree. When all the mature coconuts have been plucked, Phiphat shouts, "Come down!" and the monkey slides effortlessly down the trunk of the tree.

Dusit Roengsamot, who had hired the services of Phiphat and his monkeys, is now in possession of a motorcycle sidecar loaded with coconuts. The haul would be used in the family business, where he and his wife, Somsri, produce local-style sweets.

"We make up to ten different types of sweets a day," Somsri tells me later while pouring a molten grass-colored confection into a tray to cool and firm up. Coconut features in nearly all of Somsri's desserts, whether in the form of freshly made coconut cream or milk or the grated flesh of the nuts.

As the largest maker of sweets on the island, Somsri relies on a small team of women—mostly relatives and neighbors—to help her. Working in her open-

OPPOSITE: Phiphat Kepsap and his monkeys, Ko Yao Noi, Phang-Nga Province.
ABOVE: Grating a coconut on Ko Yao Noi, Phang-Nga Province.

A monkey climbs a tree to gather coconuts, Ko Yao Noi, Phang-Nga Province.

TOP LEFT: Bussaba Butdee squeezes grated coconut to make coconut milk in her kitchen on Ko Yao Noi, Phang-Nga Province.

BOTTOM LEFT: Freshly grated coconut, Ko Yao Noi, Phang-Nga Province.

air kitchen, they're assigned various tasks: making coconut cream and milk, steaming sticky rice, folding banana leaf pouches for steaming. Outside, standing in the sun over the heat of an open flame, Dusit smokes hand-rolled cigarettes as he takes on the job of caramelizing the coconut. He combines shredded coconut meat, the juice from immature coconuts, and generous scoops of sugar in a wok the size of a satellite dish. After forty-five minutes of constant stirring, the ingredients have melded into a rich, fragrant candy that's a crucial component of nom khawm, a triangular banana leaf package encasing steamed coconut cream and rice flour with a ball of caramelized coconut meat at its center.

Some of Somsri and Dusit's treats are sold from their home, but most are purchased by local tea shops, where they're a breakfast staple. Early the following morning, I stop into one such shop about a mile south of where they live. Like others on the island,

Phiphat Kepsap, a coconut harvester and native of Ko Yao Noi, gathering coconuts in his yard with the help of a monkey.

the tea shop is known simply by the name of its proprietor, Supranee Pradit, who locals call Ma Ya. It's essentially an extension of her front porch, with picnic tables topped with brightly patterned tablecloths and a tidy station where tea, coffee, and a few light savory dishes are served. The early-morning clientele is almost exclusively men—fishermen and rubber tappers who pair their sweets with cigarettes and rosewater-scented tea. "We come here every morning," a customer tells me. "If there's nothing fun to talk about, we talk about women!"

By the time the men have departed for their boats and plantations, women and schoolchildren are trickling in, ordering dishes such as khaao yam, rice tossed with toasted coconut, shrimp paste, and galangal; and nom jiin naam yaa, a rich, slightly spicy curry of fish and coconut milk that is ladled over thin rice noodles. The latter is served with a buffet of optional toppings, including the astringent leaves of the cashew tree, pickled cucumber, local vegetables blanched in coconut cream, preserved white radish, tiny dried fish, hard-boiled eggs, and a heap of leafy herbs that range in flavor from pungent to sweet.

I ask Ma Ya about nom jiin naam yaa, one of the most emblematic southern Thai dishes, a curry served over thin round rice noodles. The thin curry dressing, which takes on a sunny yellow tinge from fresh turmeric, "should be a bit spicy," she tells me, but adds that this heat is balanced by the sweetness of coconut milk and the salinity of soy sauce.

We speak in Ma Ya's open-air kitchen, a jumble of cooking equipment and ingredients alongside clucking chickens and sleeping cats, the whole area shaded by coconut palms. Her first step in making nom jiin naam yaa is preparing thick coconut milk. She grabs handfuls of freshly grated coconut, briefly soaks them in water, and then squeezes the stuff above a sieve set over a bowl to extract its rich, fatty liquid. Another pressing with the same grated coconut, and she has a pot of thin coconut milk. "On Ko Yao Noi," she says, nodding at the coconut tree that towers over us, "there are a lot of things we don't have to buy." Then she scatters the limp expired shreds of meat on the ground because on Ko Yao Noi even the chickens eat coconut.

The following recipes center around the coconut and its various uses, which on Ko Yao Noi range from dishes savory to sweet.

Bussaba Butdee removes the husks from
coconuts. Ko Yao Noi, Phang-Nga Province.

A coconut grove on Ko Yao Noi,
an island in Phang-Nga Province.

HOW TO MAKE COCONUT MILK AND CREAM

In the home kitchens of southern Thailand's islands, where coconut groves are often an extension of the garden, mature coconuts are grated by hand or machine, mixed with a bit of water, and simply squeezed by hand above a sieve set over a bowl—the meat so fresh and rich, it takes little effort to extract its fat and fragrance. In markets, coconuts are grated on the spot, perhaps combined with water, and then squeezed in hydraulic presses. In either case, the first pressing is known as *hua kathi*, the "head" of the coconut milk—a rich, fatty liquid that I refer to in this book as thick coconut milk. If it is left to sit, especially if exposed to cold, the fat and the water will separate; the thick part that rises to the top is known as coconut cream. The just-pressed grated coconut meat can be combined with more water and pressed again, resulting in *haang kathi*, the "tail" coconut milk—a lighter, waterier liquid that I refer to here as thin coconut milk.

Many of the recipes in this book call for coconut milk. Making it from scratch is not as difficult or time-consuming as you might think, and homemade is the closest you'll come to the consistency, flavor, and aroma of the stuff used in southern Thailand. The factor that can make or break this ingredient is the quality of the product you start with. If you have access to relatively fresh, rich coconuts, you can make your own coconut milk with little compromise. Otherwise, an alternative is to seek out frozen coconut meat at your local Asian market, although this can vary immensely in quality. In general, a good rule of thumb is to avoid shredded coconut, which has sometimes already been stripped of some of its fat, and instead seek out grated coconut. And if you don't have access to any of these, coconut milk/cream in UHT packages works, although you'll need to dilute it; see right for details.

TOP: A vendor shows freshly split coconuts, Ko Yao Noi, Phang-Nga Province.

BOTTOM: Supranee Pradit pours freshly squeezed coconut milk in her kitchen, Ko Yao Noi, Phang-Nga Province.

Kaan Khan Kathi
การคั้นกะทิ

Using Whole Fresh Coconuts

You'll need 250 g of fresh coconut meat to produce ¾ cup (180 ml) coconut cream or 1 cup (250 ml) thick coconut milk and 1 cup (250 ml) thin coconut milk.

Using a blunt, heavy object such as a pestle, crack the hard, dry, hairy exterior shell of the coconut and remove and discard it—much as you'd remove the shell from a hard-boiled egg. Using a vegetable peeler, peel away the thin brown layer of the meat—this will result in whiter coconut milk. Crack the nut itself, if it's not already broken, discard the liquid inside (the juice of mature coconuts is generally sour and unfit for drinking), and break it into pieces. Wash these pieces in a couple rinses of cool water and coarsely chop them.

Combine 250 g of the chopped coconut and ¾ cup (180 ml) room-temperature water (for older, dry coconuts, you may need to increase this to as much as 1 cup/250 ml water) and process very, very finely in a blender or food processor (or an immersion blender) until it has the consistency of a thick paste.

Lay a piece of cheesecloth or a clean tea towel over a small bowl. Pour the contents of the blender or food processor into the towel, gather the edges together, and squeeze, press, and twist, extracting as much liquid as possible. You should have ¾ to 1 cup (180 to 250 ml) liquid; this is the thick coconut milk. Set the bowl of liquid aside in the refrigerator; the fatty solids that float to the top are the coconut cream. You can simply scoop this off the surface when you're ready to use it.

Empty the contents of the towel into a small bowl and add 1 cup (250 ml) water, stirring to combine. Return the mixture to the tea towel and squeeze, press, and twist over another bowl, extracting as much liquid as possible. This should yield approximately 1 cup (250 ml) liquid; this is the thin coconut milk.

If making this in advance, remove the coconut milk/cream to airtight containers and store in the refrigerator; it should last a day if kept very cold.

Using Frozen Grated Coconut

You'll need 250 g of frozen grated coconut meat to produce ¾ cup (180 ml) coconut cream or 1 cup (250 ml) thick coconut milk and 1 cup (250 ml) thin coconut milk.

Combine the grated coconut and ¾ cup (180 ml) room-temperature water (for older, dryer frozen coconut, you may need to increase this to as much as 1 cup/250 ml water) and process very, very finely in a blender or food processor (or with an immersion blender) until it has the consistency of a watery paste.

Lay a piece of cheesecloth or a clean tea towel over a small bowl. Pour the contents of the blender or food processor into the towel, gather the edges together, and squeeze, press, and twist, extracting as much liquid as possible. You should have ¾ to 1 cup (180 to 250 ml) liquid; this is the thick coconut milk. Set the bowl aside in the refrigerator; the fatty solids that float to the top are coconut cream. You can simply scoop this off the surface when you're ready to use it.

Empty the contents of the towel into a small bowl and add 1 cup (250 ml) water, stirring to combine. Return the mixture to the tea towel and squeeze, press, and twist, extracting as much liquid as possible. This should yield approximately 1 cup (250 ml) liquid; this is the thin coconut milk.

If making this in advance, store in airtight containers in the refrigerator; it should last a day if kept very cold.

Using UHT Coconut Milk

If fresh or frozen coconut is not available, UHT coconut milk (avoid the canned stuff, which can contain emulsifiers and preservatives that will prevent it from cooking properly) can be used, but as it's essentially coconut cream, it needs to be diluted. Aroy-D brand coconut milk gets good feedback for its flavor and consistency from U.S.-based chefs and home cooks.

For coconut cream, simply use as is (or, if you want an even richer product, buy UHT cartons of coconut cream). For thick coconut milk, combine 1 part UHT coconut milk with 1 part water. For thin coconut milk, combine 1 part UHT coconut milk with 3 parts water. Set aside in the refrigerator; it should last for a few days if kept very cold.

A Soup of Coconut Milk and Melinjo Leaves

Bai Miang Tom Kathi

ใบเหมียงต้มกะทิ

Melinjo leaves are a common ingredient in southern Thailand, where in most cases they're simply plucked from a tree in the backyard. The tender, waxy green leaves don't have a great deal of flavor but, rather, a subtle, spinach-like minerality and a richness and a pleasant mouthfeel that Thais refer to as *man*—an ideal companion to the rich coconut milk–based broth in this recipe.

You probably don't have access to melinjo, but the good news is that this recipe is one of southern Thailand's most flexible. I've seen it made with cabbage, vegetable ferns (see Glossary), or Asian pennywort leaves. Spinach—or even beet greens or Swiss chard—can stand in as a rough substitute for melinjo. And the protein alternatives can include eggs, beaten and stirred into the simmering soup, or whole shrimp—or no protein at all. Regardless of what combination of ingredients you decide go with, feel free to add an extra pinch of sugar or two if your coconut milk isn't particularly sweet.

Serves 4 as part of a southern Thai meal

½ cup (50 g) salted dried anchovies

4 cups (1 L) thin coconut milk (see page 135 for instructions on how to make thin coconut milk)

2 stalks lemongrass (50 g total; see page 19 for instructions on how to prepare lemongrass for a soup)

8 shallots (80 g total), peeled and bruised

4 cloves garlic (20 g total), peeled and bruised

1 small piece heart of palm (50 g), shaved into thin 1½-to-2-inch-wide strips with a vegetable peeler

1 teaspoon table salt

2 teaspoons white sugar

70 g melinjo leaves, woody stalks discarded (this should yield around 50 g trimmed leaves)

½ cup (125 ml) thick coconut milk (see page 135 for instructions on how to make thick coconut milk)

Give the anchovies a couple rinses in cool water to reduce their saltiness. Drain.

Combine the thin coconut milk, lemongrass, shallots, and garlic in a large saucepan and bring to a boil over medium-high heat. Add the anchovies and heart of palm and reduce the heat to a rapid simmer. Add the salt and sugar and return to a simmer, then add the melinjo and return to a simmer. Add the thick coconut milk and bring to a simmer. Taste, adjusting the seasoning if necessary; the soup should taste slightly salty and sweet, with a subtle richness and a pleasant fragrance from the aromatics.

Serve warm or at room temperature with long-grain rice.

OPPOSITE: A Soup of Coconut Milk and Melinjo Leaves as made by Kanjana Maikaew, the chef/owner Tha Tondo Seafood, Ko Yao Noi, Phang-Nga Province.

Fish Curry Served over Thin Rice Noodles with Sides

Nom Jiin Naam Yaa Plaa
หนมจีนน้ำยาปลา

This is one of the most ubiquitous and beloved dishes in southern Thailand. It's a breakfast staple, and virtually every town and village has restaurants and stalls that specialize in the dish, most of which can sell out as early as 9 a.m. The curry is a brilliant intersection of rich (the coconut milk), spicy (chiles and black pepper), and herbaceous (lemongrass and turmeric) flavors, but if hard-pressed, most southern Thais would probably admit to loving most how the dish is served—that is, with a virtual buffet of sides that can range from heaping platters of herbs, vegetables, and fruit to sweet/sour quick pickles and vegetables simmered in coconut milk, making it possible to customize every bite.

Serves 6

FOR THE CURRY PASTE

½ teaspoon table salt
16 medium spicy dried chiles (8 g total)
2 teaspoons black peppercorns
6 cloves garlic (30 g total), peeled and sliced
3 stalks lemongrass (75 g total; see page 19 for instructions on how to prepare lemongrass for a curry paste)
1 finger fresh turmeric (15 g), peeled and sliced
1 tablespoon shrimp paste

FOR THE OPTIONAL QUICK-PICKLE CONDIMENT

3 tablespoons white sugar
¼ teaspoon table salt
2 tablespoons white vinegar
1 medium cucumber (approximately 150 g), halved lengthwise and sliced thin
3 shallots (3 g total), peeled, halved lengthwise, and sliced thin
2 medium spicy fresh chiles (6 g total), sliced thin

FOR THE OPTIONAL VEGETABLES SIMMERED IN COCONUT MILK CONDIMENT

1 cup (250) thin coconut milk (see page 135 for instructions on how to make thin coconut milk)
125 g long beans, cut into 1-inch pieces (alternatively, 125 g cabbage, chopped, or a mix of long beans and cabbage)
1 teaspoon white sugar
¼ teaspoon table salt

FOR THE CURRY

1 kg white-fleshed sea fish (such as 6 small threadfin bream; see Glossary), heads removed, scaled, and gutted
1 teaspoon thin soy sauce
2 cups (500 ml) thick coconut milk (see page 135 for instructions on how to make thick coconut milk)
4 cups (1 L) thin coconut milk (see page 135 for instructions on how to make thin coconut milk)
12 makrut lime leaves
1 teaspoon white sugar (optional)
½ teaspoon bouillon powder (optional)
Fish sauce (optional)

FOR SERVING

600 g thin round fresh rice noodles (khanom jiin; see Glossary) or 300 g thin round dried rice noodles (sen mii; see Glossary)

A platter that includes sliced pineapple, quartered Thai eggplants, pea eggplants, chopped long beans, krathin seed (see Glossary), Asian pennywort, tender cashew tree leaves, tender mango tree leaves, Thai basil, water celery, bai man puu (see Glossary), preserved radish, dried anchovies, and/or hard-boiled eggs

UP TO 5 DAYS IN ADVANCE, MAKE THE CURRY PASTE: Pound and grind the salt and chiles to a coarse powder with a mortar and pestle. Add the peppercorns and pound and grind to a coarse powder. Add the garlic, lemongrass, and turmeric and pound and grind to a coarse paste. Add the shrimp paste and pound and grind to a fine paste. (Alternatively, if using a food processor or blender, process the salt, chiles, peppercorns, garlic, lemongrass, turmeric, and shrimp paste to a fine paste.) If making it in advance, remove the paste to an airtight container and store in the refrigerator.

UP TO 4 HOURS IN ADVANCE, PREPARE THE OPTIONAL QUICK PICKLE CONDIMENT: Combine the sugar, 3 tablespoons water, and the salt in a small saucepan and bring to a simmer over medium heat, stirring frequently until the sugar and salt have dissolved, around 1 minute. Remove from the heat and add the vinegar, cucumber, shallots, and chile. Taste, adjusting the seasoning if necessary; the pickle should taste sweet and tart, in that order, with faint background flavors of salty and spicy. Remove to a small serving bowl and set aside for at least 2 hours to cool and marinate.

ALSO UP TO 4 HOURS IN ADVANCE, PREPARE THE OPTIONAL VEGETABLES SIMMERED IN COCONUT MILK: Combine the coconut milk, long beans, sugar, and salt in a small saucepan and bring to a rapid simmer over medium heat, then reduce the heat and simmer until the beans are tender, around 10 minutes. Taste, adjusting the seasoning if necessary; the vegetables should taste rich, followed by subtly sweet and salty. Remove to a small serving bowl and allow to cool to room temperature.

PREPARE THE FISH: Combine the fish, thin soy sauce, and 3 cups (750 ml) water in a large saucepan or a stockpot and bring to a boil over medium-high heat. Reduce the heat and simmer until the fish is cooked through, about 10 minutes. Remove the fish to a plate. Strain the stock; you need 2 cups (500 ml) for this dish.

When the fish is cool enough to handle, remove and discard the skin and bones; you should have about 300 g of flaked fish.

MAKE THE CURRY: Process the curry paste, fish, reserved fish stock, and half of the thick coconut milk in a food processor or blender until smooth. Remove to a saucepan, add the thin coconut milk, and bring to a rapid simmer over medium-high heat. Add the makrut lime leaves, the remaining thick coconut milk, the sugar (if using), and bouillon powder (if using). Reduce the heat and simmer for 20 minutes. Taste, adjusting the seasoning with fish sauce and/or additional sugar if necessary; the curry should taste rich, savory, herbal, and spicy, with a background of subtle sweet and salty flavors. Remove from the heat and keep warm, or serve at room temperature.

MEANWHILE, PREPARE THE NOODLES IF USING DRIED: While the curry is simmering, soak the dried rice noodles in a bowl of room-temperature water for 15 minutes. Drain in a sieve or colander.

Bring a couple quarts of water to a boil in a large saucepan. Add approximately one-quarter of the soaked noodles. When the water reaches a boil again, remove the noodles, drain, and set aside. Repeat with the remaining noodles.

To serve, place one-sixth (approximately 100 g) of the noodles in each of six shallow individual bowls. Top each with approximately 1½ cups (350 ml) of the curry and serve with the platter of herbs and vegetables.

Supranee Pradit making curry in her home kitchen on the island of Ko Yao Noi.

Fish Curry Served over Thin Rice Noodles with Sides as served by Supranee Pradit at her home-based restaurant Ko Yao Noi, Phang-Nga Province.

A Simple Thai-Style Rice Salad

Khaao Yam

ข้าวยำ

Rice is the headlining ingredient in this herb-forward "salad," but it wouldn't be khaao yam without the inclusion of earthy toasted coconut. The dish is a beloved breakfast on Ko Yao Noi and beyond, sold from vast bowls at Muslim-run tea shops.

This version, taught to me by Bussaba Butdee, who runs a homestay on Ko Yao Noi, includes the rather decadent addition of grilled shrimp, which she happened to have on hand. These are not standard and can be omitted. Less optional for southern Thais is the herb called *bai phaa hom*. Known colloquially as—no, I'm not making this up—"dog and pig fart herb," the leaf provides the dish with a unique, but not as unpleasant as the name might suggest, aroma. It's unlikely you'll be able to find bai phaa hom outside southern Thailand, and khaao yam made without it will still be tasty, but it, admittedly, won't have the same unique fragrance.

Serve this as a southern Thai–style breakfast or as lunch.

Serves 4

8 medium shrimp (200 g total; optional)
1½ cups (300 g) long-grain white rice
2 cups (around 150 g) finely grated coconut
    (see page 24 for tips on grating coconut)
1 tablespoon vegetable oil
1 tablespoon shrimp paste
2 stalks lemongrass (50 g total; see page 19 for
    instructions on how to prepare lemongrass for
    an herb paste)
A 4½-inch piece galangal (45 g), peeled and
    sliced thin
4 medium spicy fresh chiles (12 g total)

12 wild betel leaves (12 g total), sliced very thin
15 bai phaa hom leaves (15 g total; see Glossary),
    sliced very thin
3 makrut lime leaves, sliced very thin
6 long beans (100 g total), sliced thin
5 shallots (50 g total), peeled and sliced thin
1 small lime, peeled and chopped,
    any seeds discarded
1 small tart green mango (300 g), peeled, pitted,
    and shredded
1½ teaspoons thin soy sauce
½ teaspoon bouillon powder (optional)

PREPARE THE OPTIONAL SHRIMP: Grill or broil the shrimp, turning once, until cooked through, 12 to 15 minutes. Peel, discarding the shells and heads (if any), and thinly slice the shrimp. Set aside.

PREPARE THE RICE: Gently rinse the rice in several changes of water until the water remains clear. Combine the rice and 1½ cups (350 ml) water in a saucepan that's large enough to accommodate the bubbling and swelling grains of rice. Bring to a rolling boil over high heat and boil the rice for 3 seconds. Cover the saucepan, reduce the heat to as low as possible, and simmer, undisturbed, for 20 minutes.

RIGHT: Bussaba Butdee mixing herbs for A Simple Thai-Style Rice Salad, Ko Yao Noi, Phang-Nga Province.
OPPOSITE: A Simple Thai–Style Rice Salad as prepared by Bussaba Butdee at her homestay on Ko Yao Noi, an island in Phang-Nga Province.

Turn off the heat and remove the lid for a few seconds to release excess heat and moisture. Then replace the lid and allow the rice to rest, undisturbed, for 10 minutes. Gently stir the rice, then cover and allow to rest for a final 5 minutes.

WHILE THE RICE COOKS, MAKE THE SALAD: Toast the coconut in a wok over medium-low heat, stirring frequently, until golden and fragrant, around 15 minutes.

Pound and grind the toasted coconut to a coarse powder with a mortar and pestle. (Alternatively, process the toasted coconut to a coarse powder in a blender or food processor.) Set aside.

Heat the oil in a wok over low heat. Add the shrimp paste and fry, stirring, crushing, and mixing it, until it's toasted, well combined with the oil, and fragrant, 2 to 3 minutes. Set aside.

Pound and grind the lemongrass and galangal to a coarse paste with a mortar and pestle. Add the chiles and pound to a coarse paste. (Alternatively, if using a blender or food processor, process the lemongrass, galangal, and chiles to a coarse paste.) Set aside.

Combine the coconut, shrimp paste, shrimp (if using), wild betel leaves, bai phaa hom (if using), bai phaa hom leaves, lime leaves, long beans, shallots, lime, mango, thin soy sauce, bouillon powder (if using), and rice in a bowl, tossing to mix, being careful not to smash the grains of rice. Taste, adjusting the seasoning if necessary; the salad should be slightly spicy, herbal, and savory, in that order.

Remove to individual plates and serve at room temperature.

Steamed Packets of Sticky Rice and Banana
Khaao Niaw Haw Kluay
ข้าวเหนียวห่อกล้วย

Variations on this sweet snack—sticky rice encasing a section of banana, wrapped in a banana leaf, tied with a thread or rubber bands, and boiled or steamed—are found across Thailand. In the south, it tends to be rich and sweet, taking advantage of the region's ubiquitous coconut milk, and it is a staple at breakfast venues such as Muslim-run tea shops and Chinese coffee shops.

Serve these as a southern Thai–style breakfast, snack, or dessert.

Serves 6

2 cups (400 g) sticky rice
10 feet banana leaves
125 g white sugar
¾ cup (180 ml) thick coconut milk (see page 135 for how to make thick coconut milk)
½ teaspoon table salt
6 bananas, peeled, quartered lengthwise, and cut into 3- to 4-inch pieces around 15 g each

String or rubber bands

Thais make this sweet using kluay naam waa, a short, chubby, relatively firm, particularly fragrant variety of banana. You can use regular supermarket bananas, but ensure that they are ripe yet not mushy.

The most efficient way to steam sticky rice is with a Thai-style pot and a conical bamboo basket. If you don't have access to these tools, a steaming set can be improvised with a sieve elevated over boiling water, or a Chinese-style steamer lined with cheesecloth, although the cooking time may vary.

OPPOSITE: Steamed Packets of Sticky Rice and Banana, Ko Yao Noi, Phang-Nga Province.

AT LEAST 4 HOURS BEFORE SERVING, PREPARE THE STICKY RICE: Gently rinse the rice in several changes of water until the water remains clear. Cover with plenty of water, and soak for 4 to 6 hours.

A COUPLE OF HOURS BEFORE SERVING, STEAM THE STICKY RICE: Drain the rice, discarding the water. Bring a couple quarts of water to a boil in a Thai-style sticky rice steaming pot (or in a saucepan or a Chinese-style steamer). Put the rice in the bamboo steaming basket (or in a sieve or a Chinese-style steaming tray lined with cheesecloth) positioned a few inches above the boiling water and cover with a tea towel and then a lid, creating a relatively tight seal that allows as little steam as possible to escape. Steam the rice for 20 minutes.

Flip the entire mass of rice and steam for another 5 minutes, or until the grains are entirely cooked through, tender, and visibly stuck together. Remove the rice from the heat, transfer to a bowl or large plate, and stir it gently with a large spoon to release steam for around 10 seconds. Set aside.

WHILE THE STICKY RICE IS STEAMING, PREPARE THE BANANA LEAVES: Using a damp cloth, wipe the leaves clean of any dirt, dust, or mud. Cut away the coarse inner edge. Cut the leaves into 14 relatively uniform rectangles about 7 inches wide by 11 inches long. If the banana leaves are particularly thick, stiff, or brittle, you can briefly pass them over the flame of a gas burner to make them more pliable.

MAKE THE SWEETS: Add the sugar to the bowl of still-hot sticky rice, stirring until the sugar is dissolved and combined with the rice. Add the coconut milk and salt and stir until combined and the rice is glossy in appearance. Allow the mixture to sit for 5 minutes to absorb the excess coconut milk, then stir again to combine.

Cover the bowl with plastic wrap and allow the rice to cool to room temperature.

Make the sticky rice packets as described in the sidebar; this should yield 12 to 14 bundles. Steam the banana leaf packages in a Chinese-style steaming tray over medium heat for 20 minutes.

Serve the packets warm or at room temperature.

Making Steamed Packets of Sticky Rice and Banana at a home-bound sweets factory on Ko Yao Noi, an island in Phang-Nga Province.

HOW TO FOLD BANANA LEAVES FOR STEAMED PACKETS OF STICKY RICE AND BANANA

1 Top the matte side of a rectangle of banana leaf with approximately ¼ cup (60 ml) of the sticky rice and one banana section.

2 Shape the rice and banana mixture into a tight, relatively thin tube.

3 Tuck the far end of the banana leaf under the rice.

4 Holding the packet vertically, use your finger to compress the rice inside, then fold the near end of the leaf under the rice.

5 Lay the packet down to retain its folds. Repeat with the remaining leaves, rice, and bananas.

6 Hold two packages together with the seam sides facing each other and, using string (or two rubber bands), make two tight turns around the far end and two more around the near end, then wrap the string lengthwise between the two packages once or twice to secure.

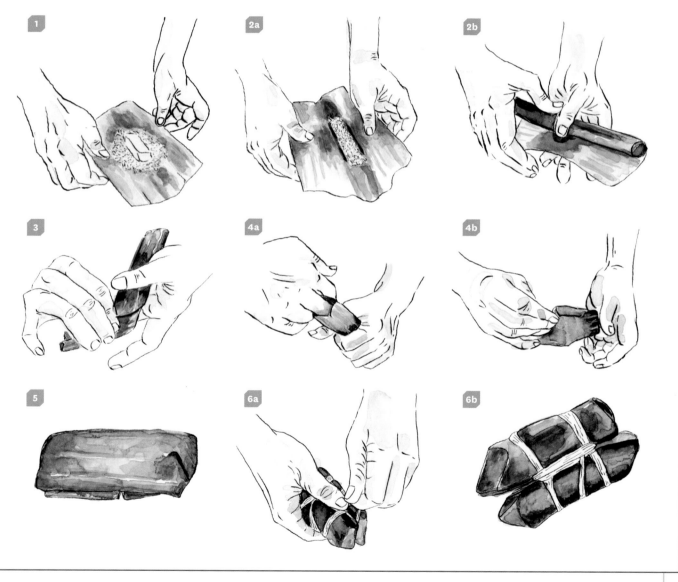

Steamed Coconut Milk Sweets with a Candied Coconut Center
Nom Khawm
หนมค่อม

This sweet—a staple in breakfast joints and coffee shops across southern Thailand—is all about hidden surprises. The banana leaf package conceals a ball of thickened coconut milk, which in turn encases a core of candied coconut. What's inside may not be obvious, but the genius of this combination of sweet and rich flavors, caramelized aromas, and soft, crunchy, chewy textures is clear to anyone who tastes it.

Serve these as a southern Thai–style breakfast, snack, or dessert.

Serves 6

FOR THE CANDIED COCONUT CENTERS

1½ cups (around 100 g) finely grated coconut (see page 24 for tips on grating coconut)
1 cup (250 ml) coconut water
½ cup (100 g) white sugar
2 tablespoons raw cane sugar
Pinch of table salt

FOR THE STICKY RICE FLOUR EXTERIOR

115 g sticky rice flour

FOR THE THICK COCONUT MILK

3 cups (750 ml) thick coconut milk (see page 135 for instructions on how to make thick coconut milk)
¾ cup (90 g) rice flour
Pinch of table salt

FOR STEAMING

10 feet banana leaves
20 toothpicks

Raw cane sugar is also known as natural brown sugar, raw sugar, or whole cane sugar; Domino brand dark brown sugar can be used as a substitute.

This sweet is steamed, and the best way to do this is with a Chinese-style steamer.

UP TO 5 DAYS IN ADVANCE, IF DESIRED, PREPARE THE CANDIED COCONUT CENTERS: Combine the grated coconut, coconut water, white sugar, raw sugar, and salt in a wok and bring to a simmer over medium-low heat, stirring frequently. After 10 minutes, the mixture should be simmering rapidly and tan in color. At 20 minutes, most of the liquid should have evaporated and the mixture should be sticky, starting to caramelize, and fragrant. After 40 minutes, the mixture should be dry, dark, and candy-like.

Remove a teaspoon of the coconut mixture and, when it is cool enough to handle, shape it into a ball. If it can be formed into a solid (though sticky) candy-like mass, the mixture is ready; if not, add a bit more sugar and continue to simmer until it tests done. Remove from the heat and allow to cool slightly.

When it is cool enough to handle, take a heaping teaspoon of the mixture and shape it into a ball about the size of a large marble (weighing approximately 10 g); remove to a plate. Repeat with the remaining coconut mixture; this should yield approximately 20 balls. Set aside, uncovered, for at least several hours, or overnight, until firm and somewhat dry (this can be done in the refrigerator).

ON THE DAY OF SERVING, PREPARE THE BANANA LEAVES: Using a damp cloth, wipe the leaves clean of any dirt, dust, or mud. Cut away the coarse inner edge. Cut the leaves into 25 relatively uniform rectangles approximately 6 inches long and 4 inches wide, snipping off the four corners to create two points at either end of each leaf. If the leaves are particularly thick, stiff, or brittle, briefly pass them over the flame of a stove to make them more pliable.

OPPOSITE LEFT: Steamed Coconut Milk Sweets with a Candied Coconut Center as made at a home-bound sweets factory on Ko Yao Noi, Phang-Nga Province.
OPPOSITE RIGHT: Caramelizing coconut for Steamed Coconut Milk Sweets with a Candied Coconut Center, Ko Yao Noi, Phang-Nga Province.

PREPARE THE STICKY RICE FLOUR EXTERIOR: Combine the sticky rice flour and ½ cup (125 ml) water in a bowl and mix with your hands until you have a heavy, slightly moist ball of dough that does not stick to your hands. Take a heaping teaspoon of the dough, roll it into a ball between your palms, and flatten it into a disk on one palm, then wrap it around a ball of the candied coconut, resulting in a ball approximately 1 inch in diameter. Repeat with the remaining dough and candied coconut.

PREPARE THE THICK COCONUT MILK: Combine the coconut milk, rice flour, and salt in a saucepan and bring to a simmer over low heat, whisking to combine. Simmer, stirring frequently, until the mixture is slightly reduced and thickened, aiming for a consistency just short of pudding, around 3 minutes. Remove from the heat and allow to cool to warm (the mixture will firm up as it cools).

MAKE THE SWEETS: Put a dough-wrapped coconut ball in the coconut milk mixture. Then, using a spoon, fish out the ball, along with a tablespoon or so of the coconut milk mixture, and place on a prepared banana leaf. Fold the leaf as described in the sidebar. Repeat with the remaining ingredients.

Steam the banana leaf packages in a Chinese-style steaming tray over medium heat. After 20 minutes, remove one package and allow to cool slightly, then open it to confirm that the thick coconut mixture is firm. If it is not, steam the packages for a bit longer.

Serve warm or at room temperature.

HOW TO FOLD BANANA LEAVES FOR STEAMED COCONUT MILK SWEETS WITH A CANDIED COCONUT CENTER

1 Place a candied coconut ball with some of the coconut milk mixture in the center of the matte side of one leaf. Bring the long edges up to cradle the ball and cream.

2 Bring the far end of the leaf up over the coconut ball and coconut mixture, folding the flaps around the exterior of the package.

3 Repeat with the near end, folding the flaps of this over the first fold and aligning the points.

4 Seal the package with a toothpick positioned vertically.

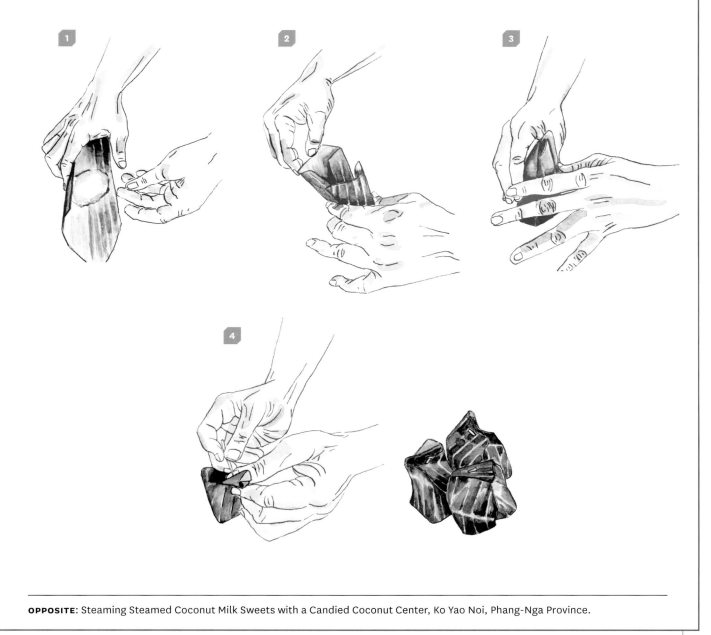

OPPOSITE: Steaming Steamed Coconut Milk Sweets with a Candied Coconut Center, Ko Yao Noi, Phang-Nga Province.

Southern Thailand's Melting Pot

FOR MANY VISITORS to Thailand, Phuket *is* Thailand. Long promoted by tourism authorities and travel guides, the island defines the country for many, and I'd guess that a fair chunk of the nearly 10 million people who visited Phuket in 2019 didn't go anywhere else in Thailand. I also think it's safe to say that, lulled by the island's picture-postcard tropical beaches, few of these people have really seen Phuket.

To find the soul of the island dubbed "The Pearl of the Andaman," it's necessary to head inland to its landlocked provincial capital. You'll find no sand and relatively few palm trees there, but, unlike most of Thailand's other urban centers, Phuket Town can offer character and charm: elegant Sino-Portuguese shophouses and ancient Chinese apothecaries; open-air markets and crumbling mansions; mosques alongside Chinese shrines; and, perhaps most important, food. Phuket Town is home to markets, decades-old restaurants, and rustic food courts serving dishes that stem from a unique blend of cuisines that one would be hard-pressed to find anywhere else in Thailand—or even a few miles away at the much-hyped beaches.

This culinary microcosm stems from the fact that Phuket Town is essentially a Chinese city. Because of its location on the Andaman Sea side of the Malay Peninsula, Phuket's links with other trading ports, such as Singapore, Malacca, and Penang, were more robust than those with Bangkok, and for centuries, sailors from around the region—particularly from China—had visited the island both to seek shelter and to do business. Phuket is also a source of tin, and when this commodity reached peak demand at the end of the nineteenth century, there weren't enough locals to mine it, so businessmen and officials recruited Hokkien Chinese laborers from China, as well as from Singapore and Penang, two of the British-controlled Straits Settlements. In a short span of time, Phuket Town went from a sleepy port town to provincial Thailand's most modern city. By 1871, the population of Phuket was more Chinese than Thai, and less than thirty years later, Phuket Town was one of the first urban centers in the country to have paved roads and automobiles.

Unlike the case in Bangkok, Phuket's Chinese community made relatively little effort to integrate with mainstream Thai culture, clinging to much of its Hokkien identity—including its food. Many of Phuket's most famous dishes still have Hokkien Chinese names and include preparations one might recognize in China's Fujian Province, the homeland of

---

OPPOSITE: A mansion in Phuket Town.

the Hokkien, or even in Penang, another important Hokkien outpost in Southeast Asia. Even today, chile is used in moderation in Phuket—a stark contrast to the rest of the south—and fish sauce takes a back seat to soy sauce.

Because so many people came to Phuket via the Straits Settlements, British colonies that were also international mixing pots, its dishes also boast influences from the Middle East, South Asia, Singapore, and Malaysia. And decades of intermingling between Hokkien immigrants and Thais resulted in an entirely new cuisine. Known locally as "Baba," it's a unique mix of Chinese dishes and cooking techniques and Southeast Asian ingredients.

So, if, like the millions who visit Phuket every year, you want a plate of phat Thai while overlooking the beach, the island is more than equipped to grant that pleasure. But in this chapter, I'm going to take you through the Phuket that you probably didn't even know existed.

A Chinese shrine in Phuket Town.

Thanon Thalang, a main street in Phuket Town.

A Fragrant Malay-Style Fish Curry

Kaeng Tuumii

แกงตูมี่

Consider everything you may have gleaned about southern Thai cookery up to this point: its love of intensely spicy, salty, flavors; its relative disdain for oil and dried spices; its obsession with turmeric. Now ignore all of this, and you're getting close to kaeng tuumii, a distinctly mild, pleasantly oily, dried spice–fragrant fish curry.

"Some people on Phuket don't like kaeng tuumii because they say that it's too oily," explains Varerat Chaisin, a native of Phuket, for thirty-five years a teacher of culinary arts, and the source of this recipe. "But it should be this way! And some people don't like dried spices. But the dish has to have dried spices; if not, then it's not kaeng tuumii."

Indeed, with its bright red hue, chunky fish steaks, and fingers of okra, kaeng tuumii doesn't even look like a Thai dish. That's because it's not; the word *tuumii* most likely stems from *tumis*, a Malay term that refers to the cooking technique of frying a curry paste in oil until fragrant.

Many of Phuket's Chinese immigrants arrived via Penang, in present-day Malaysia, during the tin mining boom of the late nineteenth century. In addition to Chinese recipes, they brought with them Malay and Baba-Nonya (dishes made with a mix of local and Chinese cooking techniques and ingredients). Kaeng tuumii is thought to stem from this influx.

Varerat tells me that the curry's distinctive richness—and some of its fragrance—comes from coconut oil, an ingredient generally only used for sweets in Thailand. Its bright red hue comes from both dried chiles and annatto (also known as achiote) seed, an ingredient otherwise unheard of in the Thai kitchen.

"If you can't get annatto seed, it's OK, but you need to include coriander and cumin," Varerat adds, bringing home that this is a dish for which fragrance is as important as flavor. (Torch ginger flowers, an optional ingredient, add a subtle fragrance and tart flavor.)

You can skip the first step here if you don't have the time or desire to make your own coconut oil; simply use ½ cup (125 ml) store-bought coconut oil. If you do choose to make your own coconut oil, note that the technique may not work with canned or UHT coconut milk.

On Phuket, this dish is generally made with steaks of white sea bass, also known as barramundi. If you don't have access to this fish, any white-fleshed sea fish, such as snapper or perch, can be substitutes.

Serves 4 as part of southern Thai meal

FOR THE COCONUT OIL (SEE HEADNOTE)

4 cups (1 L) thick coconut milk (see page 135 for instructions on how to make thick coconut milk)

FOR THE CURRY PASTE

1 teaspoon black peppercorns
2 teaspoons cumin seeds
1½ teaspoons coriander seeds
1 teaspoon annatto (also known as achiote) seeds (see Glossary)
7 large mild dried chiles (40 g total)
½ teaspoon table salt
5 shallots (50 g total), peeled and sliced
4 cloves garlic (20 g total), peeled and sliced
1 tablespoon shrimp paste

FOR THE CURRY

75 g dried tamarind paste
2 tablespoons white sugar
1 tablespoon table salt
4 teaspoons light soy sauce
700 g sea bass steaks, cut into 2-inch-wide pieces
2 torch ginger flowers (around 200 g total; see Glossary), outer petals removed, halved or quartered lengthwise, and soaked in water to prevent discoloration (optional)
150 g mature okra, caps removed

recipe continues →

OPPOSITE: A Fragrant Malay-Style Fish Curry as prepared by Varerat Chaisin, Phuket Town.

UP TO 5 DAYS IN ADVANCE, IF DESIRED, PREPARE THE COCONUT OIL: Bring the coconut milk to a boil in a wok or saucepan over high heat. When it foams, reduce the heat to a rapid simmer. After about 20 minutes, the liquid will have reduced and small bubbles of oil will have formed on the surface. At 30 minutes, most of the water in the coconut milk should have evaporated and there should be a clear separation between the oil and the solids, the latter of which will appear like curds or scrambled eggs. At 50 minutes, the solids should start to firm and appear toasted, and the oil will be clear and distinct. At around an hour, the solids should be the color and consistency of cacao nibs.

Pour the oil through a sieve set over a bowl (you can retain the crunchy solids, which are used for sweets in southern Thailand, if desired). Measure out and reserve ½ cup (125 ml) of the coconut oil. If making it in advance, remove the oil to an airtight container and store in the refrigerator.

ALSO UP TO 5 DAYS IN ADVANCE, IF DESIRED, MAKE THE CURRY PASTE: Dry-roast the peppercorns in a wok or frying pan over medium heat until fragrant, about 2 minutes. Set aside. Dry-roast the cumin, coriander, and annatto seeds until toasted and fragrant, about 1 minute. Remove from the heat.

Grind the dried spices to a fine powder with a mortar and pestle, coffee grinder, or food processor. Set aside.

Combine the dried chiles and enough water to cover by an inch or two in a saucepan and bring to a boil over high heat. Remove the saucepan from the heat, cover, and set the chiles aside to soak for 15 minutes.

Drain the chiles, discarding the water, and when they are cool enough to handle, remove and discard the seeds and stringy membranes. Slice the chiles and drain in a sieve or colander.

Pound and grind the drained chiles and salt to a coarse paste with a mortar and pestle. Add the shallots and garlic and pound and grind to a coarse paste. Add the shrimp paste and ground spices and pound and grind to a fine paste. (Alternatively, if using a food processor or blender, process the chiles, salt, shallots, garlic, shrimp paste, and ground spices to a fine paste.) If making it in advance, remove the paste to an airtight container and store in the refrigerator.

MAKE THE CURRY: Bring 1 cup (250 ml) water to a boil in a saucepan over high heat. Remove the pan from the heat, add the tamarind paste, and mash with a spoon to combine. Cover and set aside for 15 minutes.

Drain the tamarind mixture in a sieve set over a bowl, pushing on the solids to extract as much of the pulp as possible; discard the solids. You should have about ¾ cup (180 ml) tamarind pulp. Set aside.

Heat the coconut oil in a saucepan over medium heat. Add the curry paste and fry, stirring frequently, until it has amalgamated with the oil and is fragrant, about 10 minutes. Add 3 cups (710 ml) water, increase the heat to medium-high, and bring to simmer. Add the sugar, salt, soy sauce, and tamarind pulp, reduce the heat, and simmer until the liquid is reduced by about a third and is topped with a thick layer of red oil, about 15 minutes.

Add the fish, torch ginger flowers (if using), and okra. Reduce the heat to a low simmer and cook, without stirring, until the fish is just cooked and the okra is tender, about 10 minutes. Taste, adjusting the seasoning if necessary; the curry should have a near-perfect balance of sweet and tart, followed by salty; it should be subtly fragrant from the coconut oil and the spices; and it should have a relatively thick, pleasantly oily consistency and a vibrant red hue.

Remove to a serving bowl and serve warm or at room temperature with long-grain rice.

OPPOSITE: A mobile curry vendor at Phuket Town's morning market.

Pork Belly Braised with Soy Sauce, Black Pepper, and Brown Sugar

Muu Hawng

หมูฮ้อง

For the people of Phuket, soy sauce is more than a source of salt. So-called sweet and black soy sauces give dishes a subtle, pleasant sweetness and bitterness, as well as an attractive dark hue. These qualities are epitomized in muu hawng, a Phuket staple that sees fatty cuts of pork braised with soy sauce and brown sugar until those seasonings become irresistibly caramelized. Yet the most enticing aspect of the dish is arguably its fragrance, which stems not only from that soy sauce but also from a generous base of garlic and black pepper.

The recipe below, taught to me by Varerat Chaisin, a native of Phuket and longtime teacher of culinary arts, is a surefire crowd-pleaser. It's a combination of some of the elements Varerat taught me in a cooking demonstration—such as using pineapple to marinate, season, and tenderize the pork—and attributes of the dish as I'd encountered it in restaurants in Phuket Town: almost decadently generous, practically melting chunks of fatty, tender pork belly.

Serves 4 as part of a southern Thai meal

1 teaspoon table salt

6 cloves garlic (30 g total), peeled
1 scant tablespoon black peppercorns
2 tablespoons raw cane sugar
1 tablespoon white sugar
3 tablespoons light soy sauce
½ teaspoon black soy sauce
750 g pork belly (including skin and fat), cut into 1½-inch square pieces
1 small piece cored pineapple (about 120 g), sliced

MARINATE THE PORK: Pound and grind the salt, garlic, and peppercorns to a very coarse paste with a mortar and pestle. Set aside.

Combine the raw sugar, white sugar, light soy sauce, and black soy sauce in a medium bowl, stirring until the sugar has dissolved. Add the pork, pineapple, and garlic-pepper paste, stirring to combine. Set aside to marinate at room temperature for 1 hour.

MAKE THE CURRY: Remove and discard the pineapple from the pork.

Remove the pork mixture to a saucepan, add ¼ cup (60 ml) water, and bring to a rapid simmer over high heat. Reduce the heat, cover, and simmer until the pork is tender and the fat has begun to melt, around 30 minutes.

Uncover the pan and simmer until the liquid is reduced and syrupy, around 15 minutes. Taste, adjusting the seasoning if necessary; the curry should have a balance of sweet and salty flavors and be fragrant from the garlic, pepper, and sugar, with a golden-brown color and a pleasantly oily consistency.

Remove to a serving bowl and serve warm or at room temperature with long-grain rice.

OPPOSITE: Pork Belly Braised with Soy Sauce, Black Pepper, and Brown Sugar as served at Raya Restaurant, Phuket Town.

Yellow Noodles Fried with Pork, Seafood, and Yu Choy
Mii Hokkien
หมี่ฮกเกี้ยน

Ko La, located in a stained, faded shophouse, looks like one of those restaurants that's been around forever. And, well, it has. But when I stopped by, its cook, Chaiwat Chantrawibulkul, had only been working the woks there for a few months.

"I used to work in an office," Chaiwat tells me. "But I went to culinary school before that, so I quit my job and started doing this."

The dish Chaiwat makes—the only dish served at Ko La—is mii hokkien. "Hokkien noodles," thick round yellow ropes wok-fried with a combination of seafood and pork (a characteristically Hokkien mix), are a Phuket Town staple whose Chinese origins are evident in its name.

Despite only recently having taken over from Ko La's previous owner, Chaiwat works at the meticulous, intuitive pace of one who's been cooking for decades. He begins by frying the protein and vegetables until they're just short of done. After adding the noodles and a ladleful of broth, he covers the wok with a lid and blasts the heat, causing a shower of sparks to rain onto his sandaled feet. After twenty seconds or so, he reduces the flame and removes the lid, and all those elements have transformed—the noodles have absorbed the liquid and seasonings, the broth has been reduced to a gravy-like consistency. For those who want the luxury of an egg, Chaiwat will crack one into the broth and let it simmer until just cooked.

By the measuring stick of southern Thai flavors, mii hokkien is a downright plain dish, but it's one that's about unique textures—pleasantly squishy noodles, tender seafood, a thick broth, crispy vegetables—as much as it is about flavor.

Serves 6

FOR THE BROTH

8 medium head-on shrimp (200 g total)
200 g pork bones
¾ teaspoon white sugar
¾ teaspoon table salt

FOR THE NOODLES

2 tablespoons lard (or vegetable oil)
6 cloves garlic (30 g total), peeled and roughly chopped
600 g yu choy, thick stems and green leaves separated and cut into 1-inch pieces
150 g boneless lean pork, sliced thin
150 g cleaned squid, sliced into rings
120 g fish cake, sliced thin
1 tablespoon light soy sauce
600 g fresh round yellow wheat noodles
2 tablespoons black soy sauce
300 g shucked oysters
6 eggs

FOR SERVING

12 shallots (120 g total), peeled and quartered
Light soy sauce
White pepper
Chile powder

Yellow wheat noodles may be labeled yakisoba noodles in the U.S.; they are often available refrigerated.

If you only have access to frozen seafood, with the exception of the oysters, this recipe will not suffer for the use of it.

If your local butcher or supermarket doesn't have pork bones, try an Asian market.

Few home cooks—or restaurants, for that matter—have woks large enough to accommodate the ingredients for six servings, so the instructions below are for cooking one portion at a time.

---

recipe continues →

OPPOSITE: Yellow Noodles Fried with Pork, Seafood, and Yu Choy as served at Ko La, a restaurant in Phuket Town.

UP TO A FEW DAYS AHEAD, IF DESIRED, PREPARE THE BROTH: Remove the heads from the shrimp and peel the shrimp; reserve the heads and shells. Set the shrimp aside.

Combine the shrimp heads and shells, pork bones, and 2 quarts (2 L) water in a medium saucepan and bring to a boil over high heat. Reduce the heat to low, cover, and simmer for 20 minutes. Add the sugar and salt, stirring.

Strain the broth, discarding the solids. If making it in advance, transfer the broth to an airtight plastic container and store in the refrigerator. Otherwise, return the broth to the saucepan and keep at a low simmer.

PREPARE THE NOODLES: Heat 1 teaspoon of the lard in a wok over high heat. Add one-sixth of the garlic and stir. Add one-sixth each of the yu choy stems, pork, squid, shrimp, and fish cake, then add ½ teaspoon of the light soy sauce and stir. Add 1 cup (250 ml) of the broth, one-sixth of the noodles, and 1 teaspoon of the black soy sauce and stir. Add a sixth each of the oysters and the yu choy greens and stir. Spread the noodles out evenly in the bottom of the wok, cover with a lid, and simmer rapidly until the noodles are just soft and the broth is slightly reduced and amalgamated, about 1 minute. Remove the lid and reduce the heat to medium-high.

Remove the noodles and other ingredients to an individual serving bowl, leaving as much broth as possible in the wok. Return the wok to the stove and crack an egg into the broth. Cover and allow the mixture to simmer until the egg is just set, around 1 minute. Remove from the heat and top the noodles with the egg and broth, being careful not to break the yolk. Repeat with the remaining ingredients to make five more bowls.

Serve the noodles hot, with the shallots and other accompaniments.

Inside Ko La, a restaurant in Phuket Town.

Fried Thin Rice Noodles Served with a Side of Pork Broth
Mii Hun
หมี่หุ้น

Some street dishes have their origins in portability. Others are fiddly, time-consuming dishes that people no longer want to make at home. Still others are simple, quick snacks. I'd like to think that mii hun stems from homesickness.

The dish—thin round rice noodles fried in soy sauce and served with a broth of pork ribs—was most likely created by Chinese immigrants doing the best they could to replicate the flavors of home with the handful of Chinese-style ingredients they had access to.

Wannee Chunhanan, the sixty-eight-year-old daughter of Chinese immigrants, makes mii hun at a small, open-sided food court in Phuket Town. As the broth simmers, filling her cooking station with the fragrance of pepper, she scoops up the fat that rises to the top of the soup, sprinkling it on the frying noodles. "The pork is fragrant; I don't want to waste it!" she tells me.

She then presents me with two dishes: a tiny plate of slightly salty, bitter noodles and a small bowl of peppery, fragrant broth—a simple combination that lookes, tastes, and smells, unmistakably, like China.

Serves 6

FOR THE FRIED SHALLOT GARNISH

15 shallots (150 g total), peeled and sliced
1 cup (250 ml) vegetable oil

FOR THE BROTH

900 g meaty pork spareribs, cut into 2-inch pieces
2 teaspoons table salt
2 teaspoons raw cane sugar (see Note)
20 g rock sugar

6 cloves garlic (30 g total), peeled
2 teaspoons black peppercorns, coarsely ground with a mortar and pestle

FOR THE NOODLES

300 g thin round dried rice noodles (sen mii; see Glossary)
1 tablespoon black soy sauce
1 tablespoon light brown sugar
1½ teaspoons table salt

FOR SERVING

100 g preserved radish, sliced very thin
2 scallions (50 g total), chopped
Chile powder, fish sauce, white sugar, white pepper, and/or sliced tiny spicy fresh chiles in vinegar (see Note), if desired

---

The dish is garnished with shallots, deep-fried until golden, sweet, and crispy. Don't rush the deep-frying here, or the shallots will taste unpleasantly bitter.

Raw cane sugar is also known as natural brown sugar, raw sugar, or whole cane sugar; Domino brand dark brown sugar can be used as a substitute.

Few home cooks—or restaurants, for that matter—have woks large enough to accommodate the ingredients for six servings, so the instructions below are for cooking two servings at a time.

An optional condiment for this dish would be tiny spicy fresh chiles sliced and steeped in white vinegar; prepare this a day or two in advance if you'd like to serve it.

MAKE THE FRIED SHALLOT GARNISH: Combine the oil and shallots in a wok and bring to a simmer over medium-high heat. Cook at a simmer until the shallots are golden and crispy, around 45 minutes.

Remove the shallots with a mesh strainer or a sieve and set over a bowl to drain. Reserve 3 tablespoons of the shallot oil. Transfer the drained shallots to a sheet pan lined with paper towels to soak up the excess oil, then shift the shallots to another set of paper towels to cool completely.

recipe continues →

MAKE THE BROTH: Combine the spareribs, salt, and 2½ quarts (2.4 L) water in a stockpot and bring to a boil over high heat; use a ladle to scoop off any fat that floats to the top, and reserve it in a small bowl. Reduce the heat and cook at a low simmer until the ribs are tender, around 1 hour.

Add the raw sugar, rock sugar, garlic, and pepper and simmer for another 15 minutes, or until the broth is fragrant. Taste, adjusting the seasoning if necessary; the broth should taste just slightly salty and be fragrant from the garlic and black pepper. Reduce the heat and keep at a low simmer while you prepare the noodles.

MAKE THE NOODLES: Soak the rice noodles in a bowl of plenty of room-temperature water for 5 minutes. Drain thoroughly in a sieve or colander.

Heat a wok over medium heat and add 1 tablespoon of the reserved shallot oil. When it is hot, add one-third each of the noodles, soy sauce, light brown sugar, and salt, along with a tablespoon of the reserved pork fat. Fry the noodles, stirring frequently, adding a few tablespoons of fat and/or broth if the mixture is too dry, until they have soaked up the broth and seasonings and are relatively dry and just slightly singed in parts, about 5 minutes. Taste, adjusting the seasoning if necessary; the noodles should taste equal parts sweet and bitter, and slightly salty from the salt and soy sauce. Remove the noodles to two serving plates. Repeat with the remaining noodles and seasonings to make four more servings.

To serve, transfer a scant 1 cup (230 ml) of the hot broth and 2 or 3 spareribs to a small individual serving bowl and garnish with a pinch each of preserved radish and scallions. Garnish the noodles with a pinch each of the scallions and deep-fried shallots. Serve at room temperature with the seasonings and/or condiments of your choice.

OPPOSITE: Fried Thin Rice Noodles Served with a Side of Pork Broth as prepared by Wannee Chunhanan at her market stall in Phuket Town.
ABOVE: Wannee Chunhanan frying noodles at her stall in Phuket Town.

Devotees taking part in self-sacrifice during Phuket Town's vegetarian festival.

Directly in front of me, a man is enthusiastically licking the business end of a hatchet, blood dripping down his chin and splattering on his chest. Nearby, a group of young men is carrying a palanquin while bystanders toss firecrackers directly at them, shrouding them in smoke and deafening explosions. And minutes later, I encounter a man, eyes bugging out, lips trembling, in a trance-like state, with the barrel of a machine gun shoved through a gaping hole in his cheek. These scenes are played out at Phuket's annual Vegetarian Festival, arguably one of the most gruesome and ostentatious displays of asceticism around.

The story goes that, back in 1825, Phuket was in the midst of a cholera epidemic. A Chinese theater troupe was in town, and in an effort to help, the actors embarked upon a regimen of self-sacrifice. The locals pulled through, the effort was deemed successful, and the tradition has continued to this day.

Although it is associated with spectacle, for most people on Phuket, the Vegetarian Festival is largely a somber affair. For about two weeks in September/October, adherents follow seventeen precepts, the most famous of which bars the consumption of meat (as well as onions, garlic, and tobacco). The goals are purity, the expulsion of sin, and, ideally, the erasure of bad luck; only a handful take this to the extent of walking on coals, climbing a ladder made of sharp blades, or jamming firearms through their cheeks. But during the festival, which combines elements of ancestor worship, Taoism, and Mahayana Buddhism, much of Phuket Town seems to be clad in white (a symbol of purity and yet another of those precepts). The streets leading to the more important Chinese shrines are lined with stalls selling vegetarian dishes—even the normally porky local dishes are made meat-free—identified by yellow flags emblazoned with the Chinese symbol for vegetarian. In the shrines themselves, volunteers work in industrial-sized kitchens—peeling carrots, steaming rice, frying noodles—preparing the meat-free food that will be given to adherents. The acts of cooking food and its donation are regarded as making merit, and the consumption of meat-free food as a step toward purity. In the end, everybody wins—especially, tradition would say, those covered in blood.

Crab Curry Served over Thin Rice Noodles
Kaeng Nuea Puu Bai Chaphluu
แกงเนื้อปูใบชะพลู

A bright yellow curry of coconut milk, crab, fresh turmeric, and wild betel leaf served with knots of thin round rice noodles is one of Phuket's most famous specialties. Boasting chunks of crabmeat the size of canaries and costing as much as $20 per bowl, it's almost certainly the island's most decadent dish. Yet it has its roots in practicality.

"In the past, people made this with whole crabs, chopped up and put in the curry," explains Kularb Jetsadavun, the owner of Raya, the Phuket Town restaurant where the dish was allegedly invented. "My mom would pick out the crabmeat for the kids. When we opened the restaurant, I thought this was a good way to serve the dish."

Kularb's shell-free curry is essentially a tweak on nom jiin naam yaa plaa (see page 138), fish curry served over the thin fermented rice noodles known as *khanom jiin*, a breakfast staple in southern Thailand. Kularb has substituted crab for the fish and pairs the curry with *mii hun*, the local term for thin round dried rice noodles. The combo has struck a nerve; today the dish is a contemporary classic, with copycat versions served at several restaurants in Phuket Town.

Serves 4

FOR THE CURRY PASTE

½ teaspoon table salt
10 medium spicy dried chiles (4g total)
2 heaping teaspoons black peppercorns
A 1½-inch piece galangal (15 g), peeled and sliced
3 stalks lemongrass (75 g total; see page 19 for instructions on how to prepare lemongrass for a curry paste)
1 finger fresh turmeric (15 g), peeled and sliced
4 shallots (40 g total), peeled and sliced
4 cloves garlic (20 g total), peeled and sliced
2 tablespoons shrimp paste

FOR SERVING

180 g thin round dried rice noodles (sen mii; see Glossary)

FOR THE CURRY

3 cups (710 ml) thin coconut milk (see page 135 for instructions on how to make thin coconut milk)
1 cup (250 ml) thick coconut milk (see page 135 for instructions on how to make thick coconut milk)
450 g cooked lump crabmeat
8 wild betel leaves (10 g total)
1 tablespoon white sugar
2 teaspoons fish sauce

Although this recipe has the constituents of a noodle soup, it's not eaten that way. Rather, the noodles, artistically arranged in bundles, are served on a plate, and the diners ladle the curry over them, a few bites at a time.

UP TO 5 DAYS AHEAD, MAKE THE CURRY PASTE: Pound and grind the salt and chiles to a coarse powder with a mortar and pestle. Add the peppercorns and pound and grind to a coarse paste. Add the galangal and pound and grind to a coarse paste. Add the lemongrass and pound and grind to a coarse paste. Add the turmeric and pound and grind to a coarse paste. Add the shallots and garlic and pound and grind to a coarse paste. Add the shrimp paste and pound and grind to a fine paste. (Alternatively, iIf using a food processor or blender, process the salt, chiles, peppercorns, galangal, lemongrass, turmeric, shallots, garlic, and shrimp paste to a fine paste.) If making it in advance, remove the paste to an airtight container and store in the refrigerator.

PREPARE THE NOODLES: Soak the rice noodles in a bowl of room-temperature water for 15 minutes. Drain in a sieve or colander.

Bring 2 quarts (2 L) water to a boil in a large saucepan. Add the noodles. When the water reaches a boil again, drain the noodles in a colander. Rinse in plenty of cool water and, while they are still wet, use a fork or chopsticks to twist, roll, and shape the noodles into

recipe continues →

Crab Curry Served over Thin Rice Noodles
as served at Raya Restaurant, Phuket Town.

coils of about 5 g each; you should have approximately 16 coils. Remove to a sieve or colander to drain again, then remove to a plate, cover with plastic wrap, and set aside.

MAKE THE CURRY: Bring the thin coconut milk to a boil in a saucepan over medium-high heat. Add the curry paste and reduce to a simmer. Add the thick coconut milk, crabmeat, wild betel leaves, sugar, and fish sauce and simmer for 5 minutes. Taste, adjusting the seasoning if necessary; the curry should taste equal parts spicy/peppery and rich and be fragrant from the herbs and aromatics.

Place 4 coils of noodles on each serving plate and serve with a central serving bowl of the warm or room-temperature curry, or with individual bowls containing approximately 1½ cups (350 ml) of curry each.

Inside Raya Restaurant, Phuket Town.

Phuket-Style Steamed Curry with Fish

Haw Mok

ห่อหมก

Order a local-style noodle dish in Phuket Town, and it's likely to be paired with a mysterious banana leaf packet. Unfolding it will reveal a curry, steamed to the silky, soft texture of chawanmushi (Japanese-style savory egg custard), laced with tender slices of fish and boasting a yellow hue from turmeric, a subtle sting of dried chiles and black peppercorns, and a distinctly Southeast Asian aroma from fresh herbs. Anyone who's spent time in Malaysia, particularly on the island of Penang, will recognize the dish as a close cousin of otak-otak. As is the case there, the dish, which is extremely versatile, is often paired with noodle dishes, but I think it's even more delicious when eaten with rice.

The recipe below is an amalgam of the version kindly taught to me by Supakan Piyavoratham, of Khanom Jeen Jee Liu, a popular noodle restaurant in Phuket Town, and versions I encountered at other restaurants and stalls. Serve these as a side to a Phuket-style noodle dish such as Yellow Noodles Fried with Pork, Seafood, and Yu Choy (page 163) or with rice as part of a Phuket-style meal.

Serves 6

FOR THE CURRY PASTE

¼ teaspoon table salt
20 medium spicy dried chiles (10 g total)
1 heaping teaspoon black peppercorns
3 stalks lemongrass (7 g total; see page 19 for instructions on how to prepare lemongrass for an herb paste)
½ teaspoon chopped makrut lime zest
1 finger turmeric (15 g), peeled and sliced
6 cloves garlic (30 g total), peeled and sliced
1 tablespoon shrimp paste

FOR THE STEAMED CURRY

12 feet banana leaves
1 sea bass fillet (around 300 g total), any bones removed and cut into ¾-inch-thick slices
1½ cups (350 ml) coconut cream (see instructions on page 135 for how to make coconut cream)
6 makrut lime leaves, sliced very thin
½ teaspoon table salt
½ teaspoon white sugar
6 large wild tea leaves (8 g total; see Glossary)

6 toothpicks

You can substitute barracuda or kingfish for the sea bass.

UP TO 5 DAYS IN ADVANCE, MAKE THE CURRY PASTE: Pound and grind the salt and chiles to a coarse powder with a mortar and pestle. Add the peppercorns and pound and grind to a coarse powder. Add the lemongrass and pound and grind to a coarse paste. Add the makrut lime zest, turmeric, and garlic and pound and grind to a coarse paste. Add the shrimp paste and pound and grind to a fine paste. (Alternatively, if using a food processor or blender, process the salt, chiles, peppercorns, lemongrass, makrut lime zest, turmeric, garlic, and shrimp paste to a fine paste.) If making it in advance, remove the paste to an airtight container and store in the refrigerator.

ON THE DAY OF SERVING, PREPARE THE BANANA LEAVES: Using a damp cloth, wipe the leaves clean of any dirt, dust, or mud. Cut away the coarse inner edge. If the banana leaves are particularly thick, stiff, or brittle, briefly pass them over the flame of a stove to make them more pliable.

Cut 6 rectangles approximately 12 inches long and 8 inches wide, 6 rectangles 9 inches long and 5 inches wide, and 6 strips 13 inches long by 2 inches wide. Set aside.

recipe continues →

MAKE THE STEAMED CURRY: Combine the sea bass, coconut cream, makrut lime leaves, salt, sugar, and curry paste in a bowl and stir to release the gelatin in the fish until the mixture is slightly sticky in consistency, around 10 minutes.

Fill and fold the banana leaf packages as described in the sidebar, adding a wild tea leaf to each one. Steam the banana leaf packages in a Chinese-style steaming tray over medium heat for 20 minutes.

Remove the packages to small serving plates and serve warm or at room temperature.

Phuket-Style Steamed Curry with Fish as served at Som Chit, a noodle restaurant in Phuket Town.

HOW TO FOLD BANANA LEAVES FOR STEAMED CURRY WITH FISH

1 Start with one of the larger leaves, matte side up. Top with a smaller leaf, glossy side up, and top with a wild tea leaf. Top this with approximately ¼ cup (100 g) of the fish mixture.

2 Fold the leaves lengthwise around the fish mixture.

3 Fold the near end of the banana leaves up over the fish mixture, wrapping the folds around the exterior. Repeat with the far end.

4 Holding the two folds in place, wrap a narrow strip of banana leaf vertically around the package. Seal the package with a toothpick.

5 The package is ready for steaming.

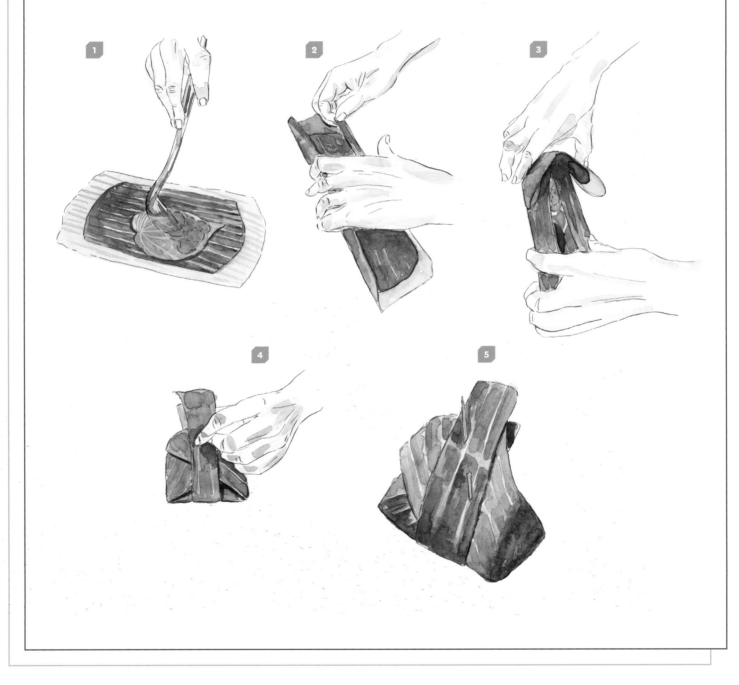

PHUKET'S SWEETS AND SNACKS

Phuket's culinary diversity is probably most evident in its sweets and savory snacks. The local term for sweet, *kohy*, is related to the Malay term *kuih*, and many of Phuket's sweets would be familiar to a native of Penang, Malaysia. Not surprisingly, several are Chinese in origin, occasionally supplemented with local ingredients or flavors. Others have culinary roots that are even more exotic: the thin, crispy pancakes known as *aapohng* can probably be traced back to the south Indian appom and most likely came to Phuket via Penang; karii pap have much in common with Indian samosas, and the pastry may have been inspired by the Portuguese, while the name ("curry puff") stems from English.

A selection of the sweet snacks available one morning at Phuket Town's Cham Cha Market:

Top Row

1 An open-faced pancake of wheat flour and eggs with a lacy consistency and a topping of crushed peanuts and sugar / *ban jian kohy* / บั้นเจียนโก้ย

2 Sticky rice mixed with coconut milk and encasing sweet fillings such as banana or taro, or savory ones such as shrimp wrapped in banana leaves and grilled over coals / *khaao niaw ping* / ข้าวเหนียวปิ้ง

3 Sticky rice, sweetened with coconut milk and sugar, supplemented with beans, wrapped in a type of palm leaf and steamed / *khanom tom* / ขนมต้ม

4 Sticky rice sweetened with coconut milk and sugar; elsewhere in Thailand, this sweet has a green hue from the addition of pandan leaf, but in Phuket it's dyed red, the color associated with Chinese offerings / *khaao niaw kaew* / ข้าวเหนียวแก้ว

5 Steamed cups of rice flour and tapioca flour and raw cane sugar, garnished with shredded coconut / *koh sui* / โกซุ้ย

Middle Row

6 Sticky rice sweetened with coconut milk and sugar; stuffed with a savory, peppery shrimp and coconut filling; wrapped in banana leaves; and grilled / *paao laang* / ป่าวหล้าง

7 Sticky rice flour, raw cane sugar, and coconut milk wrapped in banana leaves and steamed / *thawn mai* / ท่อนไม้

8 Wrappers of sticky rice dough encasing a sweet mung bean filling / *ang kuu* / อังกู๊

Bottom Row

9 The thin, crispy version of the open-faced pancake of wheat flour and eggs with a topping of crushed peanuts and sugar / *ban jian kohy* / บั้นเจียนโก้ย

10 Thin, crispy, slightly sweet pancakes made from leavened rice flour / *aapohng* / อาโป้ง

11 Rice flour, soybean paste, and alkaline water steamed in the form of a cake and served with sugarcane syrup / *kii aa kohy* / กีอาโก้ย

Compressed Sticky Rice Served with a Coconut Custard Dip

Khaao Niaw Hiip

ข้าวเหนียวหีบ

According to Maneerat Susangrat, the fourth-generation owner of Pun Tae Koy, a sweets factory based in her home in Phuket Town, khaao niaw hiip is standard at traditional weddings on the island. The tightly packed grains of sticky rice, mixed with coconut milk and sugar and stained a unique shade of cobalt, promise closeness and a sweet future. Yet unlike many sticky rice–based sweet snacks in Thailand's south, most of the sweetness doesn't stem from the rice itself, which is rich and dense, but rather from the coconut custard dip that it's paired with—yet another distinctive attribute of this dish.

Serves 6

FOR THE COMPRESSED STICKY RICE

1 cup (200 g) sticky rice
⅓ cup (80 ml) thick coconut milk (see page 135 for instructions on how to make thick coconut milk)
25 g white sugar
Pinch of table salt
6 fresh butterfly pea flowers, minced fine (or a few drops of blue food coloring)
About 1 foot banana leaf (optional)

FOR THE COCONUT CUSTARD

2 eggs
90 g white sugar
25 g palm sugar
Pinch of table salt
1 pandan leaf
2 tablespoons coconut cream (see page 135 for instructions on how to make coconut cream)

The most efficient way to steam sticky rice is with a Thai-style pot and a conical bamboo basket. If you don't have access to these tools, a steaming set can be improvised with a sieve elevated over boiling water, or a Chinese-style steamer lined with cheesecloth, although the cooking time may vary.

The butterfly pea flowers give this rice dish a light blue hue but do not contribute to its flavor or aroma. If you don't have access to the flowers, a few drops of blue food coloring will suffice.

Be patient when making the coconut custard; using too high heat will cause the eggs to cook too fast, giving it a curdled rather than smooth texture.

THE DAY BEFORE SERVING, PREPARE THE STICKY RICE: Gently rinse the rice in several changes of water until the water remains clear. Cover with plenty of fresh water and soak for 4 to 6 hours.

Drain the rice, discarding the water. Bring a couple quarts of water to a boil in a Thai-style sticky rice steaming pot (or in a saucepan or a Chinese-style steamer). Put the rice in the bamboo steaming basket (or in a sieve or a Chinese-style steamer lined with cheesecloth) positioned a few inches above the boiling water, cover with a tea towel and then a lid to create a relatively tight seal that allows as little steam as possible to escape, and steam for 20 minutes.

Flip the entire mass of rice and steam for another 5 minutes, or until the grains are entirely cooked through, tender, and visibly stuck together.

Remove the rice from the heat and transfer to a large bowl. Add the thick coconut milk, sugar, and salt to the still-hot rice, stirring until the sugar is dissolved and all the ingredients have been absorbed by the rice, which should be glossy in appearance. Transfer around one-third of the rice to a bowl and mix with the butterfly pea flowers (or the food coloring) until it is cobalt blue. Remove the remaining rice to a small square baking pan (approximately 6 by 6 by 2 inches),

recipe continues →

packing and smoothing the rice with a spatula until it is level and uniform. Cover it with the blue sticky rice, packing and smoothing the rice with a spatula until it is flat and even. Top the rice with the banana leaf, if you have it, or waxed paper and then a flat square tile or flat square dish that covers it, and top it all with something very heavy (such as a granite mortar and pestle or a stockpot filled with water). Let the rice stand for at least 5 hours to compress it.

MEANWHILE, MAKE THE COCONUT CUSTARD: Combine the eggs, white sugar, palm sugar, salt, and pandan leaf in a bowl. Using your hand, mix the ingredients, grasping, mashing, and massaging them until they are fully combined and the sugar has dissolved, around 10 minutes. Gradually add the coconut cream, continuing to mix by hand until combined.

Pour the mixture through a strainer set over a bowl and discard the pandan leaf. Fill the bottom of a double boiler with an inch or two of water, or set a heatproof bowl over a saucepan partly filled with water (the water should not touch the bottom of the bowl). Pour the custard mixture into the top of the double boiler or the bowl and bring the water to a low simmer while constantly stirring the ingredients with a whisk, which should take around 10 minutes. Continue to cook at a low simmer, stirring constantly, until the mixture has reached a consistency similar to that of a pourable pudding, around 15 minutes. Remove from the heat and allow to cool to room temperature.

MAKE THE SWEET: Turn the sticky rice out onto a cutting board and cut into strips around 1 inch wide. Then cut each strip at an angle to form diamonds around 1½ inches long; you should have around 18 sticky rice diamonds.

Serve the sticky rice on a tray or large plate with the coconut custard dip in a small serving bowl.

Phuket-Style Sugar Cookies
Khanom Naa Taek
ขนมหน้าแตก

250 g all-purpose flour
150 g white sugar
1 teaspoon ammonium bicarbonate
½ teaspoon table salt
¼ teaspoon baking powder
½ cup (125 ml) vegetable oil
1 egg
1 tablespoon water
1 to 2 drops red food coloring (optional)

Walk through Phuket Town, and you'll notice streetside stalls piled with wheat flour–based sweets and snacks. Given the city's antique shophouses and general stuck-in-time vibe, one might expect to encounter the more traditional Thai-style rice- and rice flour–based sweets. But many of Phuket Town's light bites take forms that would be familiar to someone from, say, Ohio or even rural France: Fig Newton–ish fruit-filled cookies, sweet rolls, madeleine look-alikes, and crispy wafers.

"Sweet factories in Phuket Town use wheat flour a lot," explains Mathukorn Kooramphirak, the owner of a bakery that has been making almost exclusively wheat flour–based sweets for two generations. "It's the Chinese influence."

Chinese laborers brought to Phuket to work in the tin mining industry brought with them their gluten-heavy sensibilities for noodles, as well as snacks and sweets, a preference that persists today. Mathukorn's family maintains this tradition, and one of their best sellers is *khanom naa taek*, the name a direct translation from Hokkien Chinese, meaning "cracked top."

"It's like a cookie but with Chinese ingredients," Mathukorn tells me. "Western cookies are made with butter, but we use oil."

Another particularly Chinese tweak is the use of ammonium bicarbonate, a leavening agent that results in a particularly light and crispy final product. The cookies, coin-sized, crunchy, and sweet, with a particularly inviting golden color (from eggs and yellow food coloring), are a perfect pairing with coffee or tea, or a light breakfast or a snack, Mathukorn says.

Makes approximately 54 cookies

Ammonium bicarbonate is used as a leavening agent in some cuisines and on an industrial scale in the U.S. As the chemical encounters heat, it releases both carbon dioxide and ammonia, meaning that in the oven it produces a strong, almost noxious smell. If the cookies or other product are baked at very high heat, though, the aroma will disappear entirely. If your oven can't reach temperatures as high as 500°F, crank it to its maximum and bake the cookies for a minute or two longer to ensure that they emerge crispy, toasty, and ammonia-aroma-free.

Preheat the oven to 500°F.

Combine the flour, sugar, ammonium bicarbonate, salt, and baking powder and sift into a large bowl. Add the vegetable oil, egg, water, and food coloring (if using), stirring to combine. Knead briefly by hand in the bowl.

Take heaping teaspoons/10 g portions of the dough, roll into balls, and place on a baking sheet, leaving at least ½ inch of space between the balls. Using a pen or similar object, make a shallow dimple in the top of each ball of dough.

Bake the cookies for 7 minutes, or until baked through and slightly toasted on the bottom. Let cool on the baking sheet, then remove to an airtight container for storage.

OPPOSITE: Phuket-Style Sugar Cookies as made by Mathukorn Kooramphirak's family business, Phuket Town.

Flavors of the Past

IN MANY WAYS, Ko Samui is the epitome of the modern-day Thai island: tropical, brash, and home to over-developed beaches, malls, an airport, as well as some of the country's most sophisticated and expensive resorts. But go back in time not so many decades, and Ko Samui was resolutely rustic: a remote outpost inhabited by a handful of intrepid Chinese traders and a small community of mostly Muslim fishermen and coconut farmers.

Kanitha Salim was born on the old Ko Samui. One could say that she's the dictionary-definition islander. Her parents were Thai and Chinese, and she grew up on the family fruit and coconut farm located just beyond a steep hill about two miles, as the crow flies, from the coast. At a young age, she left the island, attending college in Bangkok at a time when a trip to the capital involved an overnight boat trip to the mainland followed by a train ride of many, many hours. After several decades away, she returned to Ko Samui and to her childhood home, which she has transformed into an casual restaurant and cooking school.

"I want to preserve local recipes," she tells me. "Nowadays kids on Ko Samui eat KFC, pizza. They don't eat local food anymore! Ko Samui has changed so much."

The menu at Kanitha's restaurant paints a vivid picture of a pre–international franchise Ko Samui. Given the family business, coconut milk makes frequent appearances in soups, stir-fries, even rice. And Kanitha's Chinese background means that pork and chicken pop up occasionally—just as these proteins would

have done in her childhood. But the bulk of the menu is based on vegetables, fruit, and herbs plucked from the family garden, or shellfish or other aquatic creatures scavenged from shallow coastal waters: the kind of ingredients that speak of a past of self-sufficiency.

Culinary preservation was also a motivation for Sookhkoe Donsai.

"I used to be a lawyer and got to travel all over Thailand," explained the native of Ko Samui. "I noticed that each province had a place where one could sample its local dishes, which made me realize that Koh Samui had nothing like that. So, after coming back home, I opened this restaurant."

Nearly thirty years later, Sookhkoe's restaurant, Bangpo Seafood, is still in business, and it provides another insight into the rustic ingredients and flavors that would have been common on the Ko Samui of the past. An example of this is khoei jii, a coconut shell that is smeared with a mix of shredded coconut, shrimp paste, crabmeat, and chile, then toasted over coals and served with vegetables and herbs. Every customer who eats at Bangpo Seafood is given the dish, an item one would struggle to find anywhere else in Thailand, even just across to the mainland in Surat Thani.

Tourism has affected Ko Samui in ways that cannot be reversed, and much of its original character has been lost. But if you know where to look, you just might get a picture—and perhaps a taste—of what the island used to be like.

OPPOSITE: Elevated houses in the fishing village of Hua Thanon, Ko Samui, Surat Thani Province.
ABOVE: Drying octopus, Ko Samui, Surat Thani Province.

Shrimp Paste and Crab Toasted in a Coconut Shell

Khoei Jii

เคยจี่

This is one of those dishes that makes such clever use of local ingredients that I wonder how it doesn't exist elsewhere. But as far as I can tell, khoei jii, made with a mixture of shrimp paste, grated coconut, crabmeat, and chile pounded with a mortar and pestle, smeared on a coconut shell, and toasted over coals until fragrant, is found only on Ko Samui. Its funky, slightly spicy flavors mean it's the ideal counter to Rice Cooked in Coconut Milk with Mung Beans (page 188), another Ko Samui–only dish.

Serves 4 as part of a southern Thai meal

2 mature coconuts
Pinch of table salt
7 medium spicy fresh chiles (20 g total), chopped
8 shallots (80 g total), peeled and sliced
9 cloves garlic (40 g total), peeled and sliced
3 tablespoons shrimp paste
5 g palm sugar
50 g cooked lump crabmeat
Sides such as sliced cucumber, long beans, and/or bai man puu (see Glossary)

The shrimp paste filling is made using a granite mortar and pestle, which lends it a pleasantly coarse, chunky consistency. A food processor or blender isn't a substitute for these tools here, as it would result in a mixture with too fine a consistency.

Fresh coconuts are required here, not only for the requisite crunch, flavor, and aroma of freshly grated coconut meat, but also because the shells act as the grilling vehicle.

PREPARE THE COCONUTS: Split one coconut in half by whacking it with the back of a heavy cleaver along its widest circumference (the chubby part of the coconut, not the end with the three holes) three or four times while turning the coconut on this axis, doing your best to keep the shell in large pieces. Discard the liquid. Using a Thai coconut scraper, scrape the white flesh from the inside of the coconut (see page 24 for tips on grating coconut). Reserve ½ cup (40 g) of the grated meat for this dish and save the remainder, ideally in the freezer, for another use. Repeat with the other coconut.

Select four relatively round sections of coconut shell and, using a cleaver, chip away at the edges to arrive at relatively round disks around 5 inches in diameter. Using a cleaver or heavy knife, scrape the coarse stringy bits off the exterior of the shells.

Light a fire in a charcoal or gas grill. While the coals are reducing or the gas grill is heating, move to the next step.

MAKE THE SHRIMP PASTE FILLING: Pound and grind the salt and chiles to a coarse paste with a mortar and pestle. Add half of the reserved grated coconut and pound and grind to a coarse paste. Add the shallots and garlic and pound and grind to a coarse paste. Add the shrimp paste and pound and grind to a coarse paste. Add the palm sugar and pound and grind to a relatively fine paste. Add the crabmeat and the remaining grated coconut and pound until bruised and distributed. Set aside.

TOAST THE COCONUT SHELLS: When the coals have reduced to a low heat (approximately 250 to 350°F—you should be able to hold your palm 3 inches above the fire for 8 to 10 seconds), or with the gas flame at low, grill the coconut shells, flipping them occasionally, until toasted and fragrant but not burnt, around 15 minutes. Remove the shells from the grill.

When the shells are cool enough to handle, smear the shrimp paste filling over the concave sides of the shells. Return the shells to the grill, shrimp paste side facing up, and grill until the filling starts to become toasted and fragrant, around 15 minutes. Flip the shells and grill briefly until the filling is slightly dry, toasted, and fragrant, around 5 more minutes (if you're afraid the filling will fall out the shells, you can skip this step and simply toast the shells, face up, a bit longer). Remove from the heat and allow to cool to room temperature.

Remove the shells to a plate or tray and serve with the sides and long-grain rice (or Rice Cooked in Coconut Milk with Mung Beans).

Rice Cooked in Coconut Milk with Mung Beans
Khaao Man
ข้าวมัน

Ko Samui's legacy as a coconut plantation means that coconuts make their way into just about every local dish, including that normally unadulterated Thai staple, rice. At a handful of the more traditional homes and restaurants on the island, the grains are supplemented with coconut milk, dried mung beans, and a pinch of salt, making a plate of rice that's almost substantial enough to eat on its own.

Serve this with Shrimp Paste and Crab Toasted in a Coconut Shell (page 186) or other Ko Samui–style dishes.

Serves 4

20 g dried mung beans
1¼ cups (250 g) long-grain white rice
¼ cup (100 g) long-grain red rice (see Glossary)
1½ cups (350 ml) thin coconut milk (see page 135 for instructions on how to make thin coconut milk)
¼ teaspoon table salt

THE NIGHT BEFORE SERVING, PREPARE THE MUNG BEANS: Put the dried mung beans in a bowl with plenty of water and soak overnight.

AN HOUR BEFORE SERVING, MAKE THE RICE: Drain the mung beans, discarding the water.

Combine the white rice, red rice, and mung beans in a bowl and gently wash them in several changes of water until the water remains clear.

Transfer the rice and mung beans to a saucepan; add the coconut milk, salt, and 1½ cups (350 ml) water; and bring to a rolling boil for 3 seconds over high heat. Put a lid on the saucepan, reduce the heat to as low as possible, and simmer the rice, undisturbed, for 20 minutes.

Turn off the flame and remove the lid for a few seconds to release excess heat and steam, then cover and allow the rice to rest, undisturbed, for 10 minutes. Gently stir the rice, replace the lid, and allow the rice to rest for a final 5 minutes before serving.

Remove the rice to four plates and serve warm.

The Muslim fishing village of Hua Thanon, Ko Samui, Surat Thani Province.

Gray Mullet Grilled with Turmeric, Black Pepper, and Garlic
Plaa Krabawk Ping Hup
ปลากระบอกปิ้งหุบ

Chile, fresh turmeric, garlic, and pepper are the building blocks of Ko Samui–style cuisine, and they feature in countless dishes on the island. But where it concerns seafood, these ingredients also serve a strategic purpose.

"Turmeric and garlic counter any fishy flavors," explains Ratri, a native of Ko Samui and a cook at Bangpo Seafood, who didn't want to share her surname. She's describing one of the restaurant's most famous dishes, gray mullet coated with a paste of fresh turmeric, garlic, and peppercorns before being grilled over coals.

Practical reasons aside, the combination is also utterly delicious and fragrant, not to mention beautiful, and this just might be my favorite recipe in this book. For a Ko Samui–style meal, pair this dish with Rice Cooked in Coconut Milk with Mung Beans (page 188).

Serves 4 as part of a southern Thai meal

FOR THE HERB PASTE

Heaping ½ teaspoon table salt
2 fingers fresh turmeric (30 g total), peeled and sliced
1 heaping teaspoon black peppercorns
30 small cloves garlic (15 g total; see Note)

FOR THE FISH

1 small gray mullet (around 600 g), gutted and scaled

This recipe involves butterflying a whole fish, which is not as hard as it sounds if you have a sharp blade and some basic knife skills.

The easiest way to grill a whole butterflied fish is with a grilling basket, available at Thai or Asian markets and housewares stores.

This recipe uses tiny cloves of Thai garlic, which can be pounded up, skin and all. If you only have access to big cloves of garlic, discard the thicker, coarser skin.

PREPARE THE HERB PASTE: Pound the salt and turmeric to a coarse paste with a mortar and pestle. Add the peppercorns and pound and grind to a coarse paste. Add the garlic (skins and all if using small Thai garlic) and pound and grind to a coarse paste. Loosen the herb paste with 3 tablespoons water, stirring to combine. (Alternatively, if using a food processor or blender, process the salt, turmeric, peppercorns, garlic, and water to a coarse paste.)

PREPARE THE FISH: Follow the steps in the sidebar to butterfly the fish. Pat the fish dry with paper towels and rub the exterior with the herb paste. Set aside.

GRILL THE FISH: Prepare a medium fire in a charcoal grill (approximately 350 to 450°F—you should be able to hold your palm 3 inches above the flame for 5 to 7 seconds) or in a gas grill. Put the mullet in a grilling basket, splayed open, and grill, flipping the basket occasionally, until the fish is cooked through, golden, and fragrant, around 10 minutes.

Remove the mullet to a serving platter and serve warm with long-grain rice or Rice Cooked in Coconut Milk with Mung Beans.

The view from Bangpo Seafood, a restaurant on Ko Samui, in Surat Thani Province.

HOW TO PREPARE THE FISH FOR GRAY MULLET GRILLED WITH TURMERIC, BLACK PEPPER, AND GARLIC

1 To butterfly the fish using a sharp knife, starting at the tail of the mullet, make a deep incision along one side of spine, cutting all the way through to the bottom of the spine (but not through the bottom of the fish) and continuing this cut all the way to the head.

2 Flip the fish around and, starting at the head, repeat the cut, this time working on the opposite side of the spine.

3 Split the fish head in half and open the mullet out flat, skin side down. Chop through the base of the spine where it meets the head to disconnect it. Working from the head to the tail, cut away any skin that's connecting the spine to the fish.

4 Chop through the spine at the tail end, remove the entire spine, and discard.

5 Pat the fish dry with paper towels and rub the exterior with the herb paste.

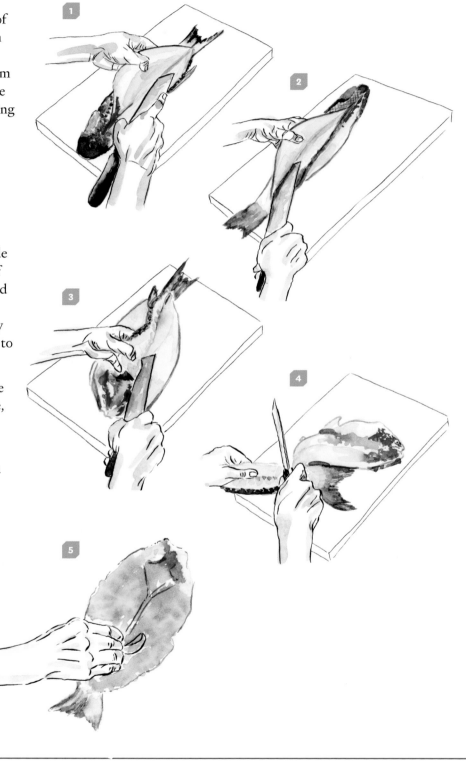

Fried Salt Pork
Muu Khoh
หมูโค

"In the old days, people didn't have refrigerators, and we didn't go to the market that often," says Kanitha Salim, a native of Ko Samui. "We didn't really eat pork or chicken—except on special occasions."

When a pig was slaughtered, usually for a Chinese holiday, Kanitha tells me, her father would coat any extra cuts with coarse salt and put them in a giant ceramic jar in the garden. When the meat was needed for a curry or stir-fry, it was pulled out, rinsed, and used. Alternatively, she tells me, they'd simmer the salted pork belly in a bit of water and then fry it, along with a bit of crushed garlic, in the lard that emerged.

Refrigerators have made the technique redundant, but this dish lives on at homes and restaurants across Ko Samui simply because it's really, really, tasty. Pair this dish with Rice Cooked in Coconut Milk with Mung Beans (page 188), if you like.

Serves 4 as part of a southern Thai meal

350 g skin-on pork belly, cut into 2-inch-wide strips
20 g table salt
20 g small cloves garlic, coarsely crushed with a
   mortar and pestle

THREE DAYS BEFORE SERVING, SALT THE PORK: Rub the salt all over the pork belly and place in a plastic container or ziplock bag. Cover or seal the bag and refrigerate for 3 days.

ON THE DAY OF SERVING, FRY THE SALT PORK: Remove the pork belly and rinse well. Cut the pork into ½-inch-thick slices that include meat, fat, and skin.

Bring the salt pork and 1 cup (250 ml) water to a boil in a wok over medium-high heat. Reduce the heat and cook at a rapid simmer until the water has completely evaporated, 15 to 20 minutes. A film of oil should have formed at the bottom of the wok.

Reduce the heat and fry the pork, stirring occasionally, until it starts to turn golden, about 20 minutes. Add the garlic and fry, stirring occasionally, until the garlic and pork are golden, fragrant, and crispy, another 10 minutes or so.

Pour off the excess fat, saving it for another use, and remove the pork and garlic to a serving plate. Serve warm or at room temperature with long-grain rice or Rice Cooked in Coconut Milk with Mung Beans.

A Dip of Green Peppercorns and Grilled Fish
Naam Chup Phrik
น้ำชุบพริก

For someone like Kanitha Salim, who grew up on a farm on Ko Samui, there might be no dish easier than this one, a dip of fresh green peppercorns pounded up with a mortar and pestle with chiles, garlic, palm sugar, shrimp paste, and some grilled fish.

"Most people here have a pepper tree at home," she tells me. "If you need pepper, you just grab it from the vine!"

Outside Southeast Asia, it's a different story, and I've been told that green peppercorns can be very hard to come across. But if you can get your hands on some, this intensely peppery, salty, savory, fishy relish is utterly delicious paired with rich, slightly sweet Rice Cooked in Coconut Milk with Mung Beans (page 188).

Serves 4 as part of a southern Thai meal

FOR THE DIP

1 horse mackerel or other small mackerel or sardines (around 100 g)
35 g fresh green peppercorns
2 cloves garlic (10 g total), peeled and sliced
5 medium spicy fresh chiles (15g total)
15 g palm sugar
2 tablespoons shrimp paste

FOR SERVING

A platter that includes a mix of leafy herbs and fresh vegetables such as Asian pennywort, young cashew tree leaves, bai man puu (see Glossary), Vietnamese coriander, water celery, young mango leaves, long beans, Thai eggplants, or cucumber, cut into bite-sized pieces

Thai-style dips such as this one are made using a granite mortar and pestle, which lends them a pleasantly coarse, chunky consistency. A food processor or blender isn't a substitute for these tools, as that would result in a dip with too fine a consistency.

To eat a Thai-style dip, take an herb, green, or vegetable, put it on your serving of rice, and top with a bit of the dip, creating a bite that combines all three elements.

A COUPLE OF HOURS BEFORE SERVING, PREPARE THE FISH: Prepare a fire in a charcoal or gas grill, with the grate around 3 inches above the coals or the flame of the gas grill. When the coals have reduced to a low heat (approximately 250 to 350°F—you should be able to hold your palm 3 inches above the flame for 8 to 10 seconds), or with the gas fire at low, add the mackerel and grill, flipping occasionally, until cooked through, fragrant, and relatively dry, approximately 20 minutes (alternatively, you can grill the fish under the oven broiler). Remove from the heat.

When the fish is cool enough to handle, remove and discard the skin and bones; you should have around 50 g fish. Set aside.

MAKE THE DIP: Scrape the peppercorns into a mortar, discarding any woody stems. Add the garlic and chiles and pound and grind to a coarse paste. Add the palm sugar and shrimp paste and pound to a coarse paste. Add the fish and pound to a coarse paste. Taste, adjusting the seasoning if necessary; the dip should taste peppery/spicy, salty, and savory, in that order. (Note that after a few minutes, the crushed peppercorns will oxidize, turning the dip almost black.)

Remove the dip to a small serving bowl and serve with the platter of herbs and vegetables and long-grain rice or Rice Cooked with Coconut Milk and Mung Beans.

FROM LEFT: Fried Salt Pork; A Soup of Coconut Milk, Vegetables, and Shrimp; and A Dip of Green Peppercorns and Grilled Fish; as prepared by Kanitha Salim, Ko Samui, Surat Thani Province.

A Soup of Coconut Milk, Vegetables, and Shrimp

Kaeng Liang Kathi

แกงเลี้ยงกะทิ

In Bangkok and central Thailand, the term *kaeng liang* refers to a cloudy, peppery soup that includes a relatively set repertoire of ingredients. On Ko Samui, the dish is based on coconut milk, is rich rather than peppery in flavor, and, at least according to Kanitha Salim, can include just about anything. The version she made for me includes papaya, sweet potato, melinjo (see Glossary), taro, and kabocha squash. You could also make it with carrots, broccoli, or potatoes. Having grown up on a coconut farm, Kanitha does emphasize the importance of using freshly squeezed coconut milk in the soup rather than the stuff in a box or can. Other than that, the only real parameters are the dish's flavors.

"It should taste salty and rich; it shouldn't be too sweet," she tells me. "Add sugar only at the end if necessary because you want the sweetness to come from the vegetables as well."

Serves 4

3 cups (710 ml) thin coconut milk (see page 135 for
    instructions on how to make thin coconut milk)
1½ cups (350 ml) thick coconut milk (see page 135 for
    instructions on how to make thick coconut milk)
1 teaspoon shrimp paste
1 teaspoon table salt
100 g peeled taro, cut into thick slices
100 g seeded peeled kabocha
    squash, cut into thick slices
50 g snake gourd (see Glossary), peeled and
    chopped into 1-inch pieces
8 medium shrimp (150 g total)
100 g barely ripe papaya, seeded, peeled, and
    cut into thick slices
50 g melinjo leaves (see Glossary), woody stalks
    removed and discarded (around 35g trimmed leaves)
¼ teaspoon white sugar (optional)

OPPOSITE: Kanitha Salim cooking in her home kitchen on Ko Samui.
LEFT: Inside a shophouse in Nathon, Ko Samui, Surat Thani Province.

Combine the thin coconut milk, thick coconut milk, shrimp paste, and salt in a saucepan and bring to a boil over medium-high heat, stirring to ensure that the shrimp paste is well distributed. Add the taro and kabocha squash, reduce the heat, and simmer until tender, around 5 minutes. Add the snake gourd and shrimp and simmer until the shrimp is cooked through and the vegetables are tender, around 5 minutes.

Add the papaya and melinjo leaves and simmer for 1 minute. Taste, adjusting the seasoning with the sugar if necessary; the soup should taste equal parts salty and rich, followed by a subtle sweetness.

Remove to a serving bowl and serve warm or at room temperature with long-grain rice.

Sunset over Phang-Nga Bay as
seen from Ko Yao Noi, an island in
Phang-Nga Province.

HUNTING WITH THAILAND'S SEA PEOPLE

Hook Klathalay is telling me about his favorite childhood meal, and he is visibly excited.

"When I was a kid, I loved sea turtle eggs!" says the thirty-five-year-old. "We'd boil them and mix them with rice and sugar."

Hook's meal would be utterly foreign to the average southern Thai, but it isn't so unusual for a Moken. Also known as the "sea gypsies," or *chao ley*, Thai for "sea people," the Moken can claim an astounding list of traits. They're one of the only groups of humans who lived predominantly at sea, in houseboats called *kabang*. Their ability to see underwater is better than anybody else's, and they can hold their breath for remarkably long periods of time. These skills were honed over centuries of sailing, hunting, and gathering among the islands of Myanmar's Mergui Archipelago and Thailand's upper Andaman Sea coast.

In recent decades, though, Moken culture has changed immensely, shifting toward a more modern and "Thai" direction. Hook is probably among the last generation of Moken to have experienced an itinerant upbringing. "I lived on a kabang with my father and brother until I was four or five years old," he tells me. "We moved to an island so I could go to school and get an education. It was strange! I lived on a boat and I spoke only Moken, so I was teased a lot."

For Hook and many other Moken, modernization accelerated in 2005, after the previous year's tsunami that killed more than 200,000 people in Southeast Asia. The Moken emerged from the disaster almost

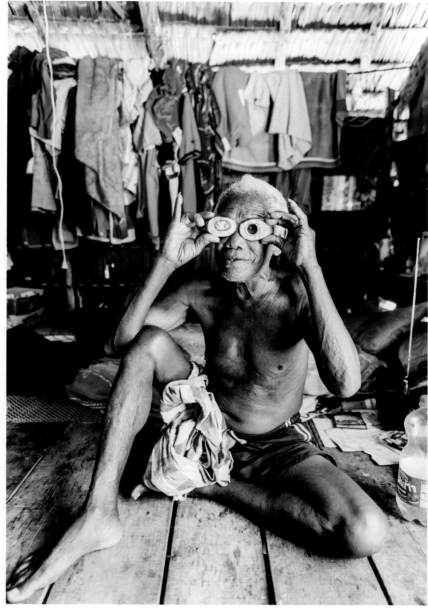

entirely unscathed, rescued by knowledge, passed down through generations, that taught them to seek high ground to avoid the deadly wave. But the Thai government ordered them to relocate to solid land, a makeshift village within Ko Surin National Park, an island-based protected area in Phang-Nga Province. Currently 315 Moken inhabit a crowded strip of wood and bamboo structures at the edge of a bay, an entirely new existence for many of them.

Feeling the pull of the old Moken ways, a few years back, Hook sought to build a houseboat, a quest documented in the 2015 documentary *No Word for Worry*. In the past, Moken boats were hollowed out of massive logs, but national park rules now prevent the Moken from cutting down trees. So, with financial assistance from the filmmakers, he designed and built a boat that blends Thai and Moken elements: made with planks and an outboard motor but equipped with a Moken-style

roof and a mast on which to raise the traditional pandan-leaf sail. For the last two years, Hook, his wife, and child have lived nearly full time on the boat, by his reckoning the only Moken in Thailand who continue to do this.

Spend some time with Hook on his boat and it doesn't take long to see that everything revolves around the hunt. As we talk, he's mending a net and lowering baited hooks into the water. One morning, I see him wading through shallow water with his son and a three-pronged spear, scanning for fish. Another evening, in mid-conversation, he leaps to the bow of his boat and casts a net into the water. Hunting is prohibited in Thailand's national parks, but officials allow the Moken to fish, hunt, and gather if they follow traditional methods, and only for their own consumption.

"As long as we have some rice, we can find the rest of what we need to live in the ocean," says Hook, who estimates that he catches the majority of the food that he and his family eat himself.

I meet with Ngoey, Hook's older brother, who has agreed to take me on a gathering trip. Although bold, impressive feats such as spearfishing, exceptional underwater vision, and the ability to hold one's breath have come to dominate popular perceptions of the Moken, the bulk of the traditional Moken diet comes from the comparatively mundane gathering of items such as shellfish and tubers.

"We live day to day," Ngoey tells me. "If we run out of food, we have to find more the next day; we don't have refrigerators!"

We jump in a tiny boat and buzz over almost impossibly clear turquoise water to a tiny, rocky island. There a handful of Moken are chipping fingernail-sized oysters off the rocks. They'll be eaten with rice—now a staple food among the Moken—for that evening's dinner.

On another day, I accompany Ngoey and his wife to a wooded island where we dig in the sandy soil for edible tubers. In the days before rice was commonplace, taro and yams were the main source of carbs for the Moken. We come across a type of large yam that requires labor-intensive soaking and rinsing to remove its toxic juices. But the real find is a type of tuber that the Moken call *marung*. Boiled and peeled, it has a texture and flavor that reminds me of water chestnuts.

"I haven't eaten marung in ten or more years!" Ngoey tells me as he bites into a tuber, clearly feeling a sense of nostalgia that seems to be as much about food as it is about a way of life.

OPPOSITE, TOP LEFT: Women collect oysters on an island in Ko Surin National Park, Phang-Nga Province.
OPPOSITE, TOP RIGHT: A Moken man returns with the day's catch, Ko Surin National Park, Phang-Nga Province.
OPPOSITE, BOTTOM: Moken childen swim in front of a Moken-style boat, Ko Surin National Park, Phang-Nga Province.
RIGHT: Hook Klathalay on his boat, Ko Surin National Park.

The Countryside

Think of Thailand, and it's likely you'll conjure a mental image of a beach. But ask a Thai person, and his mind is more likely to flit to waterlogged rice fields, sleepy villages, dense jungle, or sharp mountains. These are the rural landscapes that many Thais consider the soul of their country.

Likewise, soul food for many Thais means the type of rustic, unrefined, full-flavored dishes that also have their roots in the countryside. In the south, this could mean a salad made from ferns gathered at the edge of a rice field; a free-range chicken seasoned with a curry marinade and slowly grilled over coals; or perhaps noodles fried with local chiles, coconut milk from the tree in the yard, and a couple of duck eggs.

Even more than the dishes, it could be argued that in the south it's the ingredients from the countryside that define the cuisine. Thais from outside the region may not be able to name many southern Thai dishes, but they're inevitably familiar with at least a few southern ingredients: Cashews that are harvested from decades-old trees. Sago extracted from palms that thrive in almost impossibly thick jungle. Bitter beans plucked from massive trees at the edges of rugged mountains. Sugar tapped from palms that jut from otherwise flat landscapes. And one-of-a-kind varieties of rice—arguably the region's most important food—grown in narrow valleys or along the shore of a massive lake.

The flavors, textures, and aromas of these ingredients form the building blocks of the region's cuisine. And the stories that go into producing, harvesting, and gathering them offer us a chance to go beyond the finished dishes, as well as a glimpse of an oft-overlooked part of Thailand.

PREVIOUS SPREAD: A rural scene outside of Phatthalung.

Rare Grains

GROWING RICE the traditional way requires flat land and lots of water. Mountainous Southern Thailand lacks much of the former.

"In the south, there's very little flat land for planting rice," Patcharaporn Rakchum, an agricultural officer at Phatthalung's branch of Thailand's Rice Research Center, tells me. "Most of the rice grown in southern Thailand is consumed in the region. This isn't like central Thailand, where rice agriculture is done on a large scale and most of the rice is exported."

As a result of this challenging geography, Patcharaporn says, the residents of the country's south have been forced to develop clever methods of cultivating rice.

I was able to witness this firsthand in Phatthalung Province one late September. This is the time for the harvest, when locals cut the stalks that are top-heavy and sagging with mature grains of rice. The particular crop I've come to see is located at the edge of Songkhla Lake, a massive semi-brackish body of water. When I arrive, a group of locals are up to their shins in mud, using machetes and scythes to cut the stalks, shifting the unwieldy bundles to dry ground. Although it's hard work, the occasion is also something of a party. School kids and police are pitching in. There is an emcee, loud music, snacks, drinks, and a drone buzzing overhead. Even the provincial governor came out, donned a pair of rubber boots, and got muddy with the rest of us, all part of an effort to promote this province's unique grains.

I had been to this rice field before—ninety days previously, to be exact—when the just-sprouted seedlings had been transplanted to the muddy margins of the lake. The opposite side of the lake—more than twelve miles away—wasn't visible, and that day waves were lapping at the shore, giving the impression that people were planting rice at the edge of the ocean. And now, exactly three months later, the duration of the rainy season, after the lake level had risen, providing water and nutrients for the grains, it is harvesttime. The folks harvesting the rice are participating in a method of rice cultivation seen nowhere else in Thailand, one that doesn't require irrigation—or pesticides or fertilizer, for that matter.

Southerners have also come to rely on grains not seen elsewhere in the country. Patcharaporn tells me that researchers have identified more than 400 varieties of rice grown in southern Thailand, some with evocative names like Bird's Claw, which are kept in a seed vault at Phatthalung's Rice Research Center.

Phatthalung is the origin of what is arguably the most hyped varietal of rice in all of Thailand. Known officially as Sangyod Muang Phatthalung Rice, the heirloom grain is short and slender, with a rusty, almost purple hue if left unpolished, and it is particularly high in nutrients and antioxidants. Couple this with clever marketing and the endorsement of Thailand's royal family, and Sangyod rice has been a hit among Thailand's increasingly health-conscious middle and upper classes, selling for more than twice as much as other types of long-grain rice. Finally, after centuries, people outside of the region are recognizing southern Thailand's unique rice culture.

OPPOSITE: A waterlogged rice field in rural Phatthalung Province.
ABOVE: Sangyod Muang Phatthalung Rice, one of southern Thailand's most prized rice varieties.

SOUTHERN THAILAND'S RICE CYCLE

In Thailand, traditional rice agriculture revolves around the water-providing monsoon season, although technologies such as irrigation and genetic engineering have changed this immensely in recent years. Upcountry Thailand is largely subject to the same weather pattern, which means that rice agriculture there generally takes place between May and December. In the south, depending on what side of the Malay Peninsula the rice is being planted, it is ready to harvest between September and July.

1   When the monsoon rains begin, the fields are flooded and plowed, and a small, protected section of each plot is set aside for sowing the rice seeds.
2   After about a month, the seedlings are uprooted and transplanted into rows.
3   The seedlings are left to grow for at least 4 months.
4   At the end of the monsoon rains, the rice is harvested: the stalks of rice are cut off at the base, dried in the sun, and threshed to separate the grains from the stalks.
5   The grains of rice, with their husks still intact, are bundled into bags and left to dry in granaries for a month.
6   The rice is then milled, the process that removes the husks and the exterior layer of bran, and is ready for consumption. Rice from the most recent harvest is known as *khaao mai,* "new rice," and has a relatively high moisture content, while rice from the previous year's harvest is known as *khaao kao,* "old rice," and has less moisture, thus requiring more water to cook it.

Locals participating in the rice harvest at the edge of Songkhla Lake, Phatthalung Province.

A woman removes debris
from dried Sangyod
Muang Phatthalung Rice,
Phatthalung Province.

How to Cook Thai Long-Grain Rice

Rice and water. That's all that goes into this recipe, but it's one of the most contested, disputed, and difficult ones I've attempted as a cookbook author. Previous efforts to put in writing how to cook rice have resulted in endless back-and-forth emails with editors, lengthy phone calls with chefs, and pots of alternatingly soggy and bone-dry rice. I can't yet claim that I've cracked the code, but I have come to understand a lot more about the elements that contribute to a properly cooked pot of rice.

A significant part of the headache and ambiguity in cooking rice can be alleviated by making one rela-tively inexpensive investment: an electric rice cooker. Nearly every family in Thailand uses one, and justifi-ably: they work really, really well pretty much every single time. No waiting for that initial boil, no setting a timer for 20 minutes. Simply push a button and let the machine do all the work while you worry about other things.

Another factor is being aware of the age of your rice. Living and cooking in Thailand, I was lucky enough to have access to what is called in Thai "new rice," that is, rice from the most recent harvest that still contains a significant amount of moisture. This rice requires relatively little water for cooking, and I prefer my grains slightly dry, so I could get away with as little as a 2:1 by volume ratio of rice to water. Outside Thailand, you're most likely dealing with

214

"old rice," that is, rice that may have been harvested as many as a few years previously and has spent significant time in transit or in a warehouse. These rice grains contain less moisture, which means you have to compensate by adding more water. For "old rice" (again, most exported rice), you're going to want to start with a 1:1 ratio of rice to water, perhaps boosting it to as much as 1:1.5 as necessary. Experiment, keeping track of the particular brand of rice you have, and tweak your ratio from there, also taking into consideration, of course, how you prefer your rice. Thais are adamant about gently washing the uncooked grains of rice in several changes of water until the water runs clear, an effort to clean them of dust and other debris. This also has the effect of removing some of the rice's exterior starch, resulting in cooked grains that are more separate. You can skip this step if you like, but your rice won't have the same consistency as that served in Thailand.

If you're cooking the rice on the stove, a crucial factor is kick-starting the cooking process by bringing the water and grains to a full, rolling boil for a few seconds before reducing the heat (electric rice cookers are programmed to include this step).

I find that ½ cup (approximately 100 g, depending on how much moisture your rice contains) uncooked Thai long-grain rice makes a generous serving for one person; you can boost this to ¾ cup (approximately 150 g) if want leftover rice or simply have a big appetite.

And, finally, patience also plays an important role in cooking rice. Although many of us are aware that rice should be cooked for 20 minutes, to obtain properly cooked rice, excess heat and steam need to be relased at the end of the cooking process, after which the grains need 15 minutes of resting time. If you don't follow these steps, your rice will emerge from the pot soggy, with some of the grains stuck to the pot. These steps mean that, from beginning to end, making a pot of rice takes at least 40 minutes, not 20—so don't forget to plan ahead accordingly.

Kaan Hung Khaao Suay
การหุงข้าวสวย

Serves 4

2 cups (approximately 400 g) long-grain Thai rice

Using an Electric Rice Cooker

Gently rinse the rice in two or three changes of water in a bowl until the water remains clear. Drain the rice and add 2 cups (500 ml) water, or more as described previously, depending on the age of your rice, to the bowl. Put the rice and water in an electric rice cooker and press Start. When the rice is done, open the lid for a few seconds to release excess heat and steam. Then close the lid and allow the rice to rest, undisturbed, for 10 minutes. Gently stir the rice, replace the lid, and allow the rice to rest for a final 5 minutes before serving.

Using the Stovetop

Gently rinse the rice in two or three changes of water in a bowl until the water remains clear. Drain the rice and add 2 cups (500 ml) water, or more as described previously, depending on the age of your rice, to the bowl. Put the rice and water in a saucepan that's large enough to accommodate the bubbling and swelling grains of rice, bring the water to a rolling boil over high heat, and boil the rice for 3 seconds. Put a lid on the saucepan, reduce the heat to as low as possible, and simmer, undisturbed, for 20 minutes. After 20 minutes, turn off the heat and open the lid for a few seconds to release excess heat and steam. Then replace the lid and allow the rice to rest, undisturbed, for 10 minutes. Gently stir the rice, replace the lid, and allow the rice to rest for a final 5 minutes before serving.

BITTER BEANS

Stink beans. Or petai. Or sator. Or, least efficiently of all, "twisted cluster beans." English translations aside, bitter beans are one of southern Thailand's most emblematic foods, referred to by southerners as one of the "Three Friends," a trio of pungent but beloved pale green, bean-like ingredients that also includes djenkol beans and nitta sprouts. Technically seeds, bitter beans originate in arm's-length pods that grow on evergreen trees native to Southeast Asia. They're around the size of a chubby almond, with a pleasantly rubbery texture, a neon-green hue, and an intensely sulfurous, almost garlic-like flavor and odor (which produces the same reaction that genetically disadvantaged asparagus consumers must contend with).

I'm in the village of Lam Khanun, located at the edge of a protected zone of steep, wooded hills in the far east of Trang Province. Here bitter bean trees grow in the rugged jungle, which means that obtaining them is more an act of gathering than of harvesting—a challenge when one considers that the trees can grow to more than 100 feet tall. Bee, a twenty-one-year-old farmhand with bitter-bean-gathering experience, has agreed to show me how the pods are collected. He kicks off his sandals, squints up at the forty-foot-tall tree, and declares, "This is a short one," then effort-

lessly ascends it via a bamboo ladder. When he reaches a crook in the tree, he grabs a long bamboo pole that ends in a thin wire hook and gets to work. Wrapping his legs around the trunk of the tree and reaching for clusters of pods that are as far as twenty feet away, he plucks them, draws them back to himself, and neatly hangs them on a nearby branch. After he has accumulated perhaps six clusters, he throws a rope down to his companion and delivers the bitter beans to the ground zipline-style so the clusters don't break and the beans don't get bruised.

That evening, naturally, we eat bitter beans for dinner. My host's wife removes the stringy edges from a couple of the pods, scrapes off the astringent exterior, and cuts the pods—skin and all—into rectangular sections, adding them to a coconut milk curry as she goes.

"You can eat bitter beans raw or you can grill the entire pod. You can add them to stir-fries and curries," she explains while she preps. "We also pickle them, the beans or the whole pods. The pickled pods last longer."

From the remaining pods, she extracts the fava-like beans and peels off their thin membranes, then stir-fries them with shrimp, shrimp paste, and chile—one of southern Thailand's most famous dishes, one that fights pungency with funk and spice.

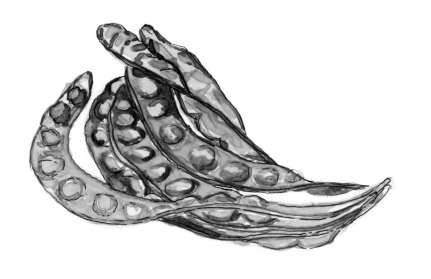

OPPOSITE: Bee, a farmhand in rural Trang Province, displays bitter beans that he has gathered.

Bitter Beans Stir-Fried with Shrimp and Shrimp Paste as prepared in Lam Khanun, Trang Province.

Bitter Beans Stir-Fried with Shrimp and Shrimp Paste

Kung Phat Luuk Taw

กุ้งผัดลูกตอ

Serves 4

2 tablespoons shrimp paste

1 tablespoon vegetable oil

2 cloves garlic (10 g total), peeled and coarsely chopped

8 medium shrimp (150 g total)

100 g bitter beans, thin membranes peeled off

1 tablespoon oyster sauce

½ teaspoon white sugar

4 medium fresh red chiles (20 g total), sliced lengthwise on a bias

---

If you're cooking anywhere outside southern Thailand, you probably won't have access to fresh bitter beans, but you can sometimes find them frozen at Asian supermarkets. Frozen bitter beans can be tossed directly into the wok from the freezer.

Peeling bitter beans at at homestay in Lam Khanun, Trang Province.

PREPARE THE SHRIMP PASTE: Combine the shrimp paste and 2 tablespoons water in a small bowl and mix until you have a watery paste. Set aside.

MAKE THE STIR-FRY: Heat the vegetable oil in a wok over high heat. Add the garlic and fry, stirring frequently, until golden and fragrant, around 10 seconds. Add the shrimp, stirring to coat with the oil. Add the bitter beans, stirring to combine, and fry until the beans are just cooked through, around 1 minute. Add the shrimp paste mixture, oyster sauce, and sugar, stirring to combine. If the mixture is too dry and risks burning, add water a tablespoon at a time to loosen it up. Add the chiles, stirring to combine.

TASTE, ADJUSTING THE SEASONING IF NECESSARY: the dish should taste equal parts savory and pungent (from the shrimp paste and bitter beans), salty, and slightly sweet and spicy. It should have a pleasantly oily, sauce-like consistency.

Remove to a serving plate and serve hot, warm, or at room temperature with long-grain rice.

In Search of Real Palm Sugar

IN THE NORTHERN PART of Songkhla Province, an almost medieval scene unfolds on a daily basis. In a smoke-filled, chaotic factory, workers stir a murky brown liquid that's bubbling away in woks the size of satellite dishes. They are making the region's famous product: tiny pucks of palm sugar. Songkhla's sugar palms can be seen just outside, their shaggy trunks and pointy leaves disrupting the otherwise flat landscape. Yet despite their proximity, the sap from these trees will not be making the short journey to the inside of this factory. The syrup produced here is a fake: a cocktail of bleached cane sugar and molasses along with food coloring and other commercial ingredients meant to emulate the dark hue of true palm sugar. When reduced sufficiently, the mixture is whipped and poured into tiny rings made from sugar palm leaves—the only part of the tree that actually figures in this particular process—and sold for a quarter of the price of the real stuff.

To understand why it's cheaper and easier to import processed ingredients and make a fake rather than use natural resources that are located literally steps away, I spend a day with Suthon Inthasara.

At the age of sixty-two, Suthon has been gather-ing palm sap in rural Songkhla Province for most of his life. His day begins in the cool morning hours, when he grabs his machete and a bundle of plastic and bamboo tubes and heads out into the fields. Slipping off his rubber sandals at the base of a sugar palm, he ascends nearly fifty feet via a bamboo ladder, the tubes dangling and knocking below him like wind chimes on a breezy day. Upon reaching the top, his first task is to remove the tubes that were hung there the previous afternoon, now loaded with fresh sap. Working in a virtual cloud of bees and wasps, he hangs these tubes on one side. He then pulls out his machete and makes a fresh cut on each budding fruit, hanging a tube that includes a few chips of wood that serve to hasten fermentation directly below it. Occasionally Suthon works a walnut cracker–like tool of two bamboo poles, "massaging" a yet-untapped bud so that it will produce sap in a few days' time.

His work on this tree done, Suthon descends, the now-heavy tubes swinging less freely. Upon reaching the ground, he offers me a taste of sugar palm sap from one of them. The liquid is fragrant and refreshing, and much less sweet than I would have expected.

OPPOSITE: Suthon Inthasara gathering palm sugar in rural Songkhla Province.
ABOVE: Suthon Inthasara taps a sugar palm tree, Songkhla Province.

The tubes are hung from a wooden pole he carries on his shoulder, and he proceeds to the next tree.

After a few more trees, when his pole is straining under the weight of so much palm sap, Suthon heads back home. There his wife has already started a fire in a large earthen stove below a giant wok, and she pours the contents of the tubes into the wok. After a couple hours of boiling, rendering the air of the outdoor kitchen humid, sweet, and yeasty, the sap has reduced to a light syrup the consistency of a slightly watery honey.

During peak season, from February to April, Suthon will climb as many as twenty trees at a time, repeating this entire process twice a day. The syrup that he and his wife make is poured into large tins and sold to sweet makers, booze distillers, or sugar producers. Yet because it's so labor-intensive to gather sugar palm sap, and because Thais have now come to prefer the lighter color of sugar made from the sap of coconut palms, today palm sugar is almost always bulked out with cane sugar or other sweeteners, and its color sometimes tweaked with food coloring. Once the standard, even in the heart of the region where it's produced, pure, unadulterated palm sugar has become an expensive rarity these days.

"I'm afraid it might disappear in the future," says Supada Tongtammachat, the head of a network of farmers and agriculturalists in this corner of Songkhla Province. "Nowadays, cane sugar is much cheaper."

Supada and a colleague offer to set up a wok and demonstrate how pure palm sugar is made. After a half hour or so of rapid simmering, the tin of sap that Suthon had gathered that very morning is reduced to a dark, fragrant puddle of syrup. She turns off the heat and, using a whisk-like tool the size of a small rake, Supada whips the syrup, coaxing the sugar to cool into a soft paste rather than hard crystals. She turns the heat back on low and scoops the sugar into small ceramic cups to cool and firm up. Supada hands me one of the tiny pucks, which has the hue of a medium roux, to taste, and it has a subtle, earthy sweetness, with a hint of a molasses-like bitterness and an immensely satisfying crunch: a unique, delicious, and beautifully inefficient product.

RIGHT: Pouring palm sugar syrup into sugar palm rings, Songkhla Province.
OPPOSITE: Suthon Inthasara returns home with tubes filled with palm sap, Songkhla Province.

MAKING PALM SUGAR

Sathing Phra and Singhanakhorn, two districts in the northern part of Songkhla Province, are known colloquially as "The Land of Sugar." Here pure palm sugar is made via the following steps:

1 Between February and April, gatherers tap and collect the sap from sugar palm trees.

2 The sap is boiled for several hours, traditionally over fires fueled by sugar palm leaves, until it has has the consistency of a syrup.

3 The syrup is reduced even further, then is whipped, via hand or machine, until it has the texture of a soft paste.

4 The warm paste is poured into rings made from dried sugar palm leaves, where it's allowed to cool and firm up.

Palm Sugar–Filled Dumplings
Khanom Khoh
ขนมโค

As a sweet, khanom khoh have a lot going for them. They look drop-dead gorgeous—the marble-sized dumplings boasting a shaggy exterior from grated coconut and a subtle green hue from the addition of pandan leaf. They run the gamut of textures—the crunchy grated coconut and toasted mung beans concealing a pillow-soft wrapper and a crunchy sugar core—and offer myriad flavors—a just-salty, rich exterior and an earthy, sweet center. Given all they offer, it's hardly surprising that khanom khoh have emerged as the flagship sweet of southern Thailand. And Phornnit Dechaphiban, a vendor in Songkhla, makes one of the most delicious versions in the south.

For more than forty years, she's sold khanom khoh from a cart in Songkhla, deftly filling and shaping the dumplings with her right hand ("My mother taught me how to make it!" She tells me, 'If you want to make this, you need to do it with one hand! If you use two, it looks dirty.'") before flinging them into a wok of simmering water. When they float to the surface, Phornnit removes and drains them, then tosses the still-warm dumplings in grated coconut and toasted mung beans. The result is warm, soft, crunchy, salty, sweet, and fragrant, green and white, all at the same time—more tastes, textures, and colors than I thought were possible in a single sweet.

Serves 6

2 tablespoons dried mung beans
1 small mature coconut (around 750 g)
1 heaping teaspoon table salt
2 large pandan leaves (20 g total), chopped
250 g sticky rice flour
½ cup (90 g) firm palm sugar chopped into scant
 ½-inch cubes

Traditionally in southern Thailand, these dumplings were made with naam phueng waen, small disks of pure palm sugar. But this is increasingly rare and expensive nowadays, so most vendors use naam taan puek, small mounds of firm coconut sugar (or a mix of sugars)—which is most likely also what anyone cooking outside of Thailand will have access to. Ideally, though, avoid naam taan piip, whipped coconut sugar, often sold in bags, which is soft and lacks the crunch associated with this dish.

Pandan leaves give the dumplings a unique hue and a subtle aroma. If you can't get the fresh leaves but still want the green color, a few drops of green food coloring will suffice.

If you have leftovers, the refrigerated dumplings reheat well in a few seconds in the microwave.

UP TO 5 DAYS IN ADVANCE, PREPARE THE TOASTED MUNG BEAN TOPPING: Dry-roast the mung beans in a wok or frying pan over medium heat until fragrant and the color of lightly roasted coffee beans, around 5 minutes. Remove from the heat.

Grind the mung beans to a very coarse texture with a mortar and pestle, coffee grinder, or food processor. Remove to an airtight container.

ON THE DAY OF SERVING, PREPARE THE COCONUT: Split the coconut in half by whacking it with the back of a heavy cleaver along its widest circumference (the chubby part of the coconut, not the end with the three holes) three or four times while turning the coconut on this axis. Discard the liquid. Using a Thai coconut grater, scrape the white flesh from the inside of the coconut into short, fine threads (see page 24 for tips on grating coconut). Reserve 2 heaping cups (200 g) of the grated meat for this dish and save the remainder, ideally in the freezer, for another use.

Combine the salt and grated coconut and transfer to a sieve set over a saucepan of boiling water, or a Chinese-style steamer lined with cheesecloth. Steam the coconut for 15 minutes, or until it is tender but still retains some crunch. Allow to cool to room temperature.

recipe continues →

PREPARE THE DUMPLING DOUGH: Combine the pandan leaves and 1 cup (250 ml) water in a blender or food processor. Process to a pulp and then strain the liquid though a sieve set over a bowl; discard the solids.

Transfer the pandan water to a bowl and add the sticky rice flour. Mix by hand until you have a light, smooth, soft dough that doesn't stick to your fingers. Add a bit more water or rice flour if necessary, to obtain this consistency. Allow the dough to rest for 30 minutes.

MAKE THE DUMPLINGS: Spread the grated coconut and ground mung beans on a round tray (a Thai-style woven bamboo tray is ideal for this) or platter.

Bring several quarts of water to a boil in a large saucepan, then reduce the heat and maintain at a simmer. Take a heaping ½ teaspoon of the dough (5 to 7 g) and roll it into a ball, flatten the ball, and top with a single cube of palm sugar, wrapping the dough around the sugar to fully encase it. Toss into the simmering water and repeat to make more dumplings, tossing them into the water as you go, without crowding the pan. Simmer until the dumplings rise to the surface of the water, around 2 minutes, removing with a sieve or slotted spoon as they are done, shaking off excess moisture, and transferring them to the tray. You should have a total of around 50 dumplings. Toss the still-warm dumplings in the coconut–mung bean mixture to coat them, then transfer them to a serving plate.

Eat warm or at room temperature; refrigerate any remaining dumplings.

Phornnit Dechaphiban selling Palm Sugar–Filled Dumplings from her stall in Songkhla.

Thin Palm Sugar Pancakes
Khanom Pam Jii
ขนมป๋าจี

Every morning on a street corner in Songkhla, Sujit Namasi makes khanom pam jii, thin, golden, crispy grated coconut–filled pancakes. The batter he uses, a mix of rice flour, tapioca starch, and palm sugar, has rested overnight, and when it hits the hot wok, it fills the air with a sweet, almost yeasty, faintly sourdough-like aroma. After about two minutes, when a palm-sized, lacy pancake has formed, he uses a fork to pry it loose and flings the limp disk across to his wife, who rolls it up around a generous pinch of grated coconut tossed with salt. As it cools, the pancake firms up, resulting in a thin, crispy, slightly sweet, barely tart tube encasing the slightly salty, crunchy, rich filling. Every step of the process—from the resting of the batter overnight to the slow cooking over coals to that final transformation—is something that can't be rushed, and the other noteworthy element of Sujit's stall is a line of customers, all wishing the process took just a little bit less time.

Serves 6

100 g rice flour
100 g tapioca starch (aka tapioca flour)
2 tablespoons white sugar
30 g palm sugar
1 small mature coconut (around 750 g)
1 scant teaspoon table salt
3 eggs
1 tablespoon vegetable oil

As the batter for this sweet must undergo a light fermentation for at least 12 hours, the recipe requires some advance planning.

Sujit Namasi making Thin Palm Sugar Pancakes at his stall in Songkhla.

TWELVE HOURS IN ADVANCE, PREPARE THE BATTER:- Combine the rice flour, tapioca starch, white sugar, palm sugar, and 1 cup (250 ml) water in a bowl. Allow to rest in a warm environment (around 75°F; if you live in a cold place, the inside of an oven with the pilot light on or a place near a radiator should suffice) for up to 12 hours.

ON THE DAY OF SERVING, PREPARE THE COCONUT: Split the coconut in half by whacking it with the back of a heavy cleaver along its widest circumference (the chubby part of the coconut, not the end with the three holes) three or four times while turning the coconut on this axis. Discard the liquid. Using a Thai coconut grater, scrape the white flesh from the inside of the coconut into short, fine threads (see page 24 for tips on grating coconut). Reserve 2 cups (150 g) of the grated meat for this recipe and save the remainder, ideally in the freezer, for another use.

Combine the salt and grated coconut. Set aside.

PREPARE THE PANCAKES: Set a wire rack over a baking sheet or line a baking sheet with paper towels.

Whisk the eggs in a small bowl. Pour approximately 1 tablespoon of the beaten eggs into another small bowl, add the vegetable oil, and stir with a fork or whisk to combine. Set aside.

Pour the remaining egg mixture into the rested batter and beat with a fork or whisk to combine. Heat a wok over medium-low heat. Dip a paper towel into the egg and oil mixture and smear over the bottom of the wok to lubricate it. Add approximately 1½ tablespoons of batter to the hot pan, lifting and quickly swirling the wok to spread the batter as evenly as possible to create a very, very thin pancake 6 or 7 inches in diameter. Return the wok to the heat and shift it occasionally to ensure that the pancake cooks evenly. After 1 minute, the edges of the pancake should start to lift from the wok and tiny holes should appear in the surface. After around 2½ minutes, the bottom of the pancake should be crispy, golden, and fragrant. Use a fork to remove the pancake to a clean counter or large plate. While it is still warm, sprinkle 1 scant tablespoon of the grated coconut across the center of the pancake, roll it up into a tube, and set it on the wire rack or baking sheet. Repeat this process with the remaining ingredients; this should yield approximately 24 pancakes.

Serve warm or at room temperature.

OPPOSITE: Thin Palm Sugar Pancakes as prepared by Sujit Namasi, Songkhla.

Southern Thai Palm Sugar Fritters

Khanom Juu Jun

ขนมจู้จุน

There's no definitive recipe for these fritters, known in southern Thailand as *khanom juu jun*. Some versions use only rice flour, while others mix rice, sticky rice, and wheat flours. Some fritters are green from the addition of pandan leaf extract, while in Muslim communities in Thailand's deep south, coffee or tea may be added to the batter, lending the fritters a subtle hue, color, and fragrance. The one constant is khanom juu jun's shape: it should look like a particularly hearty Thai-style fried egg, complete with crispy, glassy edges and a yolk-like mound in the middle.

I experimented with several different recipes, and to arrive at that ideal intersection of a crispy exterior and a chewy, lacy, crumpet-like crumb, I've gone with a combination of rice and wheat flours. As taught by Pa Lamyai, a vendor who sells the sweet in Phatthalung Province, I used real palm sugar from southern Thailand, and I allowed the batter to rest in Thailand's warm temperature for nearly 24 hours, which is not essential but had a subtle leavening effect, giving the fritters an even more complex crumb.

Serve as a southern Thai–style breakfast or snack.

Serves 6

100 g palm sugar
¼ cup (50 g) white sugar
Heaping ½ teaspoon table salt
1 cup (100 g) rice flour
1 cup (120 g) wheat flour
Vegetable oil for deep-frying

To achieve the requisite shape of this sweet, it's necessary to deep-fry the fritters in a small (less than 6 inches in diameter) wok or other cooking vessel with steep sides and a concave bottom.

UP TO 24 HOURS IN ADVANCE, PREPARE THE BATTER: Combine the palm sugar, white sugar, salt, and 1¼ cups (300 ml) water in a small saucepan and bring to just short of a simmer, stirring to ensure that the sugar has completely dissolved. Remove from the heat and let cool slightly.

Sift the flours together into a bowl. When the sugar mixture is cool enough to handle, slowly add it, stirring constantly to avoid clumps, then knead the mixture by hand to ensure it is fully blended. Cover the batter with plastic wrap and leave in a warm environment (around 75°F; if you live in a cold place, inside an oven with the pilot light on or in a place near a radiator overnight should suffice) for at least 1 hour, or up to 24 hours.

ON THE DAY OF SERVING, MAKE THE FRITTERS: Set a wire rack over a baking sheet.

Add oil to a depth of at least 2 inches to a small wok set over low heat and heat to 340°F to 350°F. Add a scant ¼ cup (60 ml) of the batter in one go (not in a slow drizzle). After a few seconds, the fritter will rise to the surface of the oil, and at about 15 seconds, you should see distinct streaks and bubbles forming in the batter. Allow the fritter to fry until golden and crispy on the bottom, 1½ to 2 minutes. Flip and fry until the bottom is golden and crispy, another 1 to 1½ minutes. Remove and drain on the wire rack. Repeat with the remaining batter, working to maintain the oil at between 340°F and 350°F the entire time. This should yield 6 or 7 fritters.

Serve warm or at room temperature.

OPPOSITE: Southern Thai Palm Sugar Fritters as made by Pa Lamyai, a vendor in Phatthalung Province.

Southern Thai Cashew and Palm Sugar "Brittle"

Hua Khrok Raa Naam Phueng

หัวครกหราน้ำผึ้ง

Every morning, starting at 4 a.m., Prasit Khabuanphon and his wife combine some of southern Thailand's most emblematic ingredients to make a sweet that, oddly enough, would be familiar to most Americans.

Working at a Thai-style charcoal stove positioned in front of their home in Songkhla, the couple simmer cashews and syrup in a large wok, filling the air with a rich, almost butter-like aroma. When the mixture is sufficiently reduced, they remove it from the heat and scoop portions of it onto leaves cut into rounds, then flatten the sticky mass and allow the disk-like sweets to cool.

The result is the most exotic nut brittle you've ever seen.

"I make them early in the morning and sell them the same day," Prasit tells me when I inquire about his particularly early work hours, explaining that the sun and southern Thailand's humid climate can alter the texture of the sweet. "You don't want these to sit overnight."

And although they may very well look like grandma's peanut brittle, the English-language name of this recipe is a relative term. Whereas peanut brittle is crispy and sweet, the goal here is something firm yet pliable, rich, and fragrant.

Serves 6

200 g palm sugar
½ cup (100 g) white sugar
½ teaspoon table salt
400 g roasted or deep-fried unsalted cashews, split lengthwise
12 cashew leaves, cut into 4-inch-diameter circles (or use a large sheet of waxed paper)

The best way to ensure that you get the correct consistency is by using a candy thermometer. In my tests, I took the sugar to the hard ball stage, just short of 250°F.

Combine the palm sugar, white sugar, salt, and 1 cup (250 ml) water in a wok and bring to a boil over high heat. Reduce the heat to a rapid simmer and cook, stirring frequently, until the sugar is dissolved and blended and the mixture is reduced by around one-third and just starting to become syrupy, around 5 minutes.

Add the cashews and bring to a rapid simmer. Reduce the heat to a simmer and cook, stirring occasionally, until the syrup is thick and the mixture smells rich and buttery (if using a candy thermometer, bring to just under 250°F, the hard ball stage), around 20 minutes. Reduce the heat to as low as possible to keep the mixture pliable while you work.

Lay the cashew leaves (or a sheet of waxed paper) out on a work surface. Transfer a scant ¼ cup (60 ml) of the cashew mixture to a leaf (or the waxed paper). If the mixture is too thin, with the syrup running far beyond the mass of cashews, reduce it for another minute or two; if the mixture is too thick to scoop easily, stir in a tablespoon of water and reduce just until it's liquid enough to work with. Dip a heatproof spatula in water and use it to press and shape the cashew mixture into a mass that sticks to the surface of the leaf (or waxed paper). Repeat with the remaining ingredients; this should yield 12 portions. Allow to cool until firm.

Remove to a serving plate or platter and serve warm or at room temperature.

OPPOSITE: Southern Thai Cashew and Palm Sugar "Brittle" as made by Prasit Khabuanphon, Songkhla.

ONE FOR THE ROAD

Located smack-dab between two provincial capitals, the town of Puyut has emerged as a de facto truck stop. But this is the overwhelmingly Muslim deep south, so rather than twenty-four-hour diners or chain burger restaurants, the people of Puyut offer murtabak.

A dish with origins in the Muslim world, *mataba*, as it's known in Thailand, takes the form of a knot of dough that is stretched thin, filled with stuff savory or sweet, and fried on a griddle until crispy. It's sometimes described in English as a stuffed pancake, but this terminology does little to convey the almost pastry-like folds that conceal a filling of minced beef seasoned with spices or a sweet filling that brings together slices of banana, sugar, and egg.

In tiny Puyut, there are at least twenty vendors serving the snack. And because of the transient nature of the consumers, Puyut's murtabak are almost exclusively sold to-go, wrapped up in sheets of waxed paper. Given that they're likely to be eaten with one hand, the other clutching the steering wheel, they're slimmed down, served with a scant amount of filling. It's a dish that was seemingly designed for a commute.

Serve these as a snack or light meal.

Making murtabak at a roadside stall in Puyut, Pattani Province.

Puyut-Style Murtabak

Mataba Baep Puyut

มะตะบะแบบปูยุด

Serves 6

FOR THE MURTABAK DOUGH

4 tablespoons butter or margarine, melted, plus melted butter or margarine for handling
1 egg
2 tablespoons sweetened condensed milk
½ teaspoon table salt
300 g all-purpose flour, plus more if needed

FOR THE SAVORY BEEF FILLING
(MAKES ENOUGH FOR 6 MURTABAK)

1 teaspoon coriander seeds
1½ tablespoons vegetable oil, plus more for handling
5 shallots (50 g total), peeled and minced
2 teaspoons mild chile powder
150 g ground beef
1 teaspoon table salt
2 teaspoons white sugar

FOR THE SWEET BANANA FILLING
(MAKES ENOUGH FOR 6 MURTABAK)

2 bananas (around 300 g total), peeled and sliced
¼ cup (50 g) white sugar
3 eggs
1 to 2 drops yellow food coloring (optional)

FOR THE MURTABAK

Butter or margarine for frying
4 eggs, beaten, if using the beef filling
1 onion (150 g), peeled, halved lengthwise, and sliced thin, if using the beef filling

---

Although shaping murtabak can be challenging, it's important to get the dough as thin as possible, or the final product can be unpleasantly doughy and undercooked.

I have provided two fillings here, one savory and one sweet; choose one, or double the amount of dough if you'd like to use both versions.

THE DAY BEFORE SERVING, PREPARE THE MURTABAK DOUGH: Combine 2 teaspoons of the melted butter, the egg, sweetened condensed milk, salt, and ½ cup (125 ml) water in a small bowl. Beat with a fork or whisk to blend.

Pour the flour into a large bowl. Slowly add the liquid mixture, using your hands to combine. The dough will be wet and sticky; if it's too sticky to handle, add another 25 to 50 g flour. Turn the dough out onto a lightly floured surface, gather it into a ball, and knead vigorously, folding the dough over onto itself until smooth, elastic, and warm, around 20 minutes.

Smear some melted butter over the inside of the bowl and return the dough to the bowl. Cover with plastic wrap and allow the dough to rest in a warm place for 1 hour.

Remove the dough from the bowl and, coating your hands liberally in melted butter, pinch off 7 pieces of dough that weigh around 70 g each, shaping them into balls and, in the process, coating them with a generous amount of melted butter; you'll have 1 ball of dough for practice and 6 for the murtabak. Put the balls of dough in a plastic container, close the lid, and allow to rest in a warm place overnight.

THE DAY BEFORE SERVING, PREPARE THE SAVORY BEEF FILLING: Dry-roast the coriander seeds in a wok or small frying pan over medium heat until fragrant and toasted, around 2 minutes. Remove from the heat.

Grind the coriander seeds to a fine power with a mortar and pestle, coffee grinder, or food processor; set aside.

Heat the oil in a saucepan over medium heat. Add the shallots and fry until translucent, around 3 minutes. Add the ground coriander and chile powder and fry until fragrant and combined, around 1 minute. Add the ground beef and cook, stirring to break up clumps, until it is cooked through and a layer of red oil has risen to the top, around 5 minutes.

Add the salt, sugar, and ½ cup (125 ml) water, bring to a simmer, and simmer to reduce slightly, 2 or 3 minutes. Taste, adjusting the seasoning if necessary; the filling should be slightly sweet, rich, salty, and fragrant from the coriander, with the consistency of a pleasantly oily Bolognese sauce. If making it in advance, remove to an airtight container and store in the refrigerator.

ALTERNATIVELY, AT LEAST 2 HOURS BEFORE SERVING, PREPARE THE SWEET BANANA FILLING: Combine the bananas and sugar in a small bowl. Set aside to macerate until the banana is soft, around 2 hours.

Add the eggs and yellow food coloring (if using) to the banana mixture and stir to combine.

ON THE DAY OF SERVING, MAKE THE MURTABAK: Rub a thin layer of oil over a large flat work surface. To shape and fill the murtabak, follow the directions in the sidebar, preparing one murtabak at a time.

Melt 2 tablespoons butter in a cast-iron frying pan over medium-low heat (if the heat is too high, the murtabak will cook too quickly, burning on the exterior but remaining undercooked and doughy on the inside). Transfer the murtabak to the pan and fry slowly until the dough is golden, crispy, and fragrant and the egg has started to set, around 1½ minutes. Flip and fry until the other side is golden, crispy, and fragrant, the egg has set, the onions are soft, and the beef filling is heated through, another 1½ minutes or so. Or, if making the sweet version, fry until the egg has just set, a total of around 3 minutes. Remove the murtabak and allow to cool slightly, then cut into 6 sections and remove to a plate. Repeat with the remaining ingredients.

Serve warm or at room temperature.

RIGHT: Puyut-Style Murtabak with a savory filling, Puyut, Pattani.

Preparing Dough for Murtabak

1 Coat your fingers with a generous amount of oil, take one ball of dough (the first ball is your tester, so just use it to practice your technique), and smear it as thin as possible on a lightly oiled surface, working from the center to the perimeter. Your fingers should be oiled enough to glide on the surface of the dough, into a circle around 8 inches across; the center should be barely thicker than the perimeter.

2 Pick up the sheet of dough with both hands: your right hand, palm down, on the edge of the dough nearest your body, and your left hand, palm up, on the left edge of the dough. Using your left hand, fling the dough away from your body, allowing its farthest edge to stick on the table, and subsequently use your right hand to pull the circle toward your body to stretch it, being careful to avoid holes or tears.

3 Shift the position of your hands on the dough a few degrees clockwise and repeat this motion 3 or 4 times, the circle growing larger with each fling, and pulling until you have a very thin circle around 12 inches in diameter. (If you find this technique too challenging, after one or two flings, simply spread the dough out on your work surface and stretch, pull, and smear it to size.)

4 If using the beef filling, put a generous pinch of the onions in the center of the circle, drizzle with 1½ tablespoons of the beef filling, and top with 1½ tablespoons of the beaten egg. Alternatively, add ¼ cup (60 ml) of the sweet banana filling. Fold the left and right sides of the dough over the filling so that they meet in the middle, then repeat with the top and bottom of the dough circle, creating a sealed rectangular package.

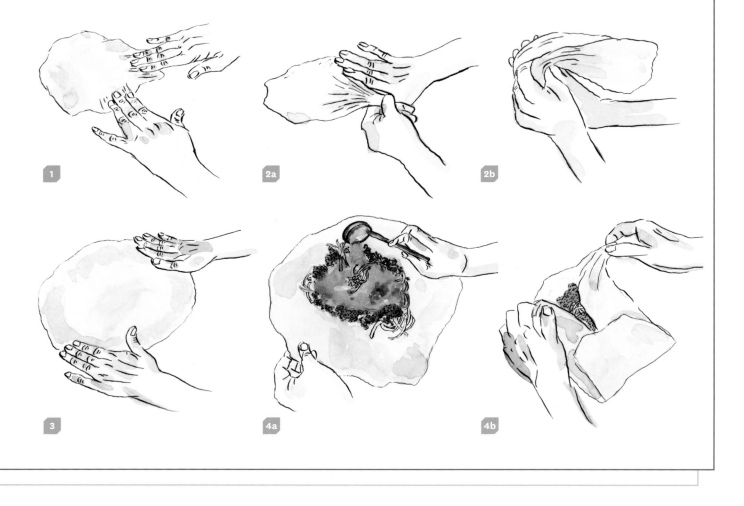

Fishing nets in Songkhla Lake, Phatthalung Province.

FROM PITH TO PEARL

At a tiny, open-air roadside restaurant in rural Phatthalung Province, Yaowanee Tancheewawong dips a spoon into a pot and then removes it, creating gloopy, sticky strands a couple of inches long. She has the tricky task of serving saakhuu ton, a dessert that in recent years has become associated with the province. Made from tiny pearls of sago that have been boiled in water with sugar, the sweet is unabashedly gelatinous in texture, but a closer look reveals tiny globes with a dry, crumbly core, not unlike minuscule dumplings. Drizzled with freshly squeezed coconut milk seasoned with a pinch of salt, the dish has five ingredients total—four if you don't count the water—yet it is one of the most delicious sweets I've encountered in Thailand.

Much of the gloop and gelatin in Asian desserts (hello, bubble tea) have their origins in tapioca, a type of tuber. Sago—subtler in consistency, more fragrant, and much more expensive—comes from the pith of a type of palm, one that is abundant in Phatthalung.

"I grew up with sago," explains Puangpen Nookeaw, a second-generation sago producer. She says this while standing in her family's sago plot, a setting less orchard and more jungle. Sago palms can grow massive and tree-like, up to eighty feet tall, taking the form of shaggy trunks with intimidating, toothed, prehistoric-looking branches. One of Puangpen's workers chose an immense tree—perhaps forty feet tall—and, using a chainsaw, had it lying on the ground in less than a minute, the tree's glaringly white pith scattered on the jungle floor as if a tiny freak Southeast Asian snowstorm had blown through. The stump has a moist, slightly waxy, almost plastic-like feel, and the shavings are fragrant, with a texture and taste similar to coconut meat or heart of palm.

The bark of the tree is removed and the stump cut into five or so sections, each of which is then quartered lengthwise. The sections are loaded onto a truck to be taken back to Puangpen's factory, essentially an extension of her home, a short drive away. From here, the sago undergoes a labor-intensive process of grating, extracting, pressing, and drying (for more on this, see right) before it becomes the tiny, deliciously gloopy pearls served at Yaowanee's restaurant—an almost magical origin for a seemingly simple dessert.

TOP: Sago pearls, Phatthalung Province.
BOTTOM: Workers preparing to cut down a sago tree, Phatthalung Province.

Making Real Sago Pearls

Puangpen Nookeaw follows these traditional steps for making sago pearls at her home factory in Phatthalung:

1 A mature sago tree is chopped down, the bark removed, and the trunk quartered lengthwise.

2 The trunk is then "grated"—in the old days, by chopping it into chunks and then pounding them in a giant mortar and pestle, later with a tool that resembles a board with nails hammered into it—and these days by custom-built machines.

3 The resulting sawdust is put in bags of fine cloth, which are massaged and squeezed in buckets of water to extract as much starch as possible. After four or five hours, when the sediment has settled, the water is poured off.

4 The sediment is packed into porous bags that are pressed overnight to expel as much moisture as possible.

5 The sediment, which at this stage has the consistency of moist, clumpy baby powder, is pushed through a sieve and rolled and tossed around in plastic basins, forming tiny pearls.

6 The pearls are spread out on mats made from a local aquatic plant and dried in the sun.

Sago Pearls Dressed with Coconut Milk

Saakhuu Ton

สาคูต้น

Although it's possible to make this dish with the more common tapioca pearls, following the directions on the package, those lack the tiny shape and subtle fragrance and texture of the real thing.

If you have access to good-quality coconuts or grated coconut, I'd encourage you to make your own thick coconut milk, as the richness and fragrance of fresh-squeezed coconut milk (as opposed to the stuff in cans or UHT boxes) contributes a great deal to this dish.

Serves 6

125 g real sago pearls
    (see headnote)
250 g white sugar
1 cup (250 ml) thick coconut milk
    (see page 135 for instructions on
    how to make thick coconut milk)
1 pandan leaf, tied in a knot
Heaping ½ teaspoon table salt

PREPARE THE SAGO: Bring 3 cups (750 ml) water to a rapid boil in a large saucepan. Very slowly add the sago pearls in a thin, gradual stream, stirring constantly (if it is added all at once, the sago will inevitably clump together). When all the sago has been added, add the sugar, stirring. Bring the mixture to a boil, reduce the heat, and simmer, stirring occasionally, for 3 minutes. Remove the saucepan from the heat, cover, and set aside to allow the sago to cool and firm up for at least 2 hours.

PREPARE THE COCONUT MILK TOPPING: While the sago is cooling, combine the thick coconut milk, pandan leaf, and salt in a small saucepan and bring to a simmer over medium heat. Reduce the heat and simmer until the coconut milk has thickened slightly, around 30 seconds. Remove from the heat. The coconut milk will taste rich and slightly salty, with a subtle fragrance from the pandan.

To serve, place about ½ cup of the sago in each small serving bowl and garnish with 1 to 1½ tablespoons of the thick coconut milk.

OPPOSITE: Yaowanee Tancheewawong serves sago pearls at her restaurant in Phatthalung Province.
ABOVE: Sago Pearls Dressed with Coconut Milk as made at Yaowanee Tancheewawong's restaurant in Phatthalung Province.

Muslim Country Cooking

BARAHOM BARZAAR is located only five miles from Pattani, the capital of the predominantly Malay-Muslim deep south province of the same name. But consisting of a few bamboo tables located under a massive tamarind tree, it's fair to say that the restaurant has a distinctly rural vibe.

"This is country food!" says Farida Klanarong, the restaurant's owner. "People from the city come here and they tell me that they're reminded of the countryside, of old dishes, of their grandparents."

Barahom is located at the edge of the village of the same name, and Farida insists on offering the type of dishes one would be more likely to find in a rural home than in a restaurant. Her menu features items such as a rustic yellow curry of fish and fresh turmeric, and a salad made from foraged ferns dressed with coconut milk. These dishes are served on banana leaves—another distinctly rural touch—and Farida discourages what might be described as more urban methods of eating.

"Eat with your hands!" she exclaims. "It tastes better that way!"

One also has to leave Pattani's city center to find ayae gawlae, chicken coated with a rich, fragrant curry marinade and grilled, or aakoh, a sweet "baked" over coconut husks. Both dishes are ubiquitous within the region, but they're generally sold outside of city centers, most likely because of the massive amount of smoke created when cooking them.

Together these venues and dishes provide a glimpse of the cuisine of Thailand's Muslim rural deep south, where Malay influences and culinary techniques, coconut milk, fresh seafood, and vibrant, rich, mild, herbaceous flavors rule.

OPPOSITE: Muslims on an excursion to the 300-year-old Al-Hussein Mosque, Narathiwat Province.
ABOVE: Southern Thai–style fishing boats, Barahom, Pattani.

Malay-Style Yellow Curry with Fish
Gula Kuning
ซูลากูนิง

The Yawi (the dialect of Malay spoken in Thailand's deep south) name of this dish translates as "yellow curry," a reference to the generous amount of fresh turmeric. Although it may be tempting, turmeric powder is not a substitute, and it won't provide the dish with its uniquely fresh, herbaceous aroma.

Serves 4 as part of a southern Thai meal

FOR THE CURRY PASTE

3 large mild dried chiles (15 g total)
1 teaspoon table salt
A 3-inch piece galangal (30 g), peeled and sliced thin
3 stalks lemongrass (75 g total; see page 19 for instructions on how to prepare lemongrass for a curry paste)
3 fingers fresh turmeric (45 g total), peeled and sliced
8 shallots (80 g total), peeled and sliced
8 cloves garlic (40 g total), peeled and sliced
1 tablespoon shrimp paste

FOR THE CURRY

3 cups (710 ml) thin coconut milk (see page 135 for instructions on how to make thin coconut milk)
1 cup (250 ml) thick coconut milk (see page 135 for instructions on how to make thick coconut milk)
4 to 6 slices dried asam fruit (see Glossary)
5 large phrik yuak or other mild fresh pale green chiles (150 g total; see Glossary)
10 medium spicy fresh chiles (30 g total)
600 g trevally or kingfish steaks, around 1 inch thick
Table salt if needed

Trevally, a fish in the jack family, is pictured here, but thick steaks of kingfish or even whole horse mackerel can be used in the dish.

UP TO 5 DAYS IN ADVANCE, PREPARE THE CURRY PASTE: Combine the dried chiles and enough water to cover by an inch or two in a saucepan and bring to a boil over high heat. Remove the saucepan from the heat, cover, and soak the chiles for 15 minutes.

Drain the chiles, discarding the water, and when they are cool enough to handle, remove and discard the seeds and stringy membranes. Slice the chiles and drain in a sieve or colander.

Pound and grind the drained chiles and salt to a coarse paste with a mortar and pestle. Add the galangal, lemongrass, and turmeric and pound and grind to a coarse paste. Add the shallots and garlic and pound and grind to a coarse paste. Add the shrimp paste and pound and grind to a fine paste. (Alternatively, if using a food processor or blender, process the chiles, salt, galangal, lemongrass, turmeric, shallots, garlic, and shrimp paste to a fine paste.) If making it in advance, remove the paste to an airtight container and store in the refrigerator.

MAKE THE CURRY: Bring the thin coconut milk and the thick coconut milk to a simmer in a saucepan over medium-low heat. Add the curry paste and asam fruit and simmer until the coconut milk has reduced slightly, around 5 minutes.

Add the large fresh chiles and simmer until just tender, around 5 minutes. Add the medium fresh chiles and the fish and simmer until the fish is cooked through, around 10 minutes. Taste, adjusting the seasoning with salt if necessary; the curry should taste rich and tart, with a vibrant yellow hue and an herbaceous flavor and fragrance from the turmeric.

Remove to a serving bowl and serve warm or at room temperature with long-grain rice.

OPPOSITE: Malay-Style Yellow Curry with Fish as served at Barahom Barzaar, Pattani Province.

A street scene in rural Narathiwat Province.

Malay-Style Salad of Vegetable Ferns and Long Beans

Kabu Pujopaku

กาบูปูโจ๊ะปากู

This salad, with origins in the Malay kitchen, revolves around a few ingredients that many American cooks may not recognize. Vegetable ferns are similar in form and taste to fiddlehead ferns, which can be used as a substitute. Long beans are, as the name hints at, roughly equivalent to elongated green beans. If you don't have access to either vegetable or fiddlehead ferns, you can go solely with long beans, or even banana blossom (which also needs to be sliced thin and parboiled beforehand), or a mix of any or all of these.

Linking these elements is a dressing based on a few more distinctly Southeast Asian ingredients—toasted coconut, mackerel, black pepper, tamarind, lime juice, and garlic—that come together in a way that will be eerily familiar to fans of American-style ranch dressing.

Serves 4 as part of a southern Thai meal

FOR THE FISH PASTE

1 mackerel or sardine (100 to 150g)
40 g finely grated coconut (see page 24 for tips on grating coconut)
1 scant teaspoon black peppercorns
2 shallots (20 g total), peeled and sliced
2 cloves garlic (10 g total), peeled and sliced

FOR THE SALAD

250 g vegetable ferns (see headnote and Glossary)
150 g long beans, chopped

FOR THE DRESSING

10 g dried tamarind paste
½ cup (125 ml) thick coconut milk (see page 135 for instructions on how to make thick coconut milk), plus more if necessary

1 tablespoon budu (or fish sauce to taste)
½ teaspoon table salt
2 teaspoons lime juice

2 to 3 medium fresh red chiles (10 g total), sliced, for garnish

---

If you don't have access to budu sauce, a less refined cousin of fish sauce (see Glossary), you can use Thai fish sauce to taste, but your dressing won't have the same subtle, unique hit of funk.

PREPARE THE FISH PASTE: Bring the mackerel and enough water to cover by an inch or two to a boil in a saucepan over high heat. Reduce the heat and simmer until the fish is cooked through, around 5 minutes. Drain, discarding the water.

When the fish is cool enough to handle, remove and discard the skin and bones; you should have around 50 g of fish flesh. Set aside.

Toast the grated coconut in a wok or frying pan over medium-low heat, stirring frequently, until golden and fragrant, around 15 minutes. Set aside.

Pound and grind the peppercorns to a coarse powder with a mortar and pestle. Add the shallots and garlic and pound and grind to a coarse paste. Add the toasted coconut and mackerel and pound and grind to a coarse paste. (Alternatively, if using a food processor or blender, process the peppercorns, shallots, garlic, toasted coconut, and mackerel to a coarse paste.) Set aside.

PREPARE THE SALAD INGREDIENTS: Pluck the tender stems and leaves from the vegetable ferns, discarding the woody stems; you should have about 150 g of vegetable ferns.

Set up an ice bath. Bring plenty of water to a boil in a saucepan over high heat. Add the long beans and simmer until just tender, around 30 seconds. Add the vegetable ferns and simmer until just tender, another 30 seconds or so. Drain the vegetables and transfer to the ice bath until cold, around 30 seconds.

Drain the vegetables again, squeeze as much moisture from them as possible, and drain in a colander.

recipe continues →

MAKE THE SALAD: Bring ¼ cup (80 ml) water to a boil in a small saucepan over high heat. Remove the pan from the heat, add the dried tamarind paste, and mash with a spoon to combine. Cover and set aside for 15 minutes.

Drain the tamarind mixture in a sieve set over a bowl, pushing on the solids to extract as much of the pulp as possible; discard the solids.

Combine the thick coconut milk, 2 tablespoons of the tamarind paste, the budu sauce, salt, and lime juice in a bowl, stirring well. Add the herb paste and the long beans and vegetable ferns, stirring to combine. Taste, adjusting the seasoning with budu (or fish sauce), salt, and/or lime juice if necessary; add a tablespoon or two more of thick coconut milk if the mixture is too dry. The salad should taste savory, rich, and slightly tart, with a strong fragrance from the black pepper and garlic, and the dressing should be relatively runny in consistency.

Remove to a serving plate, garnish with the sliced chiles, and serve with long-grain rice.

Malay-Style Salad of Vegetable Ferns and Long Beans as served at Barahom Barzaar, Pattani Province.

Thai Muslim–Style Grilled Chicken

Ayae Gawlae

อาแยฆอและ

Chicken marinated in a curry-like sauce before being grilled over coals is the superstar of Thailand's predominantly Muslim deep south. It's a staple street dish, a go-to informal meal, and also one of the few dishes from the area that people in Bangkok may have heard of. And justifiably so: it's rich, smoky, herbaceous, and even versatile, with cooks substituting ingredients such as cockles, beef, or even Japanese eggplant for the chicken.

Because the marinade is essentially a curry, this a relatively time-consuming recipe. The unique cooking process followed to grill the chicken over coals also can't be expedited. When grilling the skewers of chicken, it's helpful to keep in mind that the name of the dish, *gawlae*, means "to flip" in the local Malay dialect, a reference to the constant turning and basting required to obtain its rich, layered, smoky flavor. As such, this recipe makes a generous amount of the curry-like sauce, as it's meant to be applied in numerous layers to the chicken while grilling, as well as drizzled over the finished product.

Serves 4

FOR THE CURRY SAUCE

4 large mild dried chiles (20 g total)
10 medium spicy dried chiles (5g total)
2 teaspoons fennel seeds
1 teaspoon fenugreek seeds
1 teaspoon table salt
3 stalks lemongrass (75 g total; see page 19 for instructions on how to prepare lemongrass for a curry paste)
A 2½-inch piece ginger (25 g), peeled and sliced thin
A 2½-inch piece galangal (25 g), peeled and sliced thin
6 cloves garlic (30 g total), peeled and sliced
6 shallots (60 g total), peeled and sliced
1 tablespoon shrimp paste

1 tablespoon coconut oil (or vegetable oil)
2¼ cups (535 ml) thick coconut milk (see page 135 for instructions on how to make thick coconut milk)
4 slices dried asam fruit (see Glossary; alternatively, use 1 tablespoon dried tamarind paste)

FOR THE SKEWERS

6 to 8 boneless chicken thighs (approximately 750 g total)
1 teaspoon turmeric powder
1 teaspoon table salt
4 to 6 thick 12-inch-long bamboo skewers
2 pandan leaves

Slices of asam fruit (see Glossary) give this dish a tart flavor. If you can't find it, you can substitute dried tamarind paste.

In southern Thailand, the dish is always prepared on skewers, most likely because this makes it easy for vendors to flip many servings at a time on the grill. If you don't have access to thick bamboo skewers or pandan leaves, it's possible to grill the chicken directly on the grate, flipping it with tongs.

UP TO 5 DAYS IN ADVANCE, IF DESIRED, PREPARE THE CURRY PASTE: Combine the large and medium chiles with enough water to cover by an inch or two in a saucepan and bring to a boil over high heat. Remove the saucepan from the heat, cover, and soak the chiles for 15 minutes.

Drain the chiles, discarding the water, and when they are cool enough to handle, remove and discard the seeds and stringy membranes. Slice the chiles and drain in a sieve or colander.

Dry-roast the fennel seeds in a wok or frying pan over medium heat until toasted and fragrant, around 3 minutes. Remove and set aside. Add the fenugreek seeds to the pan and dry-roast until toasted and fragrant, around 2 minutes. Remove and set aside. Add the drained chiles and dry-roast until toasted and fragrant, around 15 minutes. Remove and set aside.

Grind the fennel seeds, fenugreek, and chiles to a fine powder with a mortar and pestle. Remove and set aside.

Pound and grind the salt, lemongrass, ginger, and galangal to a coarse paste. Add the garlic and shal-

recipe continues →

lots and pound and grind to a coarse paste. Add the shrimp paste and ground spice mixture and pound and grind to a fine paste. (Alternatively, if using a food processor or blender, process the fennel seeds, fenugreek, chiles, salt, lemongrass, ginger, galangal, garlic, shallots, and shrimp paste to a fine paste.) If making it in advance, remove the paste to an airtight container and store in the refrigerator.

UP TO 3 DAYS IN ADVANCE, IF DESIRED, PREPARE THE CURRY SAUCE: Heat the coconut oil in a wok over medium heat. Add the curry paste and fry, stirring frequently, until fragrant, around 1 minute. Add ½ cup (125 ml) of the thick coconut milk and the dried asam (or tamarind paste), stirring constantly to combine. When the mixture has reduced and the pan is almost dry, after about 5 minutes, add another ½ cup (125 ml) coconut milk. Repeat the process, using a total of 2 cups (475 ml) coconut milk (reserve the remaining coconut milk for the next step). The mixture should have the consistency of a rich, sauce-like curry. Remove from the heat and remove and discard the dried asam (or the tamarind seeds). Measure out ¼ cup (60 ml) of the curry sauce for garnish. If making the sauce in advance, remove to airtight containers and store in the refrigerator.

PREPARE THE CHICKEN: Remove and discard the bones from the chicken thighs. Combine the chicken, turmeric powder, salt, half of the curry sauce, and the reserved coconut milk in a large bowl. Set aside to marinate for 30 minutes.

While the chicken is marinating, prepare a fire in a charcoal or gas grill, with the grate around 3 inches above the coals or the gas flame. Soak the bamboo skewers in water to prevent them from burning.

While the coals are reducing or the gas grill is heating, prepare the skewers. Split each skewer almost in half lengthwise, leaving a couple inches intact as a base. Insert a thigh in a split skewer and secure the open end with a section of pandan leaf. Repeat with the remaining chicken and skewers.

GRILL THE CHICKEN: When the coals have reached medium heat (approximately 350 to 450°F—you should be able to hold your palm 3 inches above grilling level for 5 to 7 seconds), or with the gas flame at medium, add as many chicken skewers as your grill can accommodate. Grill until the curry marinade is just lightly singed and seared on one side, around 5 minutes. Flip and, using a brush, apply some of the reserved curry sauce. Repeat, flipping and applying more curry sauce, until each thigh has several layers of reduced, lightly charred paste and the chicken is cooked through but still tender, around 15 minutes total; transfer to a plate. Repeat with any remaining skewers.

When all the skewers are grilled, place the chicken on a serving dish and drizzle with the reserved curry sauce. Serve warm or at room temperature with sticky or long-grain rice.

OPPOSITE: An employee makes Thai Muslim–Style Grilled Chicken at Ayae Gawlae Ka Moh, a stall outside Pattani.

FROM PORTUGAL TO PATTANI

Take a drive outside the city limits of Pattani, in Thailand's Muslim deep south, and, especially if it's the holy month of Ramadan, you're likely to see columns of smoke towering over the road. If, like I did, you stop to take a closer look, you'll find vendors pouring a rich, fragrant batter into metal molds, which are then baked under burning coconut husks.

"During Ramadan, I can sell 300 to 400 boxes a day," explains Anas, a roadside vendor, answering my questions and working, all the while dodging errant puffs of smoke.

Anas tells me that he learned how to make the dish, known locally as *aakoh*, from his mother. He says that he mixes a batter of duck eggs, coconut milk, sugar, wheat flour, and pandanus extract. He pours this into a thick, custom-made metal mold that is elevated above coals. Once the madeleine-like oval indentations are filled, the entire mold is covered with a thin metal sheet, which is then topped with a pile of smoldering coconut husks. The heat that comes from both above and below the mold bakes the sweets, and they emerge with a rich, sweet, eggy flavor and a top that boasts some beautifully charred bits.

"My relatives make aakoh on a gas stove, but it's not as delicious as cooking with coals," Anas adds.

Yet Pattani wasn't the first place I'd encountered this sweet. Shortly before completing the research for this book, I moved to Lisbon. In the pastry shops of my new Portuguese hometown, one of my favorite breakfasts is something called a *tigelada*, a combination of eggs, milk, and sugar baked in a ceramic dish until it has a distinctly, almost decoratively charred surface along with a rich, sweet, eggy flavor. It's uncannily similar in cooking method, taste, and appearance to what I encountered on the side of the road in Pattani. Which, of course, begs the question: Is there a Portuguese connection here?

The Portuguese were the first Europeans to make contact with a Thai kingdom, way back in 1511. In a short time, it's thought, the Portuguese introduced a number of sweets to Thailand in addition to many exciting new ingredients from the Americas, including, perhaps most important of all, chiles. In Pattani, there's evidence that the Portuguese established a *feitoria*, or trading post, as early as 1538, one that employed as many as 300 Portuguese workers. Given these numbers and the Portuguese track record for culinary commerce, it's entirely possible that this sweet, beloved in far southern Thailand, actually has its origins at the western edge of the Iberian Peninsula. But without hard evidence, I'll just have to take it as a delicious culinary coincidence.

OPPOSITE: Aakoh, eggy Thai-Muslim sweets, being "baked" at the side of the road, Pattani Province.
RIGHT: Aakoh, eggy Thai-Muslim sweets, Pattani Province.

A RURAL NOODLE

Despite its small size, tiny Chaiya has it all. With a population of just under 5,000, the town center boasts a train station, a market, and two rows of ancient wooden shophouses. Located only five miles from the coast, it has easy access to a port, a source of both seafood and immigration. And it's surrounded by lush rice fields and coconut plantations. All of these elements seem to come together in the town's signature dish, a distinctly local take on phat Thai.

"Regular phat Thai is bland! I don't really like it," says Pa Phorn, for forty years a vendor of the dish, thin flat rice noodles fried with seasonings, at Chaiya's night market. "Our style is tastier."

The technique of frying noodles was most likely introduced to Thailand by Chinese immigrants, with Thais making the dish theirs by adding local seasonings such as fish sauce and dried chile. Yet despite its fascinating origin story and legions of fans around the world today, your standard Bangkok-style phat Thai isn't a particularly rich dish. Chaiya's take makes up for this via a southern-influenced, almost ketchup-like sauce that includes coconut milk, dried chiles, tamarind, and palm sugar.

"Chaiya-style phat Thai is richer; it's tart, salty, and sweet in equal measure," adds Pa Phorn.

Chaiya is also the source of Thailand's most famous salted eggs, so Pa Phorn is known to throw in a couple of local duck eggs with her noodles, adding yet another element of richness. The result is an even gutsier phat Thai, boasting flavors and influences that unite China and the best ingredients of the southern Thai countryside.

Pa Phorn making
Chaiya-Style Phat
Thai, Surat Thani
Province.

Chaiya-Style Phat Thai

Phat Thai Chaiya
ผัดไทยไชยา

Serves 6

FOR THE PHAT THAI SAUCE

50 g dried tamarind paste
5 large mild dried chiles (25 g total)
2 teaspoons table salt
8 shallots (80 g total), peeled and
    sliced
45 g palm sugar
2 cups (475 ml) thick coconut milk
    (see page 135 for instructions on
    how to make thick coconut milk)

FOR THE NOODLES

450 g thin flat dried rice noodles
2 tablespoons vegetable oil
6 duck eggs or chicken eggs
6 stalks Chinese chives (60 g total),
    trimmed of their pale, coarse
    stalks and wispy ends and cut
    into 1½-inch pieces

FOR SERVING

A platter that includes sliced
    Chinese chives, slices of
    cucumber, long beans, bean
    sprouts, and/or young cashew
    leaves or krathin leaves (see
    Glossary)
Optional seasonings such as lime
    wedges, fish sauce, sugar, and
    chile powder

The phat Thai sauce can be made in advance and kept in the refrigerator for a week or more.

The (delicious) gloopiness of the noodles and sauce means that it's necessary to fry this dish one serving at a time.

Feel free to use chicken eggs if you don't have access to duck eggs.

Few home cooks—or restaurants, for that matter—have woks large enough to accommodate the ingredients for six servings, so the instructions below are for cooking one portion at a time.

Note that this, like most Thai-style fried noodle dishes, emerges from the wok slightly underseasoned so that diners can add fish sauce, dried chile, and/or lime, as desired.

UP TO 3 DAYS IN ADVANCE, IF DESIRED, PREPARE THE PHAT THAI SAUCE: Bring 1 cup (250 ml) water to a boil in a saucepan over high heat. Remove the pan from the heat, add the dried tamarind paste, and mash with a spoon to combine. Cover and set aside for 15 minutes.

Drain the tamarind mixture in a sieve set over a bowl, pushing on the solids to extract as much of the pulp as possible; discard the solids. You should have around ¾ cup (180 ml) tamarind pulp. Set aside.

Combine the dried chiles and enough water to cover by an inch or two in a saucepan and bring to a boil over high heat. Remove the saucepan from the heat, cover, and soak the chiles for 15 minutes.

Drain the chiles, discarding the water, and when they are cool enough to handle, remove and discard the seeds and stringy membranes. Slice the chiles and drain in a sieve or colander.

Pound and grind the drained chiles and salt to a coarse paste with a mortar and pestle. Add the shallots and pound and grind to a fine paste. (Alternatively, if using a food processor or blender, process the chiles, salt, and shallots to a fine paste.)

Combine the chile and shallot paste, palm sugar, and coconut milk in a saucepan and bring to a boil over medium-high heat. Reduce the heat to a simmer and simmer, stirring occasionally, until the mixture is thick and fragrant, has reduced by nearly half, and is equal parts rich, sweet, and tart in flavor, 30 to 40 minutes. This should yield around 2 cups (500 ml) sauce. If making it in advance, remove the sauce to an airtight container and store in the refrigerator.

MAKE THE NOODLES: Soak the noodles in a bowl with plenty of water until soft, around 30 minutes. Drain the noodles in a sieve or colander.

Heat 1 teaspoon of the vegetable oil and ⅓ cup (80 ml) of the sauce in a wok over medium heat until simmering. Add around

OPPOSITE: A dish of Chaiya-Style Phat Thai as made by Pa Phorn, who has a stall in Chaiya, Surat Thani Province.

150 g of the soaked noodles and fry, stirring frequently, until they have absorbed most of the sauce, around 1 minute. Shift the noodles to one side of the wok and add one egg. Break the yolk and allow the egg to just set, around 20 seconds, then stir to combine with the noodles. Add a generous pinch of the Chinese chives and stir to combine. Remove the noodles to a plate and repeat with the remaining ingredients to make five more servings.

Serve warm or at room temperature with the vegetable platter and optional seasonings.

The Heavenly Mango Seed

IN BAN RAI YAI, in Krabi Province, they call them *met yahui* or *met thaay*. Up in Phuket, they call them *kaayii* or *kaayuu*. Elsewhere in the south, they refer to them as *hua khrok*. In Bangkok and the rest of Thailand, they're called *met mamuang himaphaan*, which can be translated as, approximately, "heavenly mango seeds."

These are all names for the cashew, a tree not related to the mango at all and with origins far, far away, in Central and South America. Ostensibly introduced to Thailand by the Portuguese a few hundred years ago, the cashew found a welcome home in the country's south. Grown, harvested, and produced predominantly by Muslims these days, cashews are an almost obligatory souvenir for Thais visiting the region. Yet they only appear in a handful of dishes in the south, and by Thai standards, they're rather expensive.

Somsak Srikoet is the second generation of his family to be in the cashew business. He describes a Ban Rai Yai of his youth that was surrounded by cashew trees. But over the last few decades, other crops have become much more lucrative. This has led villagers in Ban Rai Yai to chop down nearly all the cashew trees, planting rubber trees in their place. Today it's fair to say that Somsak is more of a cashew producer than a grower, importing raw cashews from other provinces—includ-

ing from as far afield as Thailand's northeast—and transforming them into something edible and delicious.

The cashew as we know it is the seed of a pseudofruit (one that kind of, sort of, resembles a mango). The thick shell that surrounds the seed is loaded with irritants, and the seed must undergo a messy, labor-intensive process of roasting and burning before it's edible. In Ban Rai Yai, the cashews are dried in the sun before one man, to a soundtrack of Thai country music pumped out through a massive speaker system, burns the seeds in a hot oven fueled by cashew shells, purging them of the toxic oils. The seeds are then coated in sawdust and taken to a team of women who carefully crack them, one at a time, doing their best to keep the cashews whole (large, intact seeds demand the highest prices). At this stage, the cashews are pale and only semi-roasted, sporting a paper-thin peel. They can be sold as is, ideal for inclusion in a couple different savory dishes in Thailand's south, or roasted in ovens until golden and fragrant and eaten as snacks or, occasionally, included in sweets.

Southern Thais also love to eat the tender, young, slightly astringent leaves of the cashew tree, which are sometimes included on the platters of fresh herbs and vegetables that accompany meals throughout the region. Somsak goes to gather some from one of the few trees remaining in Ban Rai Yai, and he also shakes

---

OPPOSITE: Somsak Srikoet displays fresh cashews at his farm in Ban Rai Yai, Krabi Province.
ABOVE: Cashews about to be roasted, Ban Rai Yai, Krabi Province.

a few cashew fruits loose, bringing them back to the factory. There his mother peels them and sprinkles the pieces of fruit with sugar; they're too astringent to be eaten plain. They are soft, juicy, and rich, with an almost perfume-like fragrance, and "heavenly" seems the appropriate adjective.

PROCESSING CASHEWS

At Mathaeng Cashews, a second-generation producer in Krabi Province, cashews are produced via the following steps:

1 The cashews are picked and the seeds separated from their pseudofruits, the latter of which are generally discarded in Thailand.
2 The seeds, skin and all, are dried in the sun.
3 The seeds are flame-roasted in an oven to purge them of toxic oils.
4 The cashews are shelled and the seeds sorted by size.
5 The seeds are roasted once more, if desired, and packaged.

Fish Belly Curry
Kaeng Phung Plaa
แกงพุงปลา

It's one of southern Thailand's most famous, beloved, and emblematic dishes. It's also, quite possibly, its spiciest and most intimidating. A fish curry often supplemented with vegetables, it is known within the region as *kaeng phung plaa*, "fish belly curry," and elsewhere as *kaeng tai plaa*, "fish kidney curry," both names references to the dish's defining ingredient: a funky condiment made from salted fish offal. But they neglect mention of yet another intimidating aspect of the dish: its incendiary curry paste.

"It should taste spicy—this is the main flavor," says Wanthana Jandin, a villager in Ban Rai Yai, in Krabi Province, and the source of this recipe. Indeed, her take on kaeng phung plaa was fiery, although it had as much punch from black pepper as it did from dried chile.

Kaeng phung plaa always includes generous chunks of grilled firm fish—most commonly torpedo/hardtail scad—but its vegetable ingredients can vary, ranging from crunchy joints of bamboo to tender, almost potato-like jackfruit seeds, depending on what's available. It's also one of the few savory dishes in southern Thailand that often includes cashews. Whole raw seeds can be added to the dish, providing a rich, nutty counter to all that spice, salt, and funk.

Serves 4

FOR THE CURRY PASTE

½ teaspoon table salt
16 medium spicy dried chiles (8 g total)
2 teaspoons black peppercorns
A 1½-inch piece galangal (15 g), peeled and sliced
1 finger fresh turmeric (15 g), peeled and sliced
4 cloves garlic (20 g total), peeled and sliced
1 tablespoon shrimp paste

OPPOSITE: Fish Belly Curry as made by Wanthana Jandin, Ban Rai Yai, Krabi Province.

FOR THE TAI PLAA SEASONING

½ cup (125 ml) tai plaa (see Glossary)
1 stalk lemongrass (25 g; see page 19 for instructions on how to prepare lemongrass for a soup)
1 shallot (10 g), peeled and bruised
2 makrut lime leaves

FOR THE CURRY

1 small torpedo/hardtail scad (around 300 g; see Note)
150 g green/unripe papaya, peeled, halved lengthwise, seeds removed, and sliced thick
150 g kabocha squash, peeled and cubed
150 g cassava, peeled and cubed
3 Thai eggplants (120 g total), quartered
3 long beans (60 g total), cut into 2-inch pieces
50 g raw whole cashews
6 makrut lime leaves, torn
2 teaspoons white sugar

Salted fish innards, known in Thai as *tai pla* and often labeled as such, are available in small plastic bottles; there's no substitute for this ingredient. Avoid the type that is essentially a preseasoned curry without the vegetables and protein, or the dry type that is eaten as a Thai-style dip.

If you can't find torpedo/hardtail scad, use another oily, dark-fleshed fish from the mackerel family; Pacific mackerel and horse mackerel are common substitutes.

As is the case with many southern Thai dishes, the fish is grilled until relatively dry and firm before it is added to the curry, providing a unique contrast to the soup.

The vegetable element of this dish is flexible; if you can't find green papaya—or any of the ingredients listed—it's fine to omit and compensate with another.

Wanthana used raw cashews, which she claims are best for savory dishes, but if you can't get them, toasted, roasted, or deep-fried nuts work fine.

UP TO 5 DAYS BEFORE SERVING, PREPARE THE CURRY PASTE: Pound and grind the salt and dried chiles to a coarse paste with a mortar and pestle. Add the peppercorns and pound and grind to a coarse paste. Add

recipe continues →

the galangal and turmeric and pound and grind to a coarse paste. Add the garlic and pound and grind to a coarse paste. Add the shrimp paste and pound and grind to a fine paste. (Alternatively, if using a food processor or blender, process the salt, chiles, peppercorns, galangal, turmeric, garlic, and shrimp paste to a fine paste.) If making it in advance, remove the paste to an airtight container and store in the refrigerator.

A FEW HOURS BEFORE SERVING, GRILL THE FISH: Prepare a fire in a charcoal or gas grill, with the grate around 3 inches above the coals or the gas flame. When the coals have reduced to a low heat (approximately 250 to 350°F—you should be able to hold your palm 3 inches above the fire for 8 to 10 seconds), or with the gas flame at low, add the fish and grill, flipping it occasionally, until relatively dry and firm in texture, around 40 minutes total. (Alternatively, you can grill the fish under the broiler.) Remove it to a platter.

When the fish is cool enough to handle, remove, and discard the skin and bones and separate the flesh into pinky finger–sized chunks. You should have around 150 g of fish. Set aside.

WHILE THE FISH IS GRILLING, PREPARE THE TAI PLA SEASONING: Combine the tai pla, ½ cup (125 ml) water, the lemongrass, shallot, and makrut lime leaves in a saucepan and bring to a boil over high heat. Reduce the heat and simmer for 30 seconds.

Pour the mixture through a sieve set over a bowl; discard the solids. Set the seasoning aside.

MAKE THE CURRY: Bring 3 cups (750 ml) water to a boil in a saucepan over high heat. Add the curry paste and ¼ cup (60 ml) of the tai plaa seasoning (reserve the remainder in your refrigerator for another use), stirring to combine, and heat until fragrant, around 30 seconds. Add the papaya, kabocha squash, and cassava, reduce the heat, and simmer for 2 minutes. Add the Thai eggplants and long beans and simmer until the vegetables are just starting to get tender, around 5 minutes.

Add the fish, cashews, makrut lime leaves, and sugar and bring to a simmer, around 3 minutes. Taste, adjusting the seasoning if necessary; the curry should taste equal parts salty and spicy, with a funky aroma from the tai plaa and a pleasant one from the black pepper and turmeric.

Remove to a serving bowl and serve warm or at room temperature with long-grain rice.

Sweetened Sticky Rice with Cashews

Niaw Kuan

เหนียวกวน

In contrast to South Asia, where cashews effortlessly worked their way into the repertoire of sweet snacks and desserts, in Thailand, they've remained more of an outsider, included in only a handful of dishes. For the people in southern Thailand who grow and produce cashews, perhaps the most important of these is niaw kuan, sticky rice made sweet and rich with sugar and coconut milk, then studded with cashews.

"It's a dish we eat on special occasions: Ramadan, weddings, other merit-making times," says Wanthana Jandin, a villager in Ban Rai Yai in Krabi Province. As such, she's used to making massive amounts of the dish, cooking it on outdoor stoves in satellite dish–sized woks, stirring the bubbling, fragrant mixture with giant wooden paddles. The process of simmering and stirring the sticky rice in the sugary base results in grains that retain a bit of crunch, a distinct contrast with the soft, rich cashews. The sweet boasts an almost pudding-like texture, and it is sometimes served in cups rather than on plates.

Serves 4

150 g sticky rice
4 cups (1 L) thick coconut milk (see page 135 for
   instructions on how to make thick coconut milk)
150 g white sugar
45 g palm sugar
½ teaspoon table salt
100 g roasted cashews, split lengthwise

The most efficient way to steam sticky rice is with a Thai-style pot and a conical bamboo basket. If you don't have access to these tools, a steaming set can be improvised with a sieve elevated over boiling water, or a Chinese-style steamer lined with cheesecloth, although the cooking time may vary.

Wanthana Jandin makes Sweetened Sticky Rice with Cashews, Ban Rai Yai, Krabi Province.

recipe continues →

AT LEAST 4½ HOURS BEFORE SERVING, PREPARE THE STICKY RICE: Gently rinse the rice in several changes of water until the water remains clear. Cover with plenty of fresh water and soak for 4 to 6 hours.

STEAM THE STICKY RICE: Drain the rice, discarding the water. Bring a couple quarts of water to a boil in a Thai-style sticky rice steaming pot (or in a saucepan or an Asian-style steamer). Put the rice in the bamboo steaming basket (or in a sieve or a Chinese-style steamer lined with cheesecloth) positioned a few inches above the boiling water, cover with a tea towel and then a lid to create a relatively tight seal that allows as little steam as possible to escape, and steam for 10 minutes.

Flip the entire mass of rice and steam for another 5 minutes, or until the grains are soft on the exterior but retain a bit of bite and firmness at their core.

Remove the rice from the heat, transfer to a bowl or large plate, and stir it gently with a large spoon, allowing it to release steam, for around 10 seconds. Set aside.

MAKE THE SWEET: Combine the coconut milk, white sugar, palm sugar, and salt in a wok and bring to a boil over high heat. Reduce the heat to a rapid simmer and simmer until the mixture is thick, just starting to become syrupy, and reduced by around half, approximately 20 minutes.

Add the cashews. When the mixture returns to a simmer, add the sticky rice and cook at a rapid simmer, stirring frequently, until most of the liquid has evaporated and/or has been absorbed by the rice, with the rice still retaining a bit of crunch, and the mixture is glossy, thick, and pudding-like, around 15 minutes. The flavor should be equal parts sweet and rich. Remove from the heat and pour onto a tray or into a baking pan to cool.

Remove to small bowls or cups and serve warm or at room temperature.

ABOVE: Sweetened Sticky Rice with Cashews as made by Wanthana Jandin, Ban Rai Yai, Krabi Province.
OPPOSITE: Rubber trees, rural Phang-Nga Province.

The Coast

If southern Thailand has a defining landscape, it's almost certainly its coast, which spans more than 1,200 miles along two geographically and culturally distinct sides of the Malay Peninsula. Its white sand beaches, turquoise waters, and karst cliffs are the stuff of dream vacations. It's also been an incredibly important influence on the region's cuisine.

The coast is the jumping-off point for fish and other seafood, traditionally the region's primary source of protein. These ingredients make it into an almost uncountable number of local dishes, as well as into the kitchens of a seemingly limitless number of seafood-forward restaurants that line the coast. It's here that Thais and foreigners alike pair grilled squid with a tart, spicy dip or enjoy dishes such as fist-sized prawns, deep-fried and served in a sauce that's tart from tamarind and sweet from palm sugar.

The sea is also a source of salt, a tool used to stretch the shelf life of that catch. In particular, seafood and saline meet in a number of salty, savory condiments— shrimp paste and a variety of fish sauces—that have emerged as backbones of the cuisine. And that salt, as it trickles inland in the form of brackish water, has other benefits, creating an environment for an entirely unique repertoire of fish, as well as for nipa palm trees, which have an astounding number of uses.

Southern Thailand's coastline is not limited to rural areas. The region's coastal cities have long drawn immigrants from places as far away as China and as near as Malaysia. These immigrants brought with them novel cooking techniques such as salt-preserving eggs and a taste for unusual ingredients like birds' nests, adding yet another culinary layer to southern Thailand's coastal cuisine.

PREVIOUS SPREAD: Waterside houses outside Narathiwat.

Southern Sauce

IN SOUTHERN THAILAND, you won't find a lot of fish sauce—at least not the thin, refined seasoning that many of us associate with Thai cooking. In predominantly Chinese urban centers such as Phuket Town or Trang, soy sauce rules. In coastal areas, sea salt dominates. Elsewhere, salty flavors may come from shrimp paste supplemented with salt and/or soy sauce.

In the country's deep south, cooks have their own fishy liquid. It's called *naam buuduu—budu* being a Malay term for a type of fish-based sauce produced south of the border. Like the fish sauce we're familiar with, it's made from Indian anchovies that are combined with salt and allowed to ferment in a controlled environment. Compared to standard Thai-style fish sauce, budu generally has a shorter period of fermentation, with more exposure to the sun, and is is not finely filtered, meaning that the finished products contain varying degrees of sediment. In the deep south, budu is used as an all-around seasoning agent. However, ask a Thai from Bangkok about budu, and he'll undoubtedly think of khaao yam, known by Malay speakers as *nasi kabu*, southern Thailand's salad of rice, herbs, and other ingredients. Budu is an essential ingredient in the sauce used to dress the dish (see page 282).

Saiburi, a coastal district of Pattani Province in the country's deep south, produces nearly all of Thailand's budu sauce. The vast majority of the district's inhabitants are ethnic Malay Muslims who speak a dialect of Malay and who dress in a way that's more Baghdad than Bangkok. Even the landscape feels foreign, with its mosque minarets and wandering herds of goat and sheep. In the seaside village of Nam Bo, in Saiburi District, I stop in at a home-based budu factory.

"Naam buuduu is more balanced than fish sauce," explains the owner, a middle-aged Muslim woman, who didn't want to share her name. "It's richer, more fragrant."

She lifts a plastic sheet covering a ceramic jar and scoops out some of the liquid inside, which she calls *naam buuduu khon*, "thick budu sauce." Where standard Thai fish sauce is thin, savory, and salty, this is downright rustic; still liquid, but richer and thicker. Its aroma is challenging—a hearty, in-your-face funk. It makes sense that when using this type of budu sauce, cooks are obligated to counter its scent with an arsenal of herbs and aromatics, as well as lots of sugar.

The owner then pulls out a couple bottles of *naam buuduu sai*. This translates as "clear budu sauce," which is something of a misnomer, as each bottle holds a couple of fingers of a fine silver/brown sediment below the amber-colored liquid, which is more like traditional fish sauce. However, despite having undergone an additional stage of filtering, it can still claim the funk and richness associated with budu sauce in general. This type of budu is often sweetened with a bit of sugar, and it is usually the only option available outside southern Thailand. If cooking with it, be sure to taste and accommodate for its sweetness.

OPPOSITE: Budu sauce fermenting in Saiburi, Pattani Province.
ABOVE: Freshly caught anchovies, Saiburi, Pattani Province.

MAKING NAM BUDU

Budu sauce takes a variety of forms, the main differences depending on the degree of filtration and whether it has been boiled and/or seasoned before being bottled.

1 Freshly caught Indian anchovies are mixed with at least one-third their weight in salt, then put in cement or ceramic jars, weighted down with bamboo screens and rocks to release air, and left exposed to the sun for at least five months, or as long as a year. Digestive and microbial enzymes in the fish kick-start fermentation, and salt-friendly bacteria break down the proteins, transforming the fish into a salty, savory liquid.

2 When the fish is deemed sufficiently fermented, any remaining bones and other large solids are filtered out and discarded. The liquid that results, known as *buuduu khon*, "thick budu," can be consumed as is or filtered more finely for *buuduu sai*, "clear budu."

3 Alternatively, after the larger solids have been filtered out, some budu sauce is filtered again, boiled, and seasoned with sugar, resulting in a more concentrated yet milder and slightly more refined—and less funky—seasoning.

Rice Salad with Budu Dressing
Nasi Kabu
นาซิกาบู

This is one of the more time-consuming recipes in the book, but it's also one of the most flexible. The dressing and the toasted coconut and fish toppings can be made in advance and refrigerated for days, if not weeks, and the recipe yields enough of these elements for two meals. There's seemingly an infinite variety of ways to prepare *nasi kabu*, as the dish is known among the Muslims of the deep south, and if you don't have access to noni leaves (an ingredient that gives the rice a gray tint and an herbaceous aroma) or don't have enough time to make the noodle topping, omit either or both of them. The real constants for nasi kabu are, of course, rice, an herb and vegetable topping, and the budu dressing.

Serves 6

FOR THE BUDU DRESSING

¾ cup (180 ml) unsweetened budu sauce
250 g palm sugar
2 pieces dried asam fruit (see Glossary)
10g dried tamarind paste
1 small makrut lime (around 30 g), halved
6 makrut lime leaves
A 2-inch piece ginger (20 g), peeled and sliced thick
A 2-inch piece galangal (20 g), peeled and sliced thick
2 stalks lemongrass (50 g total; see page 19 for instructions on how to prepare lemongrass for a soup)
5 shallots (50 g total), peeled and halved
5 cloves garlic (25 g total), peeled and halved

FOR THE TOASTED COCONUT TOPPING

250 g finely grated coconut (see page 24 for tips on grating coconut)

FOR THE FISH TOPPING

5 horse mackerel or other small mackerel (500 g total), gutted
2 slices dried asam fruit (see Glossary)

FOR THE NOODLE TOPPING

50 g thin rice noodles
25 g dried tamarind paste
1 large mild dried chile (5 g)
1 shallot (10 g), peeled and sliced thin
1 clove garlic (5g total), peeled and sliced
1 teaspoon vegetable oil
¼ cup (60 ml) thick coconut milk (see page 135 for instructions on how to make thick coconut milk)
1 teaspoon white sugar
1 teaspoon light soy sauce
½ teaspoon table salt

FOR THE VEGETABLE AND HERB TOPPING

150 to 200 g very thinly sliced vegetables and herbs (in Thailand's deep south, these might include bai phaa hom [see Glossary], cabbage, carrots, cucumber, lemongrass, long beans, makrut lime leaves, pomelo pips, torch ginger flowers, Vietnamese coriander, water celery, wild betel leaves, and/or young mango leaves)
150 g bean sprouts

FOR THE RICE

8 noni leaves (40 g total; see Glossary)
3 cups (500 g) long-grain white rice
2 pandan leaves, tied in a knot
2 stalks lemongrass (50 g total; see page 19 for instructions on how to prepare lemongrass for a soup)
4 makrut lime leaves
4 shallots (40 g total), peeled and halved
1 teaspoon white sugar

FOR SERVING

1½ teaspoons chile powder
1½ teaspoons coarsely ground black pepper

recipe continues →

A dish of Rice Salad with Budu Dressing as served at Thai-Islam Phochana, a restaurant in Yala.

UP TO 5 DAYS IN ADVANCE, PREPARE THE BUDU DRESS-ING: Combine 1¼ cups (300 ml) water, the budu sauce, palm sugar, asam fruit, tamarind paste, makrut lime, makrut lime leaves, ginger, galangal, lemongrass, shallots, and garlic in a saucepan and bring to a boil over high heat. Reduce the heat and simmer until the liquid is reduced by around half, fragrant, and just starting to become syrupy, around 30 minutes. The dressing should taste sweet, followed by equal parts salty and tart, with lots of fragrance from the budu and the herbs and aromatics.

Strain the dressing, discarding the solids; this should yield about 1¼ cups (300 ml), enough for two recipes. Remove to a tightly sealed container and refrigerate.

UP TO 3 DAYS IN ADVANCE, PREPARE THE TOASTED COCONUT TOPPING: Toast the coconut in a wok over medium-low heat, stirring and scraping constantly, until fragrant, golden, and toasted, around 30 minutes. Set aside to cool, then transfer to a tightly sealed container and refrigerate.

ALSO UP TO 3 DAYS IN ADVANCE, PREPARE THE FISH TOPPING: Bring the mackerel and enough water to cover by an inch or two to a boil in a saucepan over high heat. Reduce the heat and simmer until the fish is cooked through when tested with a fork, around 5 minutes.

Drain the fish, discarding the water. When the fish is cool enough to handle, remove and discard the

The fishing village of Tammalang, Satun Province.

skin and bones; you should have around 250 g of fish flesh.

Toast the mackerel and dried asam fruit in a wok over low heat, stirring and scraping constantly to break the fish into small, almost strand-like pieces, until it is fragrant, dry, and fluffy, around 30 minutes. Set aside to cool, then transfer to a tightly sealed container and refrigerate.

AGAIN UP TO 3 DAYS IN ADVANCE, PREPARE THE NOODLE TOPPING: Soak the rice noodles in a bowl of room-temperature water for 15 minutes.

Drain the noodles in a sieve or colander, discarding the water, then set aside to drain further.

Bring ¼ cup (60 ml) water to a boil in a saucepan over high heat. Remove from the heat, add the dried tamarind paste, and mash with a spoon to combine. Cover and set aside for 15 minutes.

Strain the tamarind mixture through a sieve set over a bowl, pushing on the solids to extract as much of the pulp as possible; discard the solids. You should have a scant ¼ cup (60 ml) tamarind pulp.

Combine the dried chile and enough water to cover by an inch or two in a saucepan and bring to a boil over high heat. Remove the saucepan from the heat, cover, and soak the chile for 15 minutes.

Drain the chile, discarding the water, and when it is cool enough to handle, remove and discard the seeds and stringy membranes. Slice the chile and drain in a sieve or colander.

Pound and grind the drained chile, shallots, and garlic to a fine paste with a mortar and pestle. (Alternatively, if using a food processor or blender, process the chile, shallots, and garlic to a fine paste.)

Heat the vegetable oil in a wok over medium-low heat. Add the chile paste and fry, stirring frequently, until fragrant, around 1 minute. Add the coconut milk, tamarind pulp, sugar, soy sauce, and salt, increase the heat to medium, and simmer, stirring frequently, until the ingredients are fragrant and amalgamated, around 1 minute. Add the noodles and fry, stirring constantly, until they have absorbed all the liquid and are dry, around 5 minutes. Taste, adjusting the seasonings if necessary; the noodles should taste equal parts rich and tart, with a balanced background flavor of salty, sweet, and spicy. If making the noodles ahead, remove to a tightly sealed container and refrigerate until use.

ON THE DAY OF SERVING, PREPARE THE RICE: Blend or process the noni leaves with 2 cups (475 ml) water in a blender or food processor until smooth. Strain the liquid into a bowl; discard the solids.

Gently rinse the rice in several changes of water until the water remains clear. Combine the rice, noni leaf liquid, pandan leaf, lemongrass, makrut lime leaves, shallots, and sugar in a large saucepan and bring to a rolling boil for around 3 seconds. Cover, reduce the heat, and cook at a low simmer for 20 minutes.

Turn off the heat and open the lid for a few seconds to release excess heat and steam, then replace the lid and allow the rice to rest, undisturbed, for 10 minutes. Gently stir the rice, cover, and allow to reach room temperature.

To serve, place ¾ to 1 cup (180 to 250 ml) of the rice on each plate and drizzle with 1½ to 2 tablespoons of the budu dressing. Top each portion of rice with ½ cup (25 g) of the vegetable and herb topping, ½ cup (25 g) bean sprouts, 1 heaping tablespoon of the toasted coconut topping, 2 heaping tablespoons of the noodle topping, ¼ teaspoon chile powder, and ¼ teaspoon pepper. Finish each dish with 2 heaping tablespoons of the fish topping.

Budu Dip
Ai Budu
ไอบูดู

"Even if you don't have money, you can still eat budu!" exclaims Hameedah Cheuma, a cook in the southern province of Pattani. At its most basic, it's easy to imagine why a dip of unfiltered fish sauce supplemented with palm sugar and herbs has long been enjoyed by budget-constrained southern Thai Muslims. It's easy to make, cheap, and full flavored. Hameedah, who shared this recipe, tells me that the dip can be enhanced by adding pricier ingredients, including flaked grilled fish, minced shrimp, toasted grated coconut, or even ripe durian.

This recipe is a wonderful opportunity to play and experiment with southern Thai seasonings and flavors. Do you prefer sweeter flavors? Be generous with the palm sugar. Not a fan of tartness? Go easy on the lime juice. As long as the salt and funk of the budu come through, you're on the right track.

Serves 4

FOR THE DIP

3 tablespoons thick unfiltered budu (naam buuduu khon; see Glossary)
60 g palm sugar
1 to 2 limes, cut into wedges and seeds removed
20 tiny spicy fresh chiles (10 g total), sliced thin
4 shallots (40 g total), peeled and sliced thin
1 stalk lemongrass (25 g; see page 19 for instructions on how to prepare lemongrass for an herb paste)
6 makrut lime leaves, sliced very thin

FOR SERVING

A platter that includes leafy herbs and fresh vegetables such as Asian pennywort, baby corn, cucumber, and/or Thai eggplant; parboiled or steamed vegetables such as cabbage, carrots, long beans, okra, vegetable ferns, and/or wing beans; and/or grilled items such as a pod of bitter beans, or horse or other small mackerel, rubbed with salt and turmeric powder and grilled over coals

---

To eat a Thai-style dip, take an herb, green, or vegetable, put it on your plate of rice, and top with a bit of the dip, creating a bite that combines all three elements.

Combine the budu, palm sugar, and ½ cup (125 ml) water in a saucepan and bring to a simmer, stirring to dissolve the sugar. Taste, adjusting the seasoning if necessary; at this point, the dip should taste predominately salty and funky, followed by sweet. If it's unpleasantly salty, add more water; if you like sweetness, add more sugar. Set aside to cool.

Squeeze the equivalent of the juice of 1 lime into it, working to extract the volatile oils from the zest, then leave the rinds in the dip. Taste, adjusting the seasoning if necessary with more lime juice; the dip should taste predominantly salty and tart, followed by sweet and funky, with a consistency that's just barely bordering on syrupy. Add the chiles, shallots, and lemongrass, stirring to combine.

Remove to a small serving bowl and garnish with the makrut lime leaves. Serve with the platter of sides and long-grain rice.

OPPOSITE: Budu Dip as prepared by Hameedah Cheuma, Pattani.

Preserving the Catch

COMPRISED OF HOUSES, shops, and even a mosque elevated on pillars above the water, Ban Sam Chong, in Phang-Nga Province, is one of a handful of so-called "floating villages" in southern Thailand. It's no surprise that the people here have a close connection to the sea and fishing, and I'm here to learn about that gray, salty, pungent, unglamorous staple of Thai cuisine known as shrimp paste. But my questions only seem to elicit exasperation.

"If you don't have shrimp paste, you can't cook!" exclaims Ramphai Sumalee, sixty-three, a producer of the ingredient for more than four decades.

In southern Thailand's cuisine, shrimp paste provides dishes, in particular chile-based dips, curries, and soups, with body, a boost of salt and umami, and a unique aroma. For Thais, its role is obvious and crucial. For those who didn't grow up with shrimp paste, the English name can be misleading. *Kapi*, as it's known in Thai, isn't generally made from shrimp but rather from krill, tiny crustaceans found in both salty and brackish water. These days, some types of kapi are made from larger shrimp or even fish, but the traditional highest-quality product comes from just two ingredients: krill and salt.

Ramphai tells me that good shrimp paste has a dense, firm, slightly oily texture; a salty (but not too salty) flavor; and a pleasantly funky aroma. The highest-quality shrimp paste makes its way into naam chup, the chile-based dips that are paired with vegetables and herbs and eaten with rice. Coarser, poorer-quality, saltier kapi is pounded up with aromatics such as chiles, lemongrass, shallots, and garlic as an essential ingredient in the colorful, aromatic pastes that are the building blocks of Thai curries, soups, and stir-fries. In general, and if it is used properly, one would struggle to detect the particular flavor or aroma of kapi in many Thai dishes, but without it, they would lack a subtly pungent, uniquely savory roundness and saltiness.

"It just makes food delicious," concludes Ramphai.

In Ban Bang Phat, another "floating village" in Phang-Nga Province, I meet yet one more southern Thai in the act of preservation. Crouching at a low, nearly concealed grill in front of his elevated house, Suthat Waharat is making kung siap, "skewered shrimp," an old method followed to preserve larger crustaceans.

"Only about three households in this village still make kung siap the old way," Suthat tells me. "We're the second or third generation to do it."

He tells me that to make kung siap, he takes wild shrimp ("Farmed shrimp are harder to grill, and they

OPPOSITE: A local holds a tub of shrimp paste, Ban Sam Chong, Phang-Nga Province.

289

turn black"), skewers them on bamboo, and grills them over low coals until they're dry—that's it. "It takes about an hour to grill the shrimp," says Suthat. "You have to do it carefully and turn them often so that they don't burn."

These days, according to Suthat, most kung siap are made by boiling and seasoning farmed shrimp before drying them in the sun—often they're not even skewered. But they lack the unique flavor and aroma of shrimp preserved the old-school way.

"There's no need to use salt or season the shrimp; they're already sweet," Suthat tells me of his kung siap. "They get a smoky flavor from the grill."

Today refrigeration has rendered such methods of food preservation essentially irrelevant. Yet the flavors, aromas, and textures of many traditional preserved products have become essential aspects of southern Thai cuisine, a transition from necessity to preference, in effect preserving the preserved.

MAKING SHRIMP PASTE

Three families in Ban Sam Chong still make kapi by hand, from krill, a process that can take as long as nine days.

1 Fisherman troll shallow, brackish water, locating the krill as they jump up above the water. Then they catch the krill with long, fine scoop nets, which are either perched in front of small boats or, in shallow water, dragged by hand. The krill are rinsed and sorted, and any larger shrimp or fish are discarded.
2 Then the krill are spread out in the sun to dry, which in Thailand can take as little as a couple of hours.
3 When partially dry, the krill are pounded with coarse salt in a large wooden mortar and pestle (or, increasingly these days, blitzed in a food processor) to a coarse paste.
4 The paste is pressed into containers, covered, and left to ferment for 3 to 7 days.
5 The paste is broken into clumps and dried in the sun yet again, pounded until smooth, and packaged for sale or consumption.

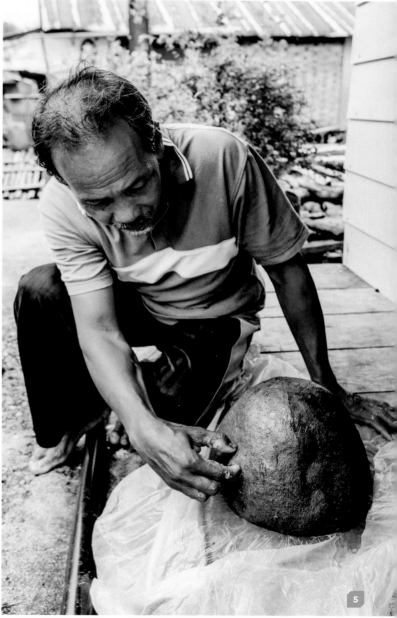

A Spicy Dip of Smoked Shrimp and Shrimp Paste

Naam Phrik Kung Siap
น้ำพริกกุ้งเสียบ

Among Thais, naam phrik kung siap is easily the most famous dish from Phuket; visitors from other parts of Thailand are practically obligated to bring tubs of the stuff back home to friends and family. Yet these days, as tourism has almost completely superseded aquaculture on the island, the dip's defining ingredients—namely, smoked shrimp and shrimp paste—are sourced from neighboring Phang-Nga Province.

Thailand's naam phrik (also known in the south as naam chup), spicy "dips" that are sort of, kind of, roughly equivalent to Mexican salsas, are the most truly regional dishes in the country. Phuket's contribution to the genre combines typically bold seasonings such as fresh chiles, shrimp paste, lime juice, and garlic. But the headlining ingredient is the kung siap, smoked shrimp that provide the dish with a crunchy, pleasantly fishy, savory punch and a campfire-like aroma (for more on this ingredient, see page 289).

"It's a dish that's somewhere between a Thai-style salad and a dip," Satja Chodchoi, the owner of a Phuket Town eatery called NC Restaurant, tells me, adding that her variation also includes strips of crispy tart green mango, giving it a uniquely hearty consistency for a naam phrik.

Serves 4

FOR THE DIP

2 cups (475 ml) vegetable oil
1 heaping cup (around 50 g) kung siap (see Glossary)
32 tiny spicy fresh chiles (16 g total)
5 cloves garlic (25 g total), peeled and sliced
2 tablespoons high-quality Thai shrimp paste
8 shallots (80 g total), peeled and sliced
1 tablespoon palm sugar
¼ cup (60 ml) lime juice
1 small sour green mango, peeled and shredded (you should have 40 g shredded mango)

FOR SERVING

A platter that includes parboiled or steamed vegetables such as bitter gourd, cabbage, carrot, and/or small eggplant, and/or raw herbs and vegetables such as cucumber, young cashew leaves, bitter beans, and/or white turmeric, cut into bite-sized pieces or sliced as appropriate

---

If you can't source authentic kung siap, opt for the largest, highest-quality dried shrimp you can find.

Thai-style dips such as this one are made using a granite mortar and pestle, which lends them a pleasantly coarse, chunky consistency. A food processor or blender would result in a dish with too fine a consistency.

To eat a Thai-style dip, take an herb, green, or vegetable, put it on your plate of rice, and top with a bit of the dip, creating a bite that combines all three elements.

DEEP-FRY THE DRIED SHRIMP: Heat the vegetable oil to 225°F in a wok over medium heat. Add the shrimp and deep-fry, stirring occasionally, until toasted and fragrant, about 30 seconds. Remove with a strainer and drain on paper towels.

MAKE THE DIP: Pound and grind the chiles, garlic, shrimp paste, and half of the shallots to a coarse paste with a mortar and pestle. Add the palm sugar and lime juice and pound and grind to a relatively fine paste. Add the deep-fried dried shrimp, mango, and the remaining shallots, gently bruising them with the pestle and then mixing with a spoon to combine; you do not want these ingredients to become mush, just slightly bruised and coated in the shrimp paste mixture. If the dip is too dry to mix this way, add a tablespoon or so of water to loosen it up. Taste, adjusting the seasoning if necessary; the dip should taste equal parts tart, spicy, and salty, as well as slightly sweet; it should be crunchy from the dried shrimp and mango, and fairly thick and dry in consistency.

Remove to a small serving bowl and serve with the platter of the vegetables and long-grain rice.

OPPOSITE: A Spicy Dip of Smoked Shrimp and Shrimp Paste as served at NC Restaurant, Phuket Town.

A Thai-Style Dip of Shrimp Paste and Coconut Milk
Kaeng Khoei
แกงเคย

Shrimp paste is strong stuff. But it only takes a bit of cooking for its aroma to shift from pungent to savory. Combine it with fragrant Thai-style aromatics and rich coconut cream, as in this southern Thai dip, and its saltiness and savoriness seem to have found natural counterparts.

Serves 4

FOR THE HERB PASTE

4 shallots (40 g total), peeled and sliced
4 cloves garlic (20 g total), peeled and sliced
7 medium spicy fresh red chiles (20 g total), sliced
2 stalks lemongrass (50 g total; see page 19 for instructions on how to prepare lemongrass for an herb paste)
½ finger turmeric (8 g), peeled and sliced

FOR THE DIP

2 cups (475 ml) thick coconut milk (see page 135 instructions on how to make thick coconut milk)
2 shallots (20 g total), peeled and sliced thin
5 tablespoons high-quality Thai shrimp paste
30 g palm sugar
6 makrut lime leaves, 4 torn, 2 sliced very fine
3 medium spicy fresh red chiles (10 g total), sliced on the bias

FOR SERVING

A platter that includes fresh vegetables such as bitter beans, cucumbers, and/or baby corn, and steamed or parboiled vegetables such as carrots, broccoli, cauliflower, and/or vegetable ferns, cut into bite-sized pieces or sliced as appropriate

---

To eat a Thai-style dip, take an herb, green, or vegetable, put it on your plate of rice, and top with a bit of the dip, creating a bite that combines all three elements.

PREPARE THE HERB PASTE: Pound and grind the shallots, garlic, chiles, lemongrass, and turmeric to a fine paste with a mortar and pestle. (Alternatively, if using a food processor or blender, process the shallots, garlic, chiles, lemongrass, and turmeric to a fine paste.)

MAKE THE DIP: Bring the coconut milk to a boil in a saucepan over high heat. Add the herb paste, shallots, and shrimp paste, stirring to combine. Reduce the heat to a rapid simmer and cook, stirring occasionally, until the mixture is reduced and fragrant and a thin layer of oil has emerged on the surface, around 15 minutes.

Reduce the heat to a simmer, add the palm sugar and torn makrut lime leaves, and cook, stirring occasionally, until the sugar has dissolved and the dip is fragrant and amalgamated, around 5 minutes. Taste, adjusting the seasoning if necessary; the dip should taste funky and salty, rich, sweet, and herbaceous, in that order.

Remove to a small serving bowl and garnish with the sliced makrut lime leaves and chiles. Serve warm or at room temperature with the platter of vegetables and long-grain rice.

OPPOSITE: A Thai-Style Dip of Shrimp Paste and Coconut Milk as made by Kaya Sumalee, Ban Sam Chong, Phang-Nga Province.

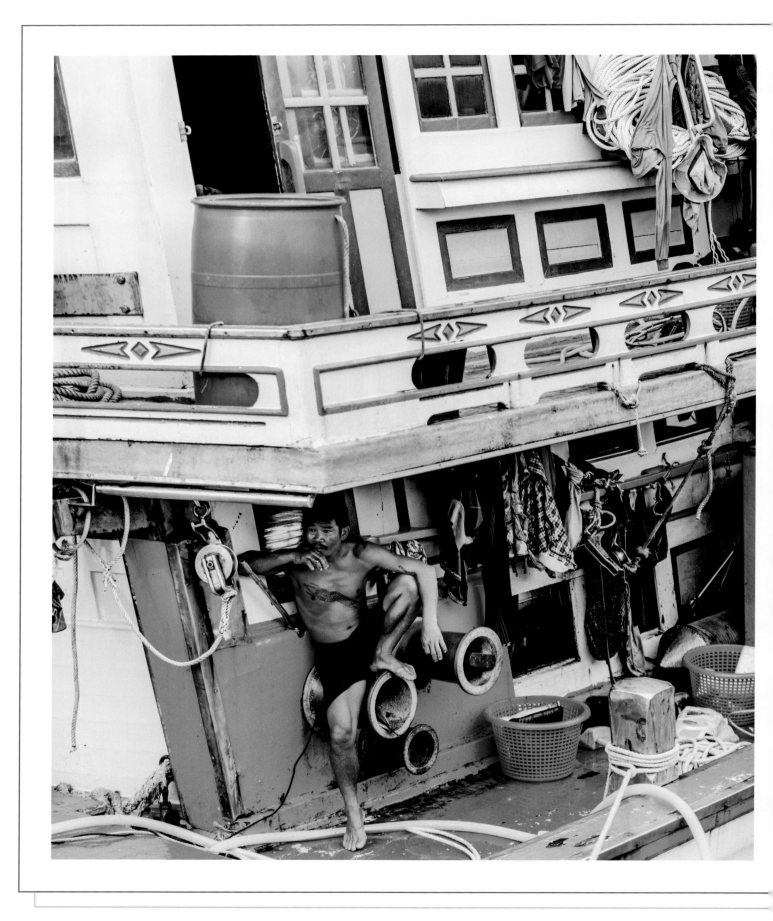

SEAFOOD SLAVERY

Visit Phuket's largest fishing pier, and you'll hear fishermen chatting openly in Khmer. The men unraveling the tangled nets on the docked boats wear the long skirt known as the *lungyi*, and the women sorting fish on shore have painted their cheeks yellow with the paste called *thanaka*—both easily identifiable markers of Burmese culture. There's little or no effort to conceal the fact that much of the workforce behind Thailand's $7 billion fishing industry is not, in fact, Thai. What's much less obvious is that some of these migrant workers are caught up in a modern form of slavery.

Compelled by the poverty they face at home and promises of money abroad, men and women in Myanmar and Cambodia pay brokers—essentially human traffickers—between $600 and $1,000 to deliver them to Thailand for work. They may have been offered jobs on farms or in factories. Instead, when they arrive in Thailand, they find that they have been duped into working in the fishing industry there. Some are "sold" to unscrupulous captains for large sums of money, which they are expected to pay back via their labors, finding themselves in a form of indentured servitude. As part of a 2012 investigation by journalist Patrick Winn, one fishing crew member said, "Once a captain is tired of a [captive], he's sold to another captain for profit. A guy can be out there for ten years just getting sold over and over."

Many of these foreign workers are virtually imprisoned on "ghost ships," small trawlers that are unregistered and that rarely return to shore. Some laborers assert that they've gone years without setting foot on land. Others describe workdays of eighteen to twenty hours, along with beatings and other physical abuse.

Some say they have witnessed much worse: "Years ago, I saw an entire foreign crew shot dead," Da, a Thai fisherman, told Winn. "There were fourteen of them. They'd been out to sea for five years straight without compensation. The boss didn't want to pay up, so he lined them up on the side of the boat and shot them one by one."

Because of the immense scale of Thailand's fishing industry—it's the second-largest supplier of seafood to the U.S.—it's possible that the fish on your table may have arrived as a result of such practices. A 2014 report by the *Guardian* found that seafood that had been procured by slaves was being sold by some of the world's largest retailers, including Walmart, Carrefour, Costco, and Tesco. This can take the form of shrimp or mackerel caught in Thailand's waters, but it may also be found in less obvious products, such as dog food, which can include the seafood bycatch known as "trash fish."

These reports have put Thailand in the international spotlight, and the threat of sanctions by the EU and U.S. has led to the creation of an industry body meant to lend more transparency to the fishing process, as well as a swath of reforms by the Thai government. But according to a 2018 report by the *Guardian*, little has changed, with many of the reforms being described as merely cosmetic.

The complicity of the Thai authorities and the fondness of Western consumers for cheap seafood have undoubtedly contributed to the status quo. But it can be argued that the key to change lies with retailers, who have the upper hand in demanding more transparency regarding how their products were caught and prepared. Until they decide to do this, it's likely that slavery will persist in Thailand's waters.

OPPOSITE: A fisherman at Phuket's largest pier.

ABOVE: Saengjan Chuaykoet prepares salted eggs in her factory in Chaiya, Surat Thani Province.
OPPOSITE: Salted duck eggs, Chaiya, Surat Thani Province.

From Sea to Salted Eggs

Chaiya, in Surat Thani Province, is little more than two parallel streets bordered by a string of old wooden shophouses and a sleepy train station. Located about five miles from the Gulf of Thailand, it has long been a destination for Chinese immigrants, who originally arrived via sea, bringing with them both domesticated ducks and novel ways of food preservation, two elements that have contributed to the town's most famous culinary export.

"Salted eggs are Chinese," asserts Saengjan Chuaykoet, who, along with her sister, is the third generation to produce the ingredient in Chaiya. "It was a way of preserving food."

On the surface, salted eggs might seem a distinctly landlubber dish, but they owe much to the ocean. In addition to probably having arrived in Thailand with Chinese sailors, salted eggs were, initially at least, prepared directly in the sea itself.

"In the old days, people used to bury the eggs in sand in mangrove forests," Saengjan tells me. We are talking in her home factory, a slightly lopsided wooden structure near the train tracks, where she and her sister preserve thousands of eggs by hand every day. "My grandma started preserving them in soil; they're not as salty, and they can be kept longer."

Saengjan and her sister have strayed little from their grandparents' technique. Every day, the pair takes fresh local duck eggs and coats them in a mixture of coarse sea salt, water, and the almost powder-like fine soil from toppled termite mounds. Why termite mounds? I wonder aloud. "Normal dirt doesn't stick to the eggs," says Saengjan matter-of-factly. (She adds that duck, rather than chicken, eggs are favored for this treatment because of their richer yolks and thicker shells.)

Encased in their muddy jackets, the eggs are layered in rice husk ash to separate and protect them, then boxed up. Wait two weeks, and you have subtly salty eggs with just-firm yolks that can be fried, sunny-side up, as the locals do; they're also excellent when steamed on a bed of minced, seasoned pork. Wait three weeks, and you have eggs with lively though not overwhelming salty whites and firm, just-salty yolks. Hard-boiled and quartered, their salinity countered via lime juice and sugar, slices of onion, chile, and Chinese celery, they are the basis of one of Thailand's favorite late-night snacks.

"It's not complicated," Saengjan tells me. "Just soil, salt, and water. The most important thing is the eggs."

She offers me a hard-boiled salted egg, sliced in half directly through the shell. "Eat a bit of the yolk with the white," she urges. "It won't taste too salty that way."

That bite combined a white with none of the overwhelming salinity or unpleasant chalkiness of lesser-quality salted eggs and a yolk with a deep orange color and a rich, rather than salty, flavor—a delicious and unexpected union of land, sea, migration, and preservation.

Simple Salted Eggs
Khai Khem
ไข่เค็ม

Chaiya's salted eggs are unique and beloved because of the diet of the ducks that produce them, which results in particularly rich yolks, and the unique way the eggs are preserved, which allows the salt to penetrate them slowly. Most likely you don't have access to ducks that are fed a seafood-heavy diet, nor to the soil from termite mounds, so the next best thing is salting eggs in brine. This method results in eggs with a less subtle salinity (and, depending on the duck eggs you have access to, probably less rich yolks) but that can still be used in a variety of recipes.

If you can't get duck eggs, chicken eggs can also be brine-salted as described below, although their thinner shells and less rich yolks mean that it takes only a week of brining to achieve the salinity and richness required in dishes such as Squid Fried with Salted Egg Yolk (page 304). Two weeks of brining, and you can boil the eggs and use them in a Salted-Egg Salad (page 303). More than two weeks in brine, though, and it's likely that chicken eggs will be unpleasantly salty.

Makes 4 to 6 salted eggs

125 g table salt
4 to 6 duck eggs

Bring 4 cups (1 L) water and the salt to a boil in a saucepan over high heat. Remove from the heat and stir to ensure that the salt is dissolved. Allow the brine to cool to room temperature.

While the water is cooling, wash the eggs thoroughly. When the brine has reached room temperature, combine the water and eggs in a sealable container and set aside at room temperature.

After 1 week, the egg whites will be semi-firm, almost pudding-like in texture, and barely salty in flavor, and the yolks will be just starting to become firm. After 2 weeks, the whites will be slightly more gelatinous and subtly salty, and the yolks will have an exterior that is just starting to firm up, with a texture like a bonbon and a subtly salty flavor (at this stage, the eggs are ideal for being fried, sunny-side up, or used in dishes such as Squid Fried with Salted Egg Yolk). After 3 weeks, the whites should be relatively gelatinous and pleasantly salty, and the yolks firm to the touch and slightly salty in flavor (at this stage, the eggs can be boiled and used in a Salted-Egg Salad). After 3 or 4 weeks of brining, depending on how salty you like your eggs, rinse any eggs you have not used of brine and put them in the refrigerator, where they can be kept for weeks longer. Brining for longer than 4 weeks will most likely result in unpleasantly salty eggs.

Making salted duck eggs, Chaiya, Surat Thani Province.

Salted-Egg Salad
Yam Khai Khem
ยำไข่เค็ม

This salad based on salted eggs is one of Thailand's most beloved dishes, a staple of the late-night Thai-Chinese–run eateries known as *khaao tom kui*. Its bold flavors mean that it's a common counterpart to Thai beer or rice booze. It's also eminently flexible: Out of onions? Use shallots. No lime juice? Use vinegar. Don't like spicy? Omit the chiles.

Serves 4

4 uncooked Simple Salted Eggs (page 302)
3 tablespoons lime juice
2 teaspoons fish sauce
1 heaping teaspoon white sugar
¼ medium onion (50 g), peeled and sliced lengthwise
2 stalks Chinese celery (30 g total), leafy parts only, chopped
4 medium spicy fresh chiles (10 g total), sliced thin

PREPARE THE SALTED EGGS: Bring a small saucepan of water to a boil, add the eggs, and boil for 10 minutes. Remove the eggs and immediately transfer to a bowl of ice-cold water. Leave them in the ice water for 15 minutes (this will make the eggs easier to peel).

Drain the eggs, peel, and quarter lengthwise. Set aside.

PREPARE THE DRESSING: Combine the lime juice, fish sauce, and sugar in a small bowl, stirring until the sugar has dissolved. Taste and adjust the seasoning if necessary; if the salted eggs are particularly salty, you may want to increase the sugar and/or lime juice.

MAKE THE SALAD: Combine the salted eggs, onion, Chinese celery, chiles, and dressing in a bowl. Toss gently to coat the ingredients with the dressing.

Remove to a small serving plate and serve the salad on its own or with long-grain rice.

Salted-Egg Salad as served at a restaurant in Surat Thani.

303

Squid Fried with Salted Egg Yolk
Plaa Muek Phat Khai Khem
ปลาหมึกผัดไข่เค็ม

This stir-fry of hearty rings of squid and salted egg yolks is a staple of seafood restaurants across the country. Dew Tharaphong, the chef/owner of Ratri Seafood, just outside Chaiya, boosts the dish's innate richness by adding ingredients such as oyster sauce, milk, and *naam phrik phao*, a condiment of deep-fried dried chiles sometimes known as Thai chile jam.

Serves 4 as part of a southern Thai meal

400 g medium whole squid

2 uncooked salted duck eggs (see Note)

2 teaspoons fish sauce

2 teaspoons oyster sauce

1 teaspoon white sugar

1 tablespoon milk

1 teaspoon Thai chile jam (naam phrik phao; see Glossary)

1 teaspoon oil reserved from the chile jam or vegetable oil

4 cloves garlic (40 g total), peeled and minced

½ medium onion (100 g), peeled and sliced lengthwise

2 stalks scallions (20 g total), cut into 2-inch pieces

2 large mild fresh chiles (50 g total), sliced on a bias

Commercially available salted duck eggs are generally already hard-boiled, which means the yolks will be solid and crumbly, not the desired texture for this recipe. If you don't have access to uncooked salted eggs, follow the recipe for Simple Salted Eggs (page 302) and use the eggs after they have been brined for 2 weeks. If you opt to go with fully salted eggs (that is, after 3 weeks of brining), you will most likely have to adjust the salty seasonings in this recipe.

When using Thai chile jam, be sure to include some of the oil, which will contribute to the dish's richness and fragrance.

PREPARE THE SQUID: Remove and discard the skin, eyes, beaks, and then the clear bones from the squid. Slice the squid bodies into rings around 1 inch wide and halve the tentacles lengthwise. Set aside.

PREPARE THE SALTED EGGS AND SEASONINGS: Crack the salted eggs open and discard the whites. Combine the yolks, fish sauce, oyster sauce, sugar, milk, and chile jam in a bowl. Whisk with a fork until the yolks are distributed and the mixture has the consistency of a thick salad dressing. Set aside.

COOK THE SQUID: Heat the oil in a wok over high heat. When it is smoking, add the squid, garlic, and onion and sear, without stirring, for around 1 minute. Then stir so the moisture that emerges from the squid can evaporate, around 30 seconds. Add the egg mixture, stirring to combine, and cook until the yolks are just set, around 15 seconds. Add the scallions and chiles and cook, stirring occasionally, until the ingredients are thoroughly combined, the dish has a relatively dry texture, and the chiles are just starting to get tender, around 30 seconds. Taste, adjusting the seasoning if necessary; the dish should taste rich and mild, subtly sweet, and salty, with a pleasant crunch from the onions and chiles.

Remove to a serving plate and serve hot with long-grain rice.

OPPOSITE: Squid Fried with Salted Egg Yolk as prepared by Dew Tharaphong, the chef/owner of Ratri Seafood outside Chaiya, Surat Thani Province.

Nipa Palm Vinegar

DESPITE HIS SEVENTY-FIVE YEARS, Kowit Jantharangsee welcomes visitors to his nipa palm plantation in the Pak Phanang District of Nakhon Si Thammarat Province with youthful enthusiasm. Standing knee-deep in mud, he hacks at nipa palm branches with a machete to demonstrate how to tap the palms for sugar, before splitting open the basketball-sized fruit to offer guests a taste of what's inside.

Pak Phanang, where land and sea meet in the form of swamps and muddy mangrove forests, is the ideal environment for the nipa palm, which grows in dense, wet stands across the district. It has long, thick, woody branches with intimidating spikes and massive fruit. It also has an astounding number of uses: its branches are used to build walls and roofs; the leaves can be dried and turned into cigarette papers, roofing material, mats, or even a type of primitive raincoat;

the fruit-bearing stalks are tapped and their sweet sap fermented and made into sugar or alcohol; and its fruit can be eaten fresh or preserved in syrup. Yet if southern Thais associate nipa palms with a single product, it's vinegar.

"We've been making vinegar from nipa palms for hundreds of years, since our early ancestors," Kowit tells me. He explains that the vinegar is made from naturally fermented nipa palm syrup, with no added sugars or yeasts, and that it is added to soups, noodle dishes, or dips. "People from our generation prefer this type of vinegar; we don't like the commercial stuff. It's sweeter, more fragrant." To prove his point, he gestures at a rustic ceramic jar and offers me a taste of raw nipa palm vinegar. It is cloudy, yeasty, heady, funky, tart, and sugary all at the same time, a mix of tastes and aromas that could seemingly only stem from this unique plant and place.

OPPOSITE: Kowit Jantharangsee holds tools used to tap nipa palms in his plantation in Pak Phanang District, Nakhon Si Thammarat Province.
ABOVE: Bottles of nipa palm vinegar made by Kowit Jantharangsee, Pak Phanang District, Nakhon Si Thammarat Province.

MAKING NIPA PALM VINEGAR

Kowit Jantharangsee, who oversees a nipa palm plantation in a rural district of Nakhon Si Thammarat Province, produces vinegar via the following steps:

1 When a nipa palm with a mature fruit is located, the fruit-bearing branch is beaten with a rubber-coated mallet exactly fifty times every two days for a total of nine times to encourage the sap to flow. Each round of beating is indicated by a mark scratched on the trunk of the palm.

2 When the branch is sufficiently bruised, the fruit is cut off it, and the fresh cut is covered with mud and left overnight.

3 In the morning, the mud-covered section is sliced off and exposed; a bamboo tube is hung below the cut to collect the dripping sap. The next morning, yet another cut is made, and that afternoon, the sap is harvested.

4 The sap is strained and transferred to ceramic jars, where it ferments for 15 to 20 days. The vinegar is then filtered through a cloth and bottled.

A Soup of Gray Mullet, Turmeric, and Nipa Palm Vinegar

Tom Som Plaa Krabawk

ต้มส้มปลากระบอก

"If you're measuring ingredients, it's a waste of time!"

This from Anna Ngoenthuam, the cook at an excellent curry stall in Nakhon Si Thammarat, who provided this recipe. I, on the other hand, encourage you to measure ingredients when making the dish, a southern Thai staple that gets its yellow hue from fresh turmeric and its distinctive tart/sweet flavor from nipa palm vinegar. But I'd also ask you to consider these measurements as a jumping-off point, using your own sense of taste to tweak the amounts and arrive at a balance of the tastes that Anna associates with the dish ("I like it to have all three flavors—sweet, tart, and salty—but sour at the front.") and those you prefer.

Serves 4 as part of a southern Thai meal

FOR THE CHICKEN STOCK

1 chicken carcass, skin and fat removed
½ medium onion
1 clove garlic

FOR THE SOUP

6 shallots (60 g total), peeled and bruised
4 cloves garlic (20 g total), peeled and bruised
4 stalks lemongrass (100 g total; see page 19 for instructions on how to prepare lemongrass for a soup)
3 fingers fresh turmeric (45 g total), peeled and bruised
1½ teaspoons fish sauce
1 teaspoon table salt
20 g palm sugar
¼ cup (60 ml) nipa palm vinegar (see Note)
3 small gray mullet (around 500 g total), scaled and gutted

6 medium spicy fresh chiles (20 g total), bruised
4 makrut lime leaves, torn

In southern Thailand, this would be made with small gray mullet that are used head and all. If you can only find larger mullet, cut them into steaks around 1 inch thick.

Nipa palm vinegar is a common ingredient in Filipino cooking, where it's known as *sukang sasa* or *sukang nipa*; look for it at Filipino markets. Otherwise, use regular white vinegar and add a bit more sugar to mimic the slightly sweet, yeasty flavor of nipa palm vinegar.

UP TO 5 DAYS IN ADVANCE, PREPARE THE CHICKEN STOCK: Combine 5 cups (1.2 L) water, the chicken carcass, onion, and garlic in a stockpot and bring to a boil over high heat. Reduce the heat and simmer for 15 minutes.

Remove from the heat and strain the stock into a bowl; discard the solids. If making it in advance, remove the stock to an airtight container and store in the refrigerator.

MAKE THE SOUP: Bring 4 cups (1 L) of chicken stock to a boil in a saucepan over high heat. Add the shallots, garlic, lemongrass, and turmeric and reduce the heat to a rapid simmer. Add the fish sauce, salt, palm sugar, and nipa palm vinegar and bring to a simmer. Add the mullet and chiles, bring to a simmer, and simmer until the fish is cooked through when tested with a fork, around 2 minutes. Taste, adjusting the seasoning if necessary; the soup should pleasantly tart, followed close behind by sweet, with a subtle, pleasing aroma from the lemongrass and turmeric. Add the chiles and makrut lime leaves and remove the soup from the heat.

Remove to a serving bowl and serve hot or at room temperature with long-grain rice.

OPPOSITE: A Soup of Gray Mullet, Turmeric, and Nipa Palm Vinegar as prepared by Anna Ngoenthuam, the chef at Khaao Kaeng Sawng Naam, a curry stall in Nakhon Si Thammarat.

A Seafood Feast

IF YOU'VE VISITED THAILAND'S SOUTH, most likely you've eaten at a seafood restaurant. Does this mean you've tasted southern food? Well, not exactly. Although these restaurants take advantage of the region's fish and shellfish and may feature a dish or two of southern origin, the vast majority of the dishes served at southern Thailand's seafood-centric restaurants are central Thai—or, more accurately, Chinese—in origin. Think grilled squid served with a spicy, tart dipping sauce; fish deep-fried whole and drizzled with a sweet/tart dressing; rice fried with chunks of crab; and soups brimming with fist-sized prawns. You'll find relatively few chiles and even less turmeric and black pepper at a Thai seafood restaurant, but even if the menu isn't necessarily regional, in recent decades, the dishes they serve have come to be associated with the region. And, perhaps most important, they're undeniably tasty and fun.

The following recipes are courtesy of Peeratat Iansakulwet, the chef/owner of Rim Thalay Seafood, a restaurant in Nakhon Si Thammarat Province. If prepared together, they make a seafood dinner that touches on both seafood-shack staples and dishes with more southern influences.

OPPOSITE, CLOCKWISE FROM TOP RIGHt: Deep-Fried Kingfish Served with a Fish Sauce Dressing and Green Mango Salad; boiled cockles served with Seafood Dipping Sauce; Sweet Squid; and Deep-Fried Prawns in Tamarind Sauce; Rim Thalay Seafood, Nakhon Si Thammarat Province.

Deep-Fried Prawns in Tamarind Sauce

Kung Thawt Raat Sawt Makhaam

กุ้งทอดราดซอสมะขาม

Prawns deep-fried until crispy and golden and drizzled with a deliciously gooey/tart/sweet sauce: this formula will be familiar to anyone who's eaten at a Chinese restaurant in the U.S. or a seafood restaurant in Thailand's south.

Serves 4 as part of a Thai seafood meal

FOR THE TAMARIND SAUCE

75 g dried tamarind paste
100 g palm sugar
1 teaspoon fish sauce
½ teaspoon table salt

FOR THE DEEP-FRIED PRAWNS

600 g medium head-on prawns
4 cups (1 L) vegetable oil, or as needed
½ cup deep-frying flour (see Glossary)
6 shallots (60 g total), peeled and sliced
4 medium spicy dried chiles (2 g total)

PREPARE THE TAMARIND SAUCE: Bring 1 cup (245 ml) water to a boil in a saucepan over high heat. Remove the pan from the heat, add the dried tamarind paste, and mash with a spoon to combine. Cover and set aside for 15 minutes.

Strain the tamarind mixture through a sieve set over a bowl, pushing on the solids to extract as much of the pulp as possible; discard the solids. You should have around ¾ cup (180 ml) tamarind pulp.

Combine the tamarind pulp, palm sugar, fish sauce, salt, and 1 cup (250 ml) water in a saucepan and bring to a boil over high heat. Reduce the heat and simmer until the liquid is reduced by around half and is thick, syrupy, and concentrated, around 40 minutes. The sauce should taste equal parts tart and sweet, followed by salty. Adjust the seasoning if necessary and keep warm.

MAKE THE DISH: Remove the heads from the prawns (this should yield around 400 g headless prawns). Using kitchen shears, cut the shells of the prawns open down their backs, from the "neck" to the base of the tail. Set aside.

Add oil to a depth of 3 inches to a wok and heat to 350°F over medium-high heat. Coat half of the prawns with the deep-frying flour, shaking them in a sieve or colander to remove excess flour. Add the prawns to the oil and deep-fry until golden and cooked through, around 3 minutes. Remove and drain on paper towels. Repeat with the remaining prawns, working to maintain the oil at 350°F.

Coat the shallots with deep-frying flour, shaking them in a sieve or colander to remove excess flour. Add the shallots and dried chiles to the oil and deep-fry until golden and crispy, around 1 minute. Remove from the oil with a wire skimmer and drain on paper towels.

Remove the shrimp to a serving plate, drizzle with the warm sauce, and garnish with the deep-fried shallots and chiles. Serve hot or warm with long-grain rice.

Seafood Dipping Sauce
Naam Jim Siifuud
น้ำจิ้มซีฟู้ด

Order grilled or boiled seafood at a seafood shack in Thailand, and without having to ask, you'll receive a bowl of this spicy/tart condiment. Entire reputations hinge on a restaurant's seafood dipping sauce, and Peeratat Iansakulwet, the chef/owner of Rim Thalay Seafood, prides himself on making a version built around a light palm sugar syrup, one of the few ingredients that can stand up to seasonings as bold as raw garlic, fish sauce, and chiles. This balance, he tells me, makes it a perfect pairing for grilled squid or parboiled cockles. Or you may find yourself scooping it over white rice.

Serves 4 as part of a Thai seafood meal

100 g palm sugar
4 medium spicy fresh chiles (8 g total)
2 cloves garlic (10 g total), peeled
2 teaspoons lime juice
1½ teaspoons fish sauce

PREPARE THE PALM SUGAR SYRUP: Bring the palm sugar and ¼ cup (60 ml) water to a boil in a saucepan over medium-high heat. Reduce the heat and simmer until the sugar is dissolved and you have a light syrup, 2 or 3 minutes. Set aside to cool.

MAKE THE DIP: Process 2 tablespoons of the palm sugar syrup, the chiles, garlic, lime juice, fish sauce, and 1 tablespoon water to a uniform consistency in a blender or food processor. Taste, adjusting the seasoning if necessary; the dipping sauce should be equal parts tart and spicy, with a subtle sweetness and a pleasant aroma of garlic.

Serve at room temperature or chilled.

Sweet Squid
Muek Khai Tom Waan
หมึกไข่ต้มหวาน

Rim Thalay Seafood's signature dish is a bowl of tiny squid, fat with eggs, simmered in sugar with a splash of fish sauce.

"It's a way of preserving seafood—the dish can be kept for several days," explains Peeratat, the chef/owner, of the dish, which has its origins in the south.

The result is syrupy, savory, and tender, an intersection of sugar and seafood that, against the odds, works, especially as a counterpart to the typically more acidic and/or spicy dishes that constitute a Thai seafood meal.

Serves 4 as part of a Thai seafood meal

500 g small squid with eggs (see Note)
2 tablespoons light brown sugar
2 teaspoons fish sauce
Pinch of MSG (optional)

If your fishmonger doesn't have access to squid with eggs, ask for the smallest, most tender squid you can find.

Remove and discard the hard beaks and ink sacs from the squid. Score each squid a couple times on one side.

Combine the squid, sugar, fish sauce, and MSG (if using) in a wok and bring to a boil over medium high heat. Within the first minute or so, the squid will release a great deal of liquid; reduce the heat and maintain at a rapid simmer until most of the liquid has evaporated, leaving a syrupy sauce, and the squid have shrunk but are still tender, a total of around 7 minutes. Taste, adjusting the seasoning if necessary; the squid should taste sweet, followed by pleasantly fishy and salty.

Remove to a serving bowl and serve warm or at room temperature with long-grain rice.

Deep-Fried Kingfish Served with a Fish Sauce Dressing and Green Mango Salad

Plaa Insii Thawt Naam Plaa Kap Yam Mamuang
ปลาอินทรีทอดน้ำปลากับยำมะม่วง

Thick steaks of kingfish, marinated in a fish sauce–based dressing and deep-fried, are a staple of seafood restaurants across Thailand. Peeratat Iansakulwet's version is served a little differently.

"It was our idea to have the dressing on the side," he says. "If you marinate the fish in fish sauce, it turns dark and doesn't look very nice. Also, people can decide how much dressing they want."

I encourage you to try it this way too, serving the fish, in typical Thai-style, with a bright, crunchy salad of shredded green mangoes but with the dressing on the side for dipping. The result is a dish that spans just about every flavor and texture.

Serves 4 as part of a Thai seafood meal

FOR THE FISH SAUCE DRESSING

2 teaspoons fish sauce
5 g palm sugar
½ teaspoon oyster sauce
½ teaspoon light soy sauce
1 dried shiitake mushroom (2 g), soaked in warm water until soft, drained, and sliced
1 large mild fresh red chile (25 g), sliced

FOR THE GREEN MANGO SALAD

2 tablespoons lime juice
2 teaspoons fish sauce
2 teaspoons white sugar
1 small semi-tart green mango (250 g)
1 small carrot (75 g)
6 shallots (60 g total), peeled and sliced thin
6 medium spicy fresh chiles (12 g total), sliced thin
40 g roasted cashews

FOR THE DEEP-FRIED KINGFISH

4 cups (1 L) vegetable oil, or as needed
3 or 4 approximately ¾-inch-thick kingfish steaks (450 g total)

The salad relies on semi-tart, green mango; if you only have access to tart green mangoes, reduce the amount of lime juice in the dressing. This salad would pair well with just about any grilled or deep-fried fish.

For convenient and uniform shredding and strands of mango with the requisite crunchy texture, use a mandoline; a box grater will result in strands that are too thin.

MAKE THE FISH SAUCE DRESSING: Combine the fish sauce, palm sugar, oyster sauce, light soy sauce, and ½ cup (125 ml) water in a saucepan and bring to a boil over medium-high heat. Reduce the heat and simmer until the sugar has dissolved and the liquid is slightly reduced, around 1 minute.

Remove from the heat and add the shiitake mushroom and chile. Taste, adjusting the seasoning if necessary; the dressing should taste equal parts savory and salty, with just enough sweetness to make it feel balanced. Set aside.

MAKE THE GREEN MANGO SALAD: Combine the lime juice, fish sauce, and sugar in a bowl and stir to ensure that the sugar dissolves. Set aside.

Peel and shred the green mango into strands roughly equivalent in thickness and width to linguine; reserve 100 g of shredded mango for the salad. Peel and shred the carrot; reserve 50 g of shredded carrot for the salad.

Combine the shredded mango, shredded carrot, shallots, chiles, cashews, and the lime juice dressing in a bowl and stir well. Taste, adjusting the seasoning if necessary; the salad should taste tart, followed by sweet and spicy, and it should be crunchy from the mango, carrot, and cashews. Set aside.

DEEP-FRY THE KINGFISH: Add oil to a depth of 3 inches to a wok and heat to 350°F over medium-high heat. Add 1 or 2 kingfish steaks and deep-fry, flipping occasionally, until golden and crispy on the exterior but still white, tender, and moist inside, around 5 minutes. Remove and drain on paper towels. Repeat with the remaining kingfish steaks, working to maintain the oil at 350°F.

Transfer the kingfish steaks to a serving plate, the fish sauce dressing to a small serving bowl, and the green mango salad to a medium serving bowl. Serve the fish hot or at room temperature with long-grain rice.

Diners eat dinner at a seafood restaurant on Ko Yao Noi, Phang-Nga Province.

Lalita Pulsil holds a rehydrated bird's nest in Thai Aroon Royal Bird's Nest, the shop she owns in Hat Yai.

IN SEARCH OF BIRDS' NESTS

In 2007, I received something of a dream assignment: I was asked to assist photographer Éric Valli, one of several photojournalists invited to Thailand to contribute to a book called *Thailand: Nine Days in the Kingdom*. For the project, Éric wanted to revisit the story he had done for *National Geographic* in 1990, "The Nest Gatherers of Tiger Cave," in which he documented the lives of birds' nest gatherers working in caves in Phang-Nga Bay in southern Thailand.

The men Éric documented then and again in 2007 spent their days in search of nests built by swiftlets, a bird native to Southeast Asia. The pale, plastic-looking nests are made from the hardened saliva of the birds, who build them on the walls of island-bound caves in the bay. The nests are considered both a delicacy and a medicine by the Chinese, who eat them in a soup. Because of their rarity and the effort it takes to gather them, swiftlet nests are incredibly expensive, sometimes selling for more than $2,000 per kilogram. Yet scientists have been unable to confirm the alleged health benefits of the nests, and environmentalists claim that the industry has had a negative impact on swiftlet reproduction, with populations in some regions having decreased dramatically.

To harvest swiftlet nests, the gatherers of Phang-Nga Bay, almost exclusively Muslims from the island of Ko Yao, relied on a complicated and seemingly haphazard network of bamboo scaffolding and bridges. The towers were sometimes hundreds of feet high, and the gatherers climbed them barefoot, jamming their toes into the knots like steps. In places where the use of scaffolding was not possible, the gatherers relied on bunches of vines, which they scaled like crude ladders, and, occasionally, rope, to reach the nests. Because the swiftlets built their nests in the highest, most remote corners of the caves, away from the reach of predators such as snakes and large insects, this infrastructure took the gatherers only part of the way, and they had to use incredibly long bamboo poles to pry the nests from the cave walls. In 2007, the gatherers were equipped with contemporary climbing harnesses and battery-powered headlamps, both of which were originally introduced by Éric. But back in the late eighties, they didn't use any safety equipment at all, and for light they relied on fiber torches that they gripped in their teeth.

Every day for a week, Éric and I would wake up before dawn and hop on a long-tailed boat that would take us to a different cave. As the nests are such a valuable commodity, the caves are controlled by competing interests and are protected by armed guards; to gain access, we first had to get the blessing of a local middleman, who we knew only as Apishat. Because of the high stakes and security, Éric suspects that we are probably among the only outsiders, Thai or foreign, to have climbed in these caves with these people.

In 2007, Éric was documenting the next generation of nest gatherers, in particular one named Sun, who at the time was thirty. Sun seemed utterly fearless, effortlessly scaling hundreds of feet on rickety bamboo towers, using his safety harness only when stationary, and he was one of the most talented natural athletes I'd ever seen. Yet despite the risks involved in the work and the value of his harvest, Sun and the other gatherers were essentially little more than manual laborers, earning very little money and living hand to mouth.

In the years since that assignment, I have lost contact with Sun, and Éric tells me that recent conflict among the interests that control the various caves means that they are currently off-limits to outsiders. In the decade and a half since we were last in the caves, there's also been a massive change in the birds' nest industry. As income has increased in China, so has demand for birds' nests, and these days the nests tend to come from a much more logistically friendly source: land-bound, ersatz caves known colloquially as "bird condos." To witness this phenomenon, I drive to Pak Phanang, in Nakhon Si Thammarat Province, a city thought to have Thailand's highest density of bird condos.

From a distance, Pak Phanang has a disproportionately tall skyline for such a small town. A closer look reveals a jagged, jarring, almost post-apocalyptic cityscape of featureless, blocky structures, some as high as nine stories, most almost entirely devoid of windows, doors, and paint, making brutalist architecture

A boat drives by a limestone island where birds's nests are gathered, Railay, Krabi Province.

A motorcylist passes by a so-called "bird condo," Pak Phanang, Nakhon Si Thammarat Province.

look warm and cozy by contrast. Most of the buildings appear to have been built from the ground up as bird condos, taking the form of sheer walls with hundreds of golf ball–sized holes that allow access to birds and air. In other cases, it appears that peoples' homes have been renovated—doors and windows bricked over, some sporting multistory extensions built directly above the homes (some of which, in fact, are still inhabited by humans). I park my car to get a closer look, and up close, the bird condos emit a distinctly cavernous, moldy, mildewy, poopy aroma, not to mention a constant soundtrack of bird chirping, piped out from loudspeakers in an effort to attract more swiftlets.

"I wouldn't want to own a bird condo," says Lalita Pulsil, the owner of Thai Aroon Royal Bird's Nest in Hat Yai. "It's a lot of work."

It's a few days later, and I am in southern Thailand's largest city to learn what happens to the nests after they're gathered. Thai Aroon Royal Bird's Nest is a typical example of the type of shop that sells this unique commodity. The ground floor consists of a showroom with brightly lit displays of birds' nests of varying quality and price—all of which Lalita purchases from bird

condos across southern Thailand—and bird nest–derived products, as well as a couple of tables where one can enjoy a bowl of birds' nest soup. Upstairs, in two clinical-feeling, air-conditioned rooms, teams of women wearing PPC-like white outfits sit at desks, using tweezers to pluck impurities and debris—mostly minuscule feathers—from limp, rehydrated birds' nests. The nests will be sorted for quality, given a deep cleaning if needed, and dried, and then are ready for sale and/or consumption.

I ask Lalita to describe what defines a good-quality birds' nest.

"People like nests with long threads," she tells me. "The best are whole nests that aren't broken or have holes; these are the most expensive."

She invites me to try a bowl of soup, and she selects a finger-sized quarter moon of a nest that weighs three grams. She soaks it in water for around twenty minutes, explaining that this will cause it to expand in mass by nearly ten times. Then she removes the nest from the water, rinses it, and simmers it in a cup or so of plain water for two or three minutes, until, as she says, the noodle-like strands are pleasantly "slippery." She supplements the soup with a couple of syrup-preserved jujubes and gingko nuts and hands it to me. I have a taste, and the flavor is so subtle it nearly escapes me, an almost imperceptible savory taste with a gelatinous, seaweed-like crunch. I catch myself wondering if I'm missing something or if I am a birds' nest philistine, when, seemingly reading my expression, Lalisa says, "It's actually very bland; it has little taste or flavor. People add things to the soup to give it flavor."

Save for a hint of supplemented sweetness, what is ostensibly one of the world's most expensive foods has all the flavor of a hospital broth. I shrug this thought off and finish the bowl, feeling grateful for those jujubes, focusing instead on all that went into this bizarre bowl—while also secretly hoping for the health benefits.

OPPOSITE, ABOVE: An employee removes impurities from a bird's nest, Thai Aroon Royal Bird's Nest, Hat Yai.
OPPOSITE, BELOW: A bowl of bird's nest soup, Thai Aroon Royal Bird's Nest, Hat Yai.
ABOVE: Dried birds' nests being sorted at Thai Aroon Royal Bird's Nest, Hat Yai.

Novice monks sit down for lunch, Trang Province.

Resources

THE FOLLOWING are some the books, websites, and other resources, both in English and Thai, that helped to guide my way around the history, culinary culture, ingredients, and dishes of southern Thailand.

For more general introductions to Thai food, consider *Pok Pok: Food and Stories from the Streets, Homes, and Roadside Restaurants of Thailand*, by Andy Ricker with JJ Goode; *Simple Thai Food: Classic Recipes from the Thai Home Kitchen*, by Leela Punyaratabandhu; or *Thai Food*, by David Thompson.

BOOKS IN ENGLISH

Baker, Chris, and Pasuk Phongpaichit. *A History of Thailand*, Port Melbourne, Australia: Cambridge University Press, 2005.

Mackay, Colin. *A History of Phuket and the Surrounding Region*, Bangkok: White Lotus, 2013.

Munro-Hay, Stuart. *Nakhon Sri Thammarat: The Archeology, History, and Legends of a Southern Thai Town*, Bangkok: White Lotus, 2001.

Osborne, Milton. *Southeast Asia: An Introductory History*, Chiang Mai, Thailand: Silkworm Books, 1997.

Ricker, Andy, with JJ Goode. *Pok Pok: Food and Stories from the Streets, Homes, and Roadside Restaurants of Thailand*, Berkeley, CA: Ten Speed Press, 2013.

Syukri, Ibrahim, translated by Conner Bailey and John N. Miksic. *The Malay Kingdom of Patani*, Chiang Mai, Thailand: Silkworm Books, 1985.

Thompson, David. *Thai Food*, Berkeley, CA: Ten Speed Press, 2002.

Van Der Cruysse, Dirk, translated by Michael Smithies. *Siam & The West: 1500–1700*, Chiang Mai, Thailand: Silkworm Books, 2002.

Various authors. *Early Metallurgy, Trade, and Urban Centres in Thailand and Southeast Asia*, Bangkok: White Lotus, 1992.

Wyatt, David K. *Thailand: A Short History*, Chiang Mai, Thailand: Silkworm Books, 2004.

BOOKS IN THAI

ข้าวแกงปักษ์ใต้ ชนิรัตน์ สำเร็จ สำนักพิมพ์แสงแดด 2557

ครัวปักษ์ใต้ สำนักพิมพ์แสงแดด 2547

คู่มืออาหารรสไทยแท้จังหวัดสงขลา สำนักงานพัฒนาชุมชนจังหวัดสงขลา

OPPOSITE: A rural scene outside of Phatthalung.

ครัวย่าหยา นวพร เรืองสกุล สารคดี 2562

ตำราอาหารสยามอันดามันสากลนิยม สารานุกรม
วัฒนธรรมและอาหารจังหวัดสตูล วิทยาลัยชุมชนสตูล
2555

ผักพื้นบ้านภาคใต้ สถาบันการแพทย์แผนไทย 2542

เมนู ปัตตานี จังหวัดปัตตานี ร่วมกับ สมาคมธุรกิจอาหาร
จังหวัดปัตตานี 2561

เมนู สตูล จังหวัดสตูล

ร้านนี้ อร่อยที่ ตรัง & ภูเก็ต สิรินทร์ วงศ์พานิช สำนัก
พิมพ์วงกลม

อาหารใต้ อาจารย์นิภา นโมการ และ อาจารย์จงทิพย์
อธิมุตติสรรค์ สำนักพิมพ์แม่บ้าน 2544

อาหารปักษ์ใต้ บาบ๋า ยาหยา ในอันดามัน อาจารย์เมฆาณี
จงบุญเรือ และ อาจารย์สมพิศ คลี่ขยาย สำนักพิมพ์เศรษฐ
ศิลป์ 2556

อาหารมุสลิม บรรณาธิการบริหาร นิตดา หงส์วิวัฒน์
สำนักพิมพ์แสงแดด 2547

อาหารอัตลักษณ์มลายู-ไทย รองศาสตราจารย์ ดี. วินัย คะห์
ลัน ศูนย์วิทยาศาสตร์ฮาลาลจุฬาลงกรณ์มหาวิทยาลัย 2553

OTHER RESOURCES

Graham, Benjamin. "Bird's Nest Soup Is More
Popular Than Ever, Thanks to Swiftlet House
Farms," www.audubon.org, October 2017.

Local Snacks of Phuket: www.wongnai.com/food
-tips/local-snacks-of-phuket

Office of the National Economic and Social
Development Council

Phuket Cuisine: phuketcuisine.com

Phuket Local Foods: www.phuketlocalfoods.com/
th-home

Thai Hua Museum, Phuket Town

Tourist Information Center, Phuket Town

CREDITS

Some of the text and images in "Cracking the Nut"
were originally featured in the July 2018 print
edition of *Saveur* in "Under the Palms."

Some of the text and photos in "From Sea to Salted
Eggs" were featured in the March 2021 edition of
Whetstone magazine's *W Journal* in an article of the
same name.

Some of the quotes and photos in "Hunting with
Thailand's Sea People" were originally featured in a
2021 CNN Travel article titled "After Centuries of
Nomadic Living, Thailand's 'Sea People' Adapt to
Life on Land."

A NOTE ABOUT PHOTOGRAPHY

All the food images in this book were shot on
location, where they were prepared in southern
Thailand, not in a studio. My primary camera
is a Nikon D800; many of the dishes were
photographed with a Nikon 60mm f/2.8 macro lens,
and when artificial lighting was necessary, I used a
Nikon SB-900 speedlight shot through a softbox.

Acknowledgments

Thank you (in chronological order) to JJ Goode, once again, for his help in the proposal process, as well as for introducing me to Melanie Tortoroli and W. W. Norton & Company; to Melanie Tortoroli for her smart, insightful feedback and for allowing me to make the book I set out to make; to Andy Ricker for his friendship, support, and immensely helpful recipe feedback; to Christopher Wise for being a travel companion and for lending his talented hand at the photo editing; to Candice Lin for her beautiful illustrations; to Jason Lang for taking the bio photo; and to Annabel Brazaitis for her work on the manuscript.

Thanks also to the following people across Thailand who contributed recipes, information, and guidance:

Adam Jeh-Uma, Pattani Province

Aisamaae Tokoi, Luukrieang, Yala Province

Anna Ngoenthuam, Khao Kaeng Sawng Naam restaurant, Nakhon Si Thammarat Province

Aree Atthan, Ban Sam Chong, Phang-Nga Province

Arjin Pornsinsiriruk, Sin Jiw restaurant, Trang Province

Bussaba Butdee, Ko Yao Noi, Phang-Nga Province

Chaiwat Chantrawibulkul, Ko La restaurant, Phuket Province

Cheusman Chetahey, Maksu Soup Chormalee restaurant, Pattani Province

Dew Tharaphong, Ratri Seafood restaurant, Surat Thani Province

Duangporn Bodart, Phatthalung Province

Dusit Roengsamot, Ko Yao Noi, Phang-Nga Province

Farida Klanarong, Barahom Barzar restaurant, Pattani Province

Farida Satsadiphan, Thai Islam Pochana restaurant, Yala Province

Hameedah Cheuma, Baan Nasi Dagae restaurant, Pattani Province

Hook Klathalay, Moo Ko Surin, Phang-Nga Province

Jaran Leangjirakan, Ranong Province

Jaruwee Jutikamol, Khrua Laa Lang restaurant, Nakhon Si Thammarat Province

Jutharat Birangrot, Satun Province

Kanitha Salim, Baan Suan Lang Sard restaurant, Ko Samui, Surat Thani Province

Katesiree Chanaphon, Yala Province

Kaya Sumalee, Ban Sam Chong, Phang-Nga Province

Ketsuda Thepsuda, Ban Lam Khanun, Trang Province

Khanaporn Janjirdsak, Trang Ko'e restaurant, Trang Province

Ko Jiw restaurant, Trang Province

Kowit Jantharangsee, Pak Phanang, Nakhon Si Thammarat Province

Kritsada Janyathiti, Burapha Bird Nest, Bangkok

Kularb Jetsadavun, Raya restaurant, Phuket Province

Lalita Pulsil, Thai Aroon Royal Bird's Nest restaurant, Songkhla Province

Lena Bumiller, Moo Ko Surin, Phang-Nga Province

Mathukorn Kooramphirak, Mae Bun Tham Bakery, Phuket Province

Maneerat Susangrat, Pun Tae Koy, Phuket Province

Meena Leangjirakan, Ranong Province

Nu Im Pannin, Ban Lam Khanun, Trang Province

Pa Phorn, Pa Phorn Phat Thai Chaiya stall, Chaiya, Surat Thani Province

Pakorn Rujiravilai, Songkhla Province

Patanan Petpirun, Yay Puad restaurant, Chumphon Province

Patcharaporn Rakchum, Rice Research Center, Phatthalung Province

Patrick Winn

Peeratat Iansakulwet, Rim Thalay Seafood restaurant, Nakhon Si Thammarat Province

Phanida Sikhao, Khaao Kaeng Phuen Baan restaurant, Nakhon Si Thammarat Province

Phiphat Kepsap, Ko Yao Noi, Phang-Nga Province

Phornnit Dechaphiban, Sonkhla Province

Prasit Khabuanphon, Songkhla Province

Puangpen Nookeaw, Kroo Jane Sago, Phatthalung Province

Raya Restaurant, Phuket Province

Ramphai Sumalee, Ban Sam Chong, Phang-Nga Province

Roti Thaew Nam restaurant, Phuket Province

Saengjan Chuaykoet, Khai Khem Chaiya Ko Tii Mae Kim, Chaiya, Surat Thani Province

Sangdow Duangkam, Betong, Yala Province

Satja Chodchoi, Khrua NC Restaurant, Phuket Province

Shukree, Yala Province

Somsak Srikoet, Mathaeng Cashews, Krabi Province

Somsri Roengsamot, Ko Yao Noi, Phang-Nga Province

Sookhkoe Donsai, Bangpo Seafood restaurant, Surat Thani Province

Sujit Namasi, Songkhla Province

Supada Tongtammachat, Singhanakhorn District, Songkhla Province

Supakan Piyavoratham, Khanom Jeen Jee Liu, Phuket Province

Supranee Pradit, Ko Yao Noi, Phang-Nga Province

Suraphon Phanusamphol, Suwalee restaurant, Nakhon Si Thammarat Province

Suthat Waharat, Ban Bang Phat, Phang-Nga Province

Suthon Inthasara, Singhanakhorn District, Songkhla Province

Taem Ninphaya, Khaao Kaeng Paa Eet restaurant, Nakhon Si Thammarat Province

Thai Sathien, Saiburi District, Pattani Province

Thanatip Boonyarat, Trang Province

Varerat Chaisin, Phuket Province

Wannee Chunhanan, Pa Phuang stall, Phuket Province

Wanthana Jandin, Ban Rai Yai, Krabi Province

Yaowanee Tancheewawong, Kanomwaan Pakee restaurant, Phatthalung Province

Yaowanee Thirakleela, Jip Khao restaurant, Trang Province

Yupha Ninphaya, Khaao Kaeng Paa Eet restaurant, Nakhon Si Thammarat Province

Index

Page numbers in italics indicate photographs/illustrations.